Current Directions
in
INTRODUCTORY PSYCHOLOGY

SECOND EDITION

EDITED BY

Abigail A. Baird, Ph.D.

Vassar College

with

Michele M. Tugade, Ph.D.

Vassar College

Heather B. Veague, Ph.D.

Vassar College

PEARSON

Upper Saddle River, NJ
Columbus, OH

Library of Congress Cataloging-in-Publication Data

Current directions in introductory psychology / edited by Abigail A. Baird, Michele M. Tugade, Heather B. Veague.

  p. cm.

"APS, Association for Psychological Science."

ISBN-13: 978-0-13-714350-4

ISBN-10:   0-13-714350-8

1. Psychology. I. Baird, Abigail A. II. Tugade, Michele M. III. Veague, Heather Barnett.

BF121.C795 2009

150—dc22   2008008189

Editorial Director: Leah Jewell
Executive Editor: Jeff Marshall
Project Manager: LeeAnn Doherty
Associate Managing Editor: Maureen Richardson
Full Service Production Liaison: Joanne Hakim
Senior Marketing Manager: Jeanette Koskinas
Marketing Assistant: Laura Kennedy
Senior Operations Supervisor: Sherry Lewis
Cover Art Director: Nancy Wells
Cover photo/illustration: "Faces '98" by Diana Ong/SuperStock, Inc.
Manager, Cover Visual Research & Permissions: Karen Sanatar
Full-Service Project Management: Doug Korb/TexTech International
Composition: TexTech International
Printer/Binder: RR Donnelley & Sons Company

Credits and acknowledgments borrowed from other sources and reproduced, with permission, in this textbook appear on appropriate page within text.

Pearson Education Ltd., London
Pearson Education Singapore, Pte. Ltd.
Pearson Education Canada, Inc.
Pearson Education–Japan
Pearson Education Australia PTY, Limited

Pearson Education North Asia Ltd., Hong Kong
Pearson Educación de Mexico, S.A. de C.V.
Pearson Education Malaysia, Pte. Ltd.
Pearson Education Upper Saddle River, New Jersey

PEARSON

10 9 8 7 6 5 4 3 2 1
ISBN 13: 978-0-13-714350-4
ISBN 10:   0-13-714350-8

Contents

Section 3: Health Psychology: Body and Brain   *89*

Section 4: Clinical Psychology: Investigation and Interpretation   *125*

Section 5: Individual Differences   *159*

Overview of this Book

This last year the American Psychological Society changed its name to the Association for Psychological Science. This change was made to reaffirm the organization's commitment to, and focus on, basic science research in the study of human behavior.

"... to identify our fundamental mission—educating the public as to why 'psychological science' is not an oxymoron. This is an uphill battle under the best of circumstances, but especially now, when all the sciences are under attack from political and religious ideologues who often seek to censor research they find threatening—and psychological research is often at the top of their hit list." (Carol Tavris, as quoted by Eric Wargo, APS Observer 19(1), January, 2006.)

The collection of papers assembled in this reader closely follows this directive. Within this volume we have assembled a group of expert researchers who review the most recent advances in psychological science.

The general purpose of this reader is to serve as a supplement to an Introduction to Psychology course, and as such we have attempted to include sections on the major sub-divisions within the larger discipline of psychological science. Perhaps as important as specific sub-areas of psychological science is the notion that all psychological questions are best approached using multiple vantage points. This philosophy embraces both crossing sub-discipline borders (e.g. how children develop moral reasoning by virtue of their social interactions), as well as looking from the neural (bottom) up through the cultural (top) levels of scientific analysis (e.g. the role of neurogenesis in the etiology of depression). It is our hope that you, the reader, are able to engage this perspective to enhance your understanding of psychological science.

Introductory psychology texts are essential because they are able to impart the fundamentals of a large and continuously expanding field. What may be hard to keep in mind while reading your textbook is that everything you read, even the most general ideas, is the product of research. This reader is meant to highlight this, by providing you with a sampling of how research works, and perhaps inspiring you to dig deeper into the psychological phenomena that most interests you.

Acknowledgment: We are deeply indebted to our undergraduate research assistant, Shari Silver, for her help in every phase of this project. Shari's contributions were essential to the completion of this reader, and we give her our sincere thanks.

Section 1: Developmental Psychology

Developmental psychology concerns itself with how individuals change across the course of the life span. Simply, the area of psychology endevours to provide the answer to the timeless question: how did you become the person you are? Historically, the debate between the deterministic influence of an individual's biology (the "Nature" argument) and the way in which an individual interacts with his/her environment (the "Nurture" argument); however, more recently, developmental science has undergone significant revision in the way the "Nature vs Nurture" debate is approached. The articles in this section present this new approach, where the synergistic influence of both nature and nurture is seen as critical to human development.

This section begins at the beginning, with a paper on the psychobiological roots of attachment by Myron Hofer (2006). Hofer offers novel insights about the nature and function of early infant attachment. He describes the way in which mothers are able to regulate a number of different physiological processes in their infants. This regulation enables the infant to learn his/her first associations between mental representations (e.g. mom's milk) and their related affects (e.g. normal heart rhythm). Hofer presents evidence for a number of regulatory functions that the attachment bond serves; and offers an updated interpretation of the emotional distress that infants display when they are separated from their caregivers. He encourages us to think about the multiple regulatory functions that attachment serves, and the individual psychobiological consequences of disrupting any of these processes. Keeping one's children healthy and happy has always been associated with notions of good parenting. While there is great debate as to "the perfect parenting techniques", most assume that children of wealthy (high socio-economic status) families are better off than children of poor (low socio-economic status) families. In the third article of this section, Luther and Latendresse (2005) suggest that this might not always be the case. The authors indicate several important ways in which the children of the affluent may be as much at risk as the children of the impoverished. The clearest of these is the social and emotional isolation that many children of affluent parents experience. This isolation often stems from parental occupations that allow these children material comforts, but often keep their parents away from home, and/or constantly pre-occupied with work. Additionally, high-achieving parents have been shown to place undue pressure to achieve on their children. Disproportionate achievement pressures have been shown to result in increased occurrence of depression, anxiety and substance abuse among children and teens. By virtue of their absence from the home, affluent parents may not be giving their children the most important thing that money cannot buy: the social and emotional support needed to develop optimally.

Although parents are most often the primary caregivers for infants and children, siblings are known to exert significant influence on an individual's development. In the fifth article in this section, Gene Brody (2004) describes both the direct and indirect influence that siblings have on an individual's development. In terms of their direct influence, siblings may serve as a source of social and emotional protection and support. Siblings also offer the opportunity to practice a variety of skills, and to teach and be taught. To benefit from relationships with siblings, these relationships do not need to be free from conflict. Much the contrary, conflict among siblings serves a vital function; it aids in the development of important problem solving skills as well as teaches children the importance of trying to understand others' points of view. Indirectly, siblings influence parental behavior; and this in turn can produce both positive and negative outcomes for the developing individual. As detailed above, optimal parenting involved close attachments that reflect and support the nature of the individual. By design, no two children will need exactly the same things from their parents, and this creates differential treatment of children in the family. Differential treatment that reflect parents ability to respond to their children's unique needs can be very positive for all members of the family, and has only been shown to be problematic when it changes from differential to preferential treatment. As is obvious by the description of sibling influence, children rely on their interactions with other children to shape their development. Children also spend increasing amounts of time with their peers. In early adolescence, peers play a critical role in teaching the developing individual "the rules of the road" for adult behavior. It is also the case that being a member of a peer group is critical to development, and being a high status member of that group is associated with positive psychosocial outcomes. Such peer groups also allow children to learn about moral reasoning. As detailed by Melanie Killen (2007), peer groups also enable children to transcend age-determined levels of moral reasoning. Inclusion and exclusion in peer groups play such a central role to child development, that developmental stage had no influence on children's ability to engage moral reasoning with regard to social exclusion. This work also details children's ability to extract and apply group norms from as early as first grade. What is made abundantly clear by the work reviewed by Killen, is that one's place in a peer group is not only critical for learning about the social world around you, but also may provide scaffolding for the development of advanced moral reasoning. In the final paper of this section Cillessen and Rose (2005) explore the actuality of popularity. First, the authors draw a distinction between two kinds of popularity, sociometric popularity and perceived popularity. Sociometrically popular individuals are well-liked, exhibit high levels of cooperative behavior and low levels of aggression; importantly, these individuals show long-term positive effects of their social status. Sociometrically popular youths, however, are not always "popular" in the traditional sense of the category. Perceived popular individuals are the "cool kids", individuals who possess a great deal of social influence, are liked by some of their peers and disliked by others, and exert their social influence through both prosocial and aggressive means. Perhaps most interesting about this group of perceived popular youths, is that although youth strive to be more like these individuals (rather than those who are sociometrically popular) they seem to have achieved this status through methods that are highly effective for the short term context of early adolescence, but not well-suited to later life socio-emotional success. As a result, Cillessen and Rose report that these youths are likely afflicted with more negative long-term outcomes than sociometrically popular individuals.

Together, the papers in the following section underscore not only the fundamental importance of human relationships, but also their truly pro-found and long-lasting developmental influence. Finally, and perhaps most importantly, these papers represent the emerging notion that nature and nurture are two dynamic forces that have independent and synergistic effects on the developing individual.

Children's Social and Moral Reasoning About Exclusion

Melanie Killen[1]
University of Maryland

Abstract

Developmental research on social and moral reasoning about exclusion has utilized a social-domain theory, in contrast to a global stage theory, to investigate children's evaluations of gender- and race-based peer exclusion. The social-domain model postulates that moral, social-conventional, and personal reasoning coexist in children's evaluations of inclusion and exclusion, and that the priority given to these forms of judgments varies by the age of the child, the context, and the target of exclusion. Findings from developmental intergroup research studies disconfirm a general-stage-model approach to morality in the child, and provide empirical data on the developmental origins and emergence of intergroup attitudes regarding prejudice, bias, and exclusion.

Keywords

social reasoning; exclusion; intergroup attitudes; moral judgment

How early do individuals become capable of moral reasoning? What is the evidence for morality in the child? Over the past two decades, research on children's moral judgment has changed dramatically, providing new theories and methods for analysis. In brief, the change has been away from a global stage model toward domain-specific models of development. According to Kohlberg's foundational stage model of moral development (Kohlberg, 1984), which followed Piaget's research on moral judgment (Piaget, 1932), children justify acts as right or wrong first on the basis of consequences to the self (preconventional), then in terms of group norms (conventional), and finally in terms of a justice perspective in which individual principles of how to treat one another are understood (postconventional). This approach involved assessing an individual's general scheme (organizing principle) for evaluating social problems and dilemmas across a range of contexts.

By the mid-1980s, however, studies of contextual variation in judgments provided extensive evidence contesting broad stages (Smetana, 2006; Turiel, 1998). For example, young children's evaluations of transgressions and social events reflect considerations of the self, the group, and justice; these considerations do not emerge hierarchically (respectively) but simultaneously in development, each with its own separate developmental trajectory (e.g., self-knowledge, group knowledge, and moral knowledge). Thus, multiple forms of reasoning are applied to the evaluations of social dilemmas and interactions. Social judgments do not reflect one broad template or stage, such as Kohlberg's preconventional stage to characterize childhood morality. Instead, children use different forms of reasoning, moral, conventional, and psychological, simultaneously when evaluating transgressions and social events.

One area of recent empirical inquiry pertains to social and moral evaluations of decisions to exclude others, particularly on the basis of group membership (such as gender, race, or ethnicity), referred to as *intergroup exclusion*. What makes this form of exclusion a particularly compelling topic for investigation from a moral viewpoint is that it reflects, on the one hand, prejudice, discrimination, stereotyping, and bias about groups, and, on the other hand, judgments about fairness, equality, and rights (Killen, Lee-Kim, McGlothlin, & Stangor, 2002). Conceptually, these judgments are diametrically opposed; prejudice violates moral principles of fairness, discrimination violates equality, and stereotyping restricts individual rights. Do both forms of reasoning exist within the child? What do children do when confronted with an exclusion decision that involves moral considerations of fairness and equal treatment, on the one hand, and stereotypic and social-conventional expectations, on the other?

A social-domain model proposes that morality includes fairness, justice, rights, and others' welfare (e.g., when a victim is involved; "It wouldn't be fair to exclude him from the game"); social-conventional concerns involve conventions, etiquette, and customs that promote effective group functioning (e.g., when disorder in the group occurs; "If you let someone new in the group they won't know how it works or what it's about and it will be disruptive"); and psychological issues pertain to autonomy, individual prerogatives, and identity (e.g., acts that are not regulated but affect only the self; "It's her decision who she wants to be friends with"). Social-domain-theory approaches to moral reasoning, along with social-psychological theories about intergroup attitudes, provide a new approach to understanding social exclusion.

Social exclusion is a pervasive aspect of social life, ranging from everyday events (e.g., exclusion from birthday parties, sports teams, social organizations) to large-scale social tragedies (e.g., exclusion based on religion and ethnicity resulting in genocide). These forms of interindividual and intergroup exclusion create conflict, tension, and, in extreme cases, chronic suffering. In the child's world, exclusion has been studied most often in the context of interindividual, rather than intergroup, conflict. Research on peer rejection and victimization, for example, has focused on individual differences and the social deficits that contribute to being a bully (lack of social competence) or a victim (wariness, shyness, fearfulness; Rubin, Bukowski, & Parker, 1998). The findings indicate that the long-term consequences for children and adults who experience pervasive exclusion are negative, resulting in depression, anxiety, and loneliness.

DEVELOPMENTAL APPROACHES

Recently, developmental researchers have investigated children's evaluations of intergroup exclusion (e.g., "You're an X and we don't want Xs in our group"). Decisions to exclude others involve a range of reasons, from group norms and stereotypic expectations to moral assessments about the fairness of exclusion. Much of what is known about group norms has been documented by social psychologists, who have conducted extensive studies on intergroup relationships. The findings indicate that social categorization frequently leads to intergroup bias and that explicit and implicit attitudes about others based on group membership contribute to prejudicial and discriminatory attitudes and behavior (Dovidio, Glick, & Rudman, 2005). Few researchers, however, have examined the developmental trajectory of exclusion from a moral-reasoning perspective.

Social-domain theory has provided a taxonomy for examining the forms of reasoning—moral, social-conventional, and psychological—that are brought to bear on intergroup exclusion decisions. One way that a social-domain model differs from the traditional stage model of moral reasoning, as formulated by Kohlberg in the late 1960s, is that the former provides a theory and a methodology for examining how individuals use different forms of reasons when evaluating everyday phenomena.

SOCIAL REASONING ABOUT EXCLUSION

One of the goals of social-domain research is to identify the conditions under which children give priority to different forms of reasons when evaluating social decisions, events, and interactions. What are the major empirical findings on intergroup exclusion decisions by children? Most centrally, children do not use one scheme ("stage") to evaluate all morally relevant intergroup problems and scenarios; moreover, although some types of decisions are age related, others are not. In a study with children in the 1st, 4th, and 7th grades, the vast majority of students (95%) judged it wrong to exclude a peer from a group solely because of gender or race (e.g., a ballet club excludes a boy because he's a boy; a baseball club excludes a girl because she's a girl), and based their judgment on moral reasons, such as that such exclusion would be unfair and discriminatory (Killen & Stangor, 2001); there were no age-related differences, contrary to what a stage-model approach would predict.

Introducing complexity, however, revealed variation in judgments and justifications. As shown in Figure 1, in an equal-qualifications condition ("What if

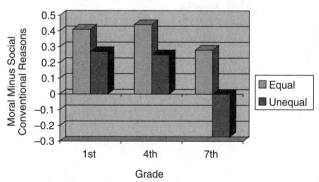

Fig. 1. Proportion of moral minus social-conventional reasons given by 1st, 4th, and 7th graders for peer-exclusion judgments based on gender or race. In one condition (equal), participants stated which of two children should be excluded from an after-school club with only one available opening when a stereotypical and nonstereotypical applicant both were equally qualified. In the other (unequal) condition, participants stated which child should be excluded if the child who fit the stereotype for that activity was also more qualified. After-school clubs were baseball/ballet and basketball/math, reflecting gender- and race-associated stereotypes, respectively. Reprinted from Killen & Stangor (2001).

7

there was only room for one more to join the club, and a girl and a boy both were equally qualified, who should the group pick?"), most children used moral reasons ("You should pick the person who doesn't usually get a chance to be in the club because they're both equally good at it"); but in an unequal-qualification condition ("What if X was more qualified, who should the group pick?"), age-related increases in the use of social-conventional reasons ("The group won't work well if you pick the person who is not very good at it") were found. Young adolescents weighed individual merits and considered the functioning of the club or team. Qualifications (e.g., good at ballet or baseball) were considered to be more salient considerations than preserving the "equal opportunity" dimensions (e.g., picking a girl for baseball who has not had a chance to play).

In fact, how children interpret their group's ingroup and out-group norms (conventions) appears to be related to prejudice and bias (moral transgressions; Abrams, Rutland, Cameron, & Ferrell, in press). Abrams et al. (in press) showed that children's view of whether exclusion is legitimate or wrong was contingent on whether they viewed an individual as supporting or rejecting an ingroup-identity norm. In other related developmental intergroup research, children's lay theories (conventional knowledge) about what it means to work in a group, and whether effort or intrinsic ability is what counts, have been shown to be significantly related to whether they view the denial of allocation of resources as fair or unfair (moral decision making); focusing on intrinsic ability in contrast to effort results in condoning prejudicial treatment (Levy, Chiu, & Hong, 2006). Moreover, adolescents' perceptions of the social status of membership in peer cliques (conventional knowledge) determine whether they view exclusion (e.g., excluding a "goth" from the cheerleading squad) as fair or legitimate (Horn, 2003). These findings demonstrate the nuanced ways in which children make judgments about groups and how group knowledge and group norms bear directly on moral judgments about exclusion and inclusion.

Research on intergroup contact in childhood provides information regarding how social experience influences the manifestation of children's stereotypes and conventional reasoning to justify exclusion. Intergroup-contact theory states that under certain conditions, contact with members of outgroups decreases prejudice (Pettigrew & Tropp, 2005). In a developmental study with participants enrolled in 13 public schools ($N = 685$) of varying ethnic diversity (see Fig. 2), European American students enrolled in heterogeneous schools were more likely to use explicit stereotypes to explain why interracial interactions make their peers uncomfortable, and were less likely to use moral reasons to evaluate peer exclusion, than were European Americans enrolled in homogeneous schools (Killen, Richardson, Kelly, Crystal, & Ruck, 2006). Children's positive experiences with students who are different from themselves, under certain conditions, facilitate moral reasoning about intergroup exclusion and suppress stereotypic expectations as a reason for an exclusion decision.

These findings support a domain-model view of social and moral judgment and challenge stage theory, which proposes that children are limited in their ability to make moral judgments by a general-processing scheme for assimilating information (their "stage"). From a stage view, one would expect children to use conventional or stereotypic (group-expectations) reasons, and expect older children to use

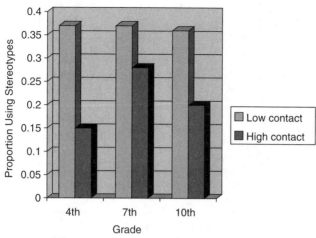

Fig. 2. Proportion of European American students who explicitly used stereotypes to explain what it is about interracial interactions that makes their peers uncomfortable, as a function of positive intergroup contact. Positive intergroup contact included cross-race friendship in classrooms, schools, and neighborhoods (based on data reported in Killen et al., 2006).

moral reasons. Instead, researchers now find that children's reasoning varies by the context and a balance of priorities.

Context has many variables, and determining it involves investigating the role of the target of exclusion as well as participant variables (age, gender, race/ethnicity) on exclusion decisions. Regarding the target of exclusion, a series of findings reveals that gender exclusion is viewed as more legitimate than exclusion based on ethnicity, with more social-conventional reasons and stereotypic expectations used to support the former than the latter (Killen et al., 2002). As shown in Figure 3, children used fewer moral reasons to evaluate exclusion in a peer-group music context with a gender target ("What if the boys' music club will not let a girl join?") than with a race target ("What if the white students in a music club will not let a black student join?"). A significant proportion of students used social-conventional reasons, such as: "A girl/black student likes different music, so she/he won't fit in with the group." Not surprisingly, though, European American females, and minority participants (both males and females), were more likely to reject these forms of exclusion and to use moral reasons than were European American males. This inclusive orientation may be due to the perspective, empathy, and reciprocity that result from experiencing prior exclusion. Thus, these findings support social-domain-theory propositions that the target of exclusion is influential on evaluations of exclusion, and that specific types of peer experiences may contribute to judgments that exclusion is wrong.

Children reject atypical peers based on stigmatized group identity (Nesdale & Brown, 2004). This finding further indicates that peer experience with exclusion is an important variable for investigation. Nesdale and Brown propose that children who experience extensive exclusion may be at risk for demonstrating prejudicial behavior toward others, and for perpetuating a cycle of negative intergroup

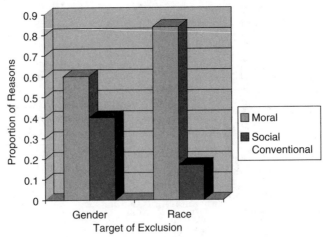

Fig. 3. Proportion of moral and social-conventional reasons for gender and racial targets of exclusion in peer-group contexts. Peer-group contexts referred to after-school music clubs that excluded a target child from joining the club due to his or her gender or race. Reasons were moral (unfairness) or social-conventional (group functioning; based on data from Killen, Lee-Kim, McGlothlin, & Stangor, 2002).

attitudes. At the same time, however, adolescents are cognizant of the wrongfulness of discrimination regarding stigmatized peers (Verkuyten & Thijs, 2002).

Although stereotypes and conventions are powerful forces that legitimize exclusion, there is also extensive evidence of how adolescents explain the wrongfulness of discrimination in terms of social justice. Social-reasoning categories provide evidence for the types of norms that children use to justify or reject exclusion decisions and for the conditions that promote children's change from a priority on morality to group functioning, which may, at times, occur at the expense of fairness.

NEW DIRECTIONS

Adults frequently use traditions and customs to justify exclusion. Tiger Woods' initial response to playing at the Augusta (Georgia) National Golf Club (host of the legendary Masters Tournament), which excludes women, was "That's just the way it is" (Brown, 2002)—categorized as social-conventional reasoning. More recently, Woods has stated, "Is it unfair? Yes. Do I want to see a female member? Yes" ("Woods Thinks Masters Debate Deserves a Private Meeting," 2005)—categorized as moral reasoning. Yet, he refuses to give up his participation in the event: "They're asking me to give up an opportunity to win the Masters three straight years" (Smith, 2003)—personal priority over the wrongfulness of exclusion. These quotes, which do not reflect coded responses from an in-depth systematic interview, nonetheless, reveal how an individual can give different priorities to exclusion decisions and how these priorities change depending on the context (Killen, Sinno, & Margie, in press). Social-conventional or personal reasons do not necessarily reflect a developmentally "primitive" response (as put forth by stage theory).

Are children moral? Yes, children demonstrate spontaneous and elaborated reasons for why it is wrong to exclude others based on group membership, referring to fairness, equality, and rights. Do children have stereotypes about others? Yes; how these stereotypes enter into moral decision making requires an in-depth analysis of how children weigh competing considerations, such as group functioning, traditions, customs, and cultural norms, when evaluating exclusion. What changes as children age is how these considerations are weighed, the contexts that become salient for children and adolescents, and the ability to determine when morality should take priority in a given situation.

What is not well known is how children's intergroup biases (those that are not explicit) influence their judgments about exclusion; what it is about intergroup contact that contributes to children's variation in reliance on stereotypes to evaluate exclusion; and how early intergroup attitudes influence children's awareness of justice, fairness, and equality. Given that stereotypes are very hard to change in adulthood, interventions need to be conducted in childhood. Understanding when children resort to stereotypic expectations is crucial information for creating effective interventions. Developmental findings on social reasoning about exclusion provide a new approach for addressing these complex issues in childhood and adulthood and for creating programs to reduce prejudice.

Recommended Reading

Aboud, F.E., & Amato, M. (2001). Developmental and socialization influences on intergroup bias. In R. Brown & S. Gaertner (Eds.), *Blackwell handbook of social psychology: Intergroup relations* (pp. 65–85). Oxford, England: Blackwell.

Gaertner, S.L., & Dovidio, J.F. (2000). *Reducing intergroup bias: The common ingroup identity model*. New York: Psychology Press.

Killen, M., Margie, N.G., & Sinno, S. (2006). Morality in the context of intergroup relationships. In M. Killen & J. Smetana (Eds.), *Handbook of moral development* (pp. 155–183). Mahwah, NJ: LEA.

Rutland, A. (2004). The development and self-regulation of intergroup attitudes in children. In M. Bennett & F. Sani (Eds.), *The development of the social self* (pp. 247–265). East Sussex, England: Psychology Press.

Turiel, E. (2002). *Culture and morality*. Cambridge, England: Cambridge University Press.

Acknowledgments—The author would like to thank Judith G. Smetana, Stefanie Sinno, and Cameron Richardson, for helpful comments on earlier drafts of this manuscript, and the graduate students in the Social and Moral Development Laboratory for collaborative and insightful contributions to the research reported in this paper. The research described in this manuscript was supported, in part, by grants from the National Institute of Child Health and Human Development (1R01HD04121-01) and the National Science Foundation (#BCS0346717).

Note

1. Address correspondence to Melanie Killen, 3304 Benjamin Building, Department of Human Development, University of Maryland, College Park, MD 20742-1131; e-mail: mkillen@umd.edu.

References

Abrams, D., Rutland, A., Cameron, L., & Ferrell, A. (in press). Older but wilier: Ingroup accountability and the development of subjective group dynamics. *Developmental Psychology.*

Brown, J. (2002, August 16). Should Woods carry the black man's burden? *The Christian Science Monitor* [electronic version]. Retrieved January 5, 2007, from http://www.csmonitor.com/2002/0816/p01s01-ussc.html

Dovidio, J.F., Glick, P., & Rudman, L. (Eds.). (2005). *Reflecting on the nature of prejudice: Fifty years after Allport.* Malden, MA: Blackwell.

Horn, S. (2003). Adolescents' reasoning about exclusion from social groups. *Developmental Psychology,* 39, 11–84.

Killen, M., Lee-Kim, J., McGlothlin, H., & Stangor, C. (2002). How children and adolescents evaluate gender and racial exclusion. *Monographs for the Society for Research in Child Development* (Serial No. 271, Vol. 67, No. 4). Oxford, England: Blackwell.

Killen, M., Richardson, C., Kelly, M.C., Crystal, D., & Ruck, M. (2006, May). *European-American students' evaluations of interracial social exchanges in relation to the ethnic diversity of school environments.* Paper presented at the annual convention of the Association for Psychological Science, New York City.

Killen, M., Sinno, S., & Margie, N. (in press). Children's experiences and judgments about group exclusion and inclusion. In R. Kail (Ed.), *Advances in child psychology.* New York: Elsevier.

Killen, M., & Stangor, C. (2001). Children's social reasoning about inclusion and exclusion in gender and race peer group contexts. *Child Development,* 72, 174–186.

Kohlberg, L. (1984). *Essays on moral development: Vol. 2. The psychology of moral development—The nature and validity of moral stages.* San Francisco: Harper & Row.

Levy, S.R., Chiu, C.Y., & Hong, Y.Y. (2006). Lay theories and intergroup relations. *Group Processes and Intergroup Relations,* 9, 5–24.

Nesdale, D., & Brown, K. (2004). Children's attitudes towards an atypical member of an ethnic ingroup. *International Journal of Behavioral Development,* 28, 328–335.

Pettigrew, T.F., & Tropp, L.R. (2005). Allport's intergroup contact hypothesis: Its history and influence. In J.F. Dovidio, P. Glick, & L. Rudman (Eds.), *Reflecting on the nature of prejudice: Fifty years after Allport* (pp. 262–277). Malden, MA: Blackwell.

Piaget, J. (1932). *The moral judgment of the child.* New York: Free Press.

Rubin, K.H., Bukowski, W., & Parker, J. (1998). Peer interactions, relationships and groups. In W. Damon (Ed.), *Handbook of child psychology: Vol. 3. Social, emotional, and personality development* (5th ed., pp. 619–700). New York: Wiley.

Smetana, J.G. (2006). Social domain theory: Consistencies and variations in children's moral and social judgments. In M. Killen & J.G. Smetana (Eds.), *Handbook of moral development* (pp. 119–154). Mahwah, NJ: Erlbaum.

Smith, T. (2003, February 20). A Master's challenge. *Online NewsHour.* Retrieved July 16, 2006, from http://www.pbs.org/newshour/bb/sports/jan-june03/golf_2-20.html

Turiel, E. (1998). The development of morality. In W. Damon (Ed.), *Handbook of child psychology: Vol. 3. Social, emotional, and personality development* (5th ed., pp. 863–932). New York: Wiley.

Verkuyten, M., & Thijs, J. (2002). Racist victimization among children in the Netherlands: The effect of ethnic group and school. *Ethnic and Racial Studies,* 25, 310–331.

Woods thinks Masters debate deserves a private meeting. (2005, February 14). *USA Today* [electronic version]. Retrieved January 10, 2007, from http://www.usatoday.com/sports/golf/2002-10-16-woodsmasters_x.htm

This article has been reprinted as it originally appeared in *Current Directions in Psychological Science*. Citation information for this article as originally published appears above.

Psychobiological Roots of Early Attachment

Myron A. Hofer[1]

Sackler Institute for Developmental Psychobiology and Department of Psychiatry, Columbia University College of Physicians & Surgeons

Abstract

New laboratory research has revealed a network of simple behavioral, physiological, and neural processes that underlie the psychological constructs of attachment theory. It has become apparent that the unique features of early infant attachment reflect certain unique features of early infant sensory and motor integration, learning, communication, and motivation, as well as the regulation of biobehavioral systems by the mother–infant interaction. In this article, I will use this new knowledge to answer three major questions that have remained unsettled in our understanding of early human attachment: What creates an attachment bond? Why is early maternal separation stressful? How can early relationships have lasting effects? I will discuss the implications of these new answers for human infants and for the development of mental processes. Attachment remains useful as a concept that, like hunger, describes the operation of subprocesses that work together within the frame of a vital biological function.

Keywords

attachment; separation; bond; maternal behavior; early experience; learning

The word *attachment* has assumed new meanings as it has spread from literature to psychology, and most recently to biology. These changes have spanned the half century since the Second World War, when the vast numbers of displaced and orphaned children made the importance of a child's early tie to its mother evident to all. As different groups within psychology used the concept, there developed champions and detractors of one or another formulation. I think that a crucial change came when Bowlby's (1982) concept of attachment as a unique motivational system was gradually found to be incapable of generating testable hypotheses that could explain several puzzling observations. Developmental psychobiology researchers focused instead on simpler processes at work within the interactions between infant and parent—such as orientation, nursing, early learning, thermoregulation, and sensorimotor-system development. There was a period between the early 1970s and late 1980s when *attachment* was seldom used by developmental psychobiologists. In the last decade, however, the word has found a new usefulness as a general descriptive term for the processes that maintain and regulate sustained social relationships, much the same way that *appetite* refers to a cluster of behavioral and physiological processes that regulate food intake.

The concept of attachment provides a good example of how a psychological construct can be analyzed at the level of the component processes that underlie it. This approach does not attempt to reduce psychological questions to the most basic units of biological organization. Rather, the focus is on the processes of behavioral and physiological regulation that closely underlie psychological constructs, providing a much-needed link between psychology and the cellular/molecular mechanisms of brain function. New knowledge at the level of behavior and integrative physiology promises to deepen our understanding of psychological constructs rather than eliminate the need for them.

In order to illustrate this point, I will describe how new research using animal models has helped resolve three questions left unanswered by psychological theories of attachment, and I will relate these findings to human psychology, as I see it.

WHAT CREATES AN ATTACHMENT BOND?

This question asks what processes are responsible for the development of the behaviors, and inferred mental states, that we refer to as the "bond" between infant and mother. Research has shown that predispositions can be created prenatally, in the fetus, to respond preferentially to specific maternal scents and sounds, and that these predispositions prepare the way for the next phase in the development of attachment.

Regina Sullivan, Steve Brake, and I (Sullivan, Hofer, & Brake, 1986) discovered an experimental learning paradigm in newborn rats that revealed a rapid and powerful learning capacity by which neonates acquire the ability to discriminate, prefer, approach, and maintain proximity to their own mother. A specific neutral odor was presented to newborns while the pups were stroked with an artist's brush for 5 to 15 minutes. The odor was later applied to shavings under mesh in a two-compartment box. The neonates then turned preferentially to that odor and remained on the mesh over the scented compartment for the duration of testing. Control subjects were presented with the same stimuli but separated in time. They showed no later preference for the odor. Such rapid and specific associative learning had not been anticipated in rats of such an early age. Indeed Bowlby and others in the 1960s thought that even human newborns and young infants interacted with their mothers entirely through reflex and fixed-action-pattern behaviors (simple, rigidly stereotyped action sequences). We now know that human newborns also can distinguish their own mother's smell, apparently on the basis of prenatal experience, and add vocal and visual recognition postnatally—probably by similar early-learning systems (Winberg, 2005).

Next, Sullivan (reviewed in Moriceau and Sullivan, 2005) discovered that for the first 10 days after birth, an aversive level of stimulation (e.g., tail pinch, mild shock) that itself elicits vigorous escape behavior will paradoxically induce approach and preference for an odor previously associated with it. After those 10 days, such associative pairing results in avoidance of the odor. The unexpected early aversive-preference learning has an obvious parallel in the strong attachments frequently observed in abused human infants. In this animal model, Sullivan and coworkers have mapped out the critical period for the effect, have shown that the critical period can be extended in time by daily repetitions of the associative experience, and have related the normal close of this period to developmental transitions in specific brain systems that are regulated by circulating adrenocortical hormones.

In these studies, the questions of the nature of a psychological bond, its specificity, and how it is formed, can be answered in terms of an unexpected rapid early-learning process with properties that can be related to brain and hormone-system development. Experiments testing alternative hypotheses led us to a new way to understand the paradoxically close attachments of children to abusive parents.

WHY IS EARLY MATERNAL SEPARATION STRESSFUL?

In most conceptual formulations of attachment, the separation response is explained as deriving from the strong affective nature of the bond, which when severed or "ruptured" by separation results in a series of traumatic emotional reactions: the "biphasic protest–despair response," in which an initial burst of calling and active search behavior is followed by a long decline in behavioral responsiveness (Bowlby, 1982; see Fig. 1). But there is circularity in this line of reasoning, as the evidence for the existence of the bond itself, and for its strength, lies in the dramatic response to its being broken by separation.

I was led to an entirely different way of thinking about separation by unexpected results in our laboratory (reviewed in Hofer, 1994). Initially, we did not believe that infant rats were capable of the complex cognitive-affective processes thought to underlie the separation response seen in infant monkeys and humans. But to our surprise, we found that, like primate infants, infant rats show a complex biphasic protest–despair response to maternal separation, as well as a number of other responses that were entirely unexpected. We found that these changes were not the expression of an integrated psychophysiological response (like the increase in heart rate and respiration during exercise) to the stressful event, but were the result of a novel mechanism I will now describe (see Fig. 2). Our experiments showed that each of the individual behavioral and physiological systems of the infant rat was responding to the loss of one or another of the components (e.g., nutrient, thermal/metabolic, or sensorimotor) of the infant's previous interaction with its mother and that the complex response to separation was due to the withdrawal of all these components at once.

For example, we found that providing one of these components, warmth, to a separated pup prevented the slow decline in the pups' general activity level (a response similar to Bowlby's "despair" phase), but this had no effect on responses in other systems. The pup's cardiac rate continued to fall by 40%, regardless of whether supplemental heat or tactile stimulation was provided. But we found that

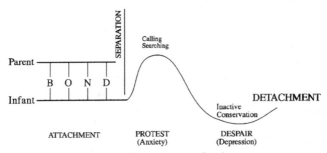

Fig. 1. Schematic representation of the dynamics of early-separation responses based on the concept of an attachment bond as described by John Bowlby (Bowlby, 1982).

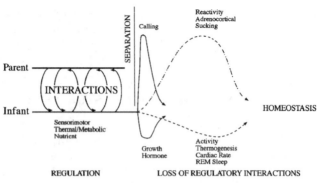

Fig. 2. Schematic representation of the dynamics of early-separation responses resulting from the loss of regulatory interactions within the mother–infant relationship.

we could maintain cardiac rate in separated pups at normal levels by continuous infusion of milk to the pup's stomach. Supplying enough milk to prevent weight loss had no effect, but if enough was given to produce a normal range of weight gain, the cardiac rate at the end of a 24-hour separation was proportional to the amount of nutrient that had been infused. In other words, the supplied milk regulated the pups' heart rate. The physiological mechanism, we found, was not gastric distention or any effect of absorbed nutrients, but an effect of specific nutrients on receptors in the lining of the stomach that are connected to the brain.

We concluded from these surprising results that warmth provided by the mother normally maintained the pup's activity level and that her milk maintained her pup's heart rate. Maternal separation withdrew these regulatory influences that were hidden within the ordinary mother–infant interactions, resulting in slowed behavior and low heart rate. We began to look for other effects of separation and the specific regulators that could prevent them. We found that sufficient levels of tactile stimulation during a 24-hour separation period prevented the increase in the pup's behavioral response to being moved into a novel test chamber, a behavioral hyper-reactivity that we had found in separated pups with normal body temperatures. Graded levels of tactile stimulation during separation produced graded levels of quieting of pups. For the rate of sucking on an artificial teat and for the immediate vocal "protest" phase of vocalization (Hofer, 1996), both of which increased in separated pups, more specific types of sensorimotor experience were necessary to reduce these behaviors to normal levels. We also studied sleep/wake states using an electroencephalograph and found that the durations of bouts of sleeping and waking and the smooth transitions between them were maintained (regulated) by the periodicity or rhythm of maternal milk supply and tactile interactions, rather than simply by their level. After 24 hours of separation, the REM-sleep time of pups remaining in their home cage was sharply decreased and slow-wave sleep was fragmented by frequent short awakenings. Only scheduled periodic bouts of nutrient infusion and tactile stimulation prevented this. Soon, other investigators were able to define other maternal regulatory effects: Saul Schanberg for growth hormone and Seymour Levine for adrenocortical system control (reviewed in Hofer, 1994).

In thinking about the implication of these findings for human infants, one can suppose that these kinds of simple maternal regulators would be found early in a baby's postnatal period, but that soon more subtle and intricate interactions would become important. Reciprocity, imitation, attunement, and play are now being investigated for their roles in regulating the baby's affective state and his or her developing capacity to self-regulate and later engage in complex social interactions outside the parental relationship. But we should be aware that regulatory interactions at the simpler levels of touch, warmth, and smell may continue to be important for humans (as well as other animals), even into adult life, with implications for human grief (Hofer, 1984).

In trying to understand responses to separation in infants (as well as in adults), we should look carefully for exactly what was lost, not simply regard separation as an affective response to stress. The discovery of numerous regulatory processes hidden within the mother–infant interaction provides a novel causative explanation for the response of infants to maternal separation that does not depend upon the metaphorical concept of a "bond" that is "broken." Furthermore, the discovery of these regulatory processes at work within an ongoing mother–infant relationship raises the question of whether, in addition, they might be responsible for regulating the course of development over time.

HOW CAN EARLY RELATIONSHIPS HAVE LASTING EFFECTS?

An immediate implication of our discovery of multiple hidden regulators within the mother–infant interaction was the possibility that different patterns of early parent–infant interaction might differentially shape the course of development of offspring. The first pattern that we investigated was the early termination of the relationship, before the usual time of weaning (reviewed in Hofer, 1994). We found that if rat pups are separated from their mothers at 15 days instead of the usual 21 to 30 days, they can survive, but they will have been deprived of maternal regulation during that period of their development. We assessed the effect of this early weaning on the vulnerability of adults to a known stressor, 24 hours of immobilization, which had been reported to produce gastric ulceration in about 50% of normally reared adult rats. We found that early weaning did not affect the expected percent vulnerability when rats were stressed in adulthood (120 days); but in early adolescence (25 and 35 days), 80% of the early-weaned rats developed ulcers, and these were larger and deeper than those occurring in adults; however, no normally reared rats developed ulcers at these ages. In the immediate aftermath of maternal separation, at 17 days of age, no rat ulcerated. Even more surprising, as rats matured into later adulthood (160 days), the early-weaned rats were actually less vulnerable than the normally reared ones were.

What I believe this experiment illustrates is that when all maternal regulators are withdrawn early, a number of physiological and behavioral systems are altered in their developmental paths and in their relation to each other, creating a complex, changing pattern of vulnerability over the life span.

We then decided to study a more discrete form of change in the pattern of early mother–infant interactions by taking advantage of naturally occurring variations in the relative frequency of different maternal behaviors, what might be called different "qualities" of the relationship. Michael Myers, Harry Shair, and I (Myers, Shair, & Hofer, 1992) were studying two strains of rats created by selective breeding, the spontaneously hypertensive strain and the normotensive-progenitor strain. We found a range of variation between litters in their mean adult blood pressure. We then observed a range of variation in the levels of 10 different maternal behaviors as we studied litters over the preweaning period. Within each strain, the offspring of mothers with high levels of three of these behaviors (licking-grooming, high-arched nursing posture, and time in contact) had significantly higher levels of blood pressure as adults than did offspring of mothers with low levels of those behaviors. (Since the animals in each strain had been inbred to the point that they were genetically identical, these differences could not be simply due to genetic covariation in maternal behavior and in blood pressure within each strain.) Furthermore, the mothers of the spontaneously hypertensive strain, as a group, showed higher levels of these maternal behaviors than did the mothers of the normotensive strain.

Finding such a strong correlation of levels of specific maternal behaviors with levels of offspring blood pressure in adulthood strongly supported our inference that certain components of the mother–infant interaction serve to regulate the later developmental paths of certain systems in their offspring. Subsequent research by Michael Meaney and his group, recently reviewed in this journal (Parent et al., 2005), found that two of these same behaviors (licking-grooming and high-arched nursing posture) predicted levels of adult offspring responses in a wide variety of other systems (e.g., adrenocortical and fear responses, cognitive function, and even maternal behavior in the next generation).

Variations in qualities of mother–infant relationships among humans thus appear to have deep biological roots in the form of their capacity to shape children's psychological and biological responses to their environment—effects that extend into adulthood.

LINKS TO HUMAN MENTAL PROCESSES

In applying these experimental results to early human development, we can begin to see how the psychological constructs of the attachment "bond" and the "traumatic" effects of maternal separation originate, in one case, in an unusual form of rapid early learning and, in the other, in the unexpected developmental regulatory functions being carried out by specific mother–infant interactions. These processes can be thought of as "underlying" the psychological concepts that people have invented to help think about complex behaviors and mental experiences. In humans, the early-learning processes and the many different regulating interactions that I have described above are the first experiences out of which mental representations and their associated affects arise. It seems likely that these mental structures combine the infants' newly developing capacities to remember and anticipate events and respond to symbolic cues with traces of the earlier functions of the maternal regulatory interactions, through processes similar to the functional links involved in the associative conditioning of physiological responses. Thus, the "internal working model" of attachment theory is constructed as early biological regulatory interactions become linked to later-developing memories, expectations, and affect states by the many associations of physical and psychological events during this developmental transition period between infancy and childhood, in the same way that the salivation of Pavlov's dogs became linked to the expectation of food through a series of prior associations. This may help explain the visceral sensations accompanying the vicissitudes of close human relationships even after the development of self-regulation of affect and motivation come to supplant the sensorimotor, thermal, and nutrient-based regulatory systems that are hidden within the observable interactions of younger infants with their mothers (Polan and Hofer, 1999).

The future directions of this research are, first, to extend our understanding of the actual links connecting specific mother–infant interactions (such as touch, voice, imitation) with developing psychological processes (on the one hand) and with cellular/molecular brain processes via neural and hormonal pathways (on the other); and, second, to find out how these interactions exert their effects on the developmental paths of behavior and biological systems, from infancy into adulthood.

Recommended Reading

Bowlby, J. (1982). (See References)
Cassidy, J., & Shaver, P.R. (Eds.). (1999). *Handbook of attachment theory and research.* New York: Guilford Publications.
Hofer, M.A. (2002). The riddle of development. In D.J. Lewkowicz & R. Lickliter (Eds.), *Conceptions of Development* (pp. 5–30) Philadelphia: Psychology Press.
Insel, T.R., & Fernald, R.D. (2004). How the brain processes social information: Searching for the social brain. *Annual Review of Neuroscience, 27,* 697–722.

Acknowledgments—This work was supported by project grants and a Research Scientist Award from the National Institutes of Mental Health and by the Sackler Institute for Developmental Psychobiology at Columbia University.

Note

1. Address Correspondence to Myron A. Hofer, MD, Professor and Director, The Sackler Institute for Developmental Psychobiology, Columbia University College of Physicians and Surgeons, New York State Psychiatric Institute, 1051 Riverside Drive, Unit #40, New York, NY 10032; e-mail: mah6@columbia.edu.

References

Bowlby, J. (1982). *Attachment* (2nd ed.). New York: Basic Books.
Hofer, M.A. (1984). Relationships as regulators: A psychobiologic perspective on bereavement. *Psychosomatic Medicine, 46,* 183–197.
Hofer, M.A. (1994). Early relationships as regulators of infant physiology and behavior. *Acta Paediatrica, 397*(Suppl.), 9–18.
Hofer, M.A. (1996). Multiple regulators of ultrasonic vocalization in the infant rat. *Psychoneuroendocrinology, 21,* 203–217.
Moriceau, S., & Sullivan, R. (2005). Neurobiology of infant attachment. *Developmental Psychobiology, 47,* 230–246.
Myers, M.M., Shair, H.N., & Hofer, M.A. (1992). Feeding in infancy: Short- and long-term effects on cardiovascular function. *Experientia, 48,* 322–333.

Parent, C., Zhang, T., Caldji, C., Bagot, R., Champagne, F., Pruessner, J., & Meaney, M. (2005). Maternal care and individual differences in defensive responses. *Current Directions in Psychological Science, 14,* 229–233.

Polan, H.J., & Hofer, M.A. (1999). Psychobiological origins of infant attachment and separation responses. In J. Cassidy & P.R. Shaver (Eds.), *Handbook of attachment theory and research* (pp. 162–180). New York: Guilford Publications.

Sullivan, R.M., Hofer, M.A., & Brake, S.C. (1986). Olfactory-guided orientation in neonatal rats is enhanced by a conditional change in behavior state. *Developmental Psychobiology, 19,* 615–623.

Winberg, J. (2005). Mother and newborn baby: Mutual regulation of physiology and behavior— A selective review. *Developmental Pychobiology, 47,* 219–229.

This article has been reprinted as it originally appeared in *Current Directions in Psychological Science*. Citation information for this article as originally published appears above.

Children of the Affluent: Challenges to Well-Being

Suniya S. Luthar and Shawn J. Latendresse[1]
Teachers College, Columbia University

Abstract

Growing up in the culture of affluence can connote various psychosocial risks. Studies have shown that upper-class children can manifest elevated disturbance in several areas—such as substance use, anxiety, and depression—and that two sets of factors seem to be implicated, that is, excessive pressures to achieve and isolation from parents (both literal and emotional). Whereas stereotypically, affluent youth and poor youth are respectively thought of as being at "low risk" and "high risk," comparative studies have revealed more similarities than differences in their adjustment patterns and socialization processes. In the years ahead, psychologists must correct the long-standing neglect of a group of youngsters treated, thus far, as not needing their attention. Family wealth does not automatically confer either wisdom in parenting or equanimity of spirit; whereas children rendered atypical by virtue of their parents' wealth are undoubtedly privileged in many respects, there is also, clearly, the potential for some nontrivial threats to their psychological well-being.

Keywords

affluence; risk; contextual influences; socioeconomic status

Children of upper-class, highly educated parents are generally assumed to be at "low risk," but recent evidence suggests that they can face several unacknowledged pressures. In this article, we describe programmatic research relevant to this issue. We begin by characterizing the samples of youth we have studied across suburban communities in the Northeast. We then provide an overview of findings of problems in various spheres of adjustment and discuss associated implications for research, practice, and policy.

RESEARCH INVOLVING UPPER-CLASS SAMPLES

Since the late 1990s, our group has accumulated data on three cohorts of youth from high-income communities; characteristics of these cohorts are summarized in Table 1. The first, which we refer to as Cohort I, consisted of 264 tenth graders attending a suburban high school serving three contiguous towns.[2] These students were followed annually through their senior year, and as sophomores, we contrasted them with 224 tenth graders in an inner-city school.

Cohort II encompassed 302 middle school students from another high-income town, whom we studied when they were in the sixth and seventh grades (Luthar & Becker, 2002). Cohort III, subsequently recruited from the same community as Cohort II, incorporated all children attending the sixth grade during the 1998–1999 academic year, and these students were then followed annually (11th-grade assessments had been completed at the time of writing this

Table 1. *Characteristics of the Samples*

Source and sample	N	Minority ethnicity in sample (%)	Eligible for free or reduced lunch in school (%)	Median annual family income in region (census)	Adults with graduate or professional degrees in region (%; census)
Luthar & D'Avanzo (1999)					
Suburban Cohort I: 10th graders followed through high school	264	18	1	$80,000–$102,000	24-37
Comparison sample: inner-city 10th graders	224	87	86	$35,000	5
Luthar & Becker (2002)					
Suburban Cohort II: 6th and 7th graders	302	8	3	$120,000	33
Luthar & Latendresse (in press)					
Suburban Cohort III: 6th graders followed annually through high school (ongoing)	314	7	3	$125,000	33
Comparison sample: inner-city 6th graders followed through 8th grade	300	80	79	$27,000	6

report). In parallel, we obtained annual assessments of an inner-city middle school sample, enabling further comparisons of youngsters from widely disparate sociodemographic settings.

EVIDENCE OF ADJUSTMENT DISTURBANCES

The first set of questions addressed with Cohort I was focused on substance use and related problems (Luthar & D'Avanzo, 1999), and descriptive analyses showed many signs of trouble among the suburban students. These youngsters reported significantly higher use of cigarettes, alcohol, marijuana, and hard drugs than did their inner-city counterparts, and also showed elevations in comparison with national norms. Suburban teens also reported significantly higher anxiety and somewhat higher depression than did inner-city youth. In comparison with normative samples, girls in the suburbs were three times more likely to report clinically significant levels of depression.

Also disturbing were findings on correlates of substance use. Among affluent (but not inner-city) youth, substance use was linked with depression and anxiety, suggesting efforts to self-medicate; this "negative affect" type of substance use tends to be sustained over time, rather than remitting soon after the teen years. In addition, among suburban boys (but not other subgroups in the study), popularity with classmates was linked with high substance use, suggesting that the peer group may endorse and even encourage substance use among affluent teenage boys.

In Cohort II, we saw no evidence of disturbance among the sixth graders, but among the seventh graders, some problems were beginning to emerge (Luthar & Becker, 2002). Among the older girls, for example, rates of clinically significant depressive symptoms were twice as high as those in normative samples. Whereas no boys in the sixth grade had used alcohol or marijuana, 7% of seventh-grade boys reported having drunk alcohol until intoxicated or using marijuana about once a month. Finally, results supported the earlier findings on correlates of substance use, which had significant links with depression and anxiety in this middle school sample, and with peer popularity among the seventh-grade boys.

In Cohort III, as well, preliminary data showed that suburban sixth graders scored below national norms on depression and anxiety, and also had lower scores than inner-city comparison youth. Once again, however, some signs of trouble began to emerge by the seventh grade, with popular students, for example, reporting significantly higher levels of substance use than others (Luthar & Sexton, 2004). We are currently examining different developmental pathways to problems and to well-being from pre- through midadolescence.

WHY MIGHT "PRIVILEGED" YOUTH BE TROUBLED?

In exploring pathways to maladjustment in affluent suburbia, we considered two sets of potential antecedents in our study of Cohort II. The first encompassed *achievement pressures*. Statistical analyses showed, in fact, that children with very high perfectionist strivings—those who saw achievement failures as personal failures—had relatively high depression, anxiety, and substance use, as did those who indicated that their parents overemphasized their accomplishments, valuing them disproportionately more than their personal character (Luthar & Becker, 2002).

The second potential antecedent was *isolation from adults,* both literal and emotional. Among upper-middle-class families, secondary school students are often left home alone for several hours each week, with many parents believing that this promotes self-sufficiency. Similarly, suburban children's needs for emotional closeness may often suffer as the demands of professional parents' careers erode relaxed "family time" and youngsters are shuttled between various after-school activities. Again, results showed that both literal and emotional isolation were linked to distress as well as substance use.

We next sought to explore family functioning in greater depth among sixth graders in Cohort III and, simultaneously, their inner-city counterparts. A common assumption is that parents are more accessible to high- than to low-income youth, but our data showed otherwise (Luthar & Latendresse, in press). We considered children's perceptions of seven aspects of parenting, and average ratings on four of these dimensions were similar for the two sets of students: felt closeness to mothers, felt closeness to fathers, parental values emphasizing integrity, and regularity of eating dinner with parents. Inner-city students did fare more poorly than suburban students on two of the remaining three dimensions—parental criticism and lack of after-school supervision—but at the same time, they did significantly better than suburban students on the last dimension, parental expectations.

Results also revealed the surprising unique significance of children's eating dinner with at least one parent on most nights. Even after the other six parenting dimensions (including emotional closeness both to mothers and to fathers) were taken into account, this simple family routine was linked not only to children's self-reported adjustment, but also to their performance at school. Striking, too, were the similarities of links involving family dining among families ostensibly easily able to arrange for shared leisure time and those who had to cope with the sundry exigencies of everyday life in poverty.

Subsequent analyses with Cohort III students and their inner-city counterparts when they were in the seventh grade revealed similarities in peer-group influences as well (Luthar & Sexton, 2004). Early adolescents at both socioeconomic extremes showed admiration for classmates who openly flouted authority. In the suburban context, high peer status was linked with overt displays of low academic effort, disobedience at school, aggressiveness among girls, and substance use among boys, and in the urban context, high peer status was associated with aggression and substance use among both boys and girls. Also noteworthy were startlingly strong links between physical attractiveness and peer popularity among affluent girls. This variable alone explained more than half the variation in their popularity scores, suggesting particularly high emphasis on physical appearance among this subgroup of girls (the links between attractiveness and popularity were substantially weaker among inner-city girls and among both groups of boys). All in all, the substantive message was that affluent adolescents, just like their inner-city counterparts, valued some peer attributes that could potentially compromise overall competence or well-being.

DOES REBELLION AMONG AFFLUENT TEENS REALLY "MATTER"?

All adolescents might be drawn to overt forms of rebellion, but it is quite plausible that wealthy youth, unlike their poor counterparts, can dabble in drug use or delinquency without any substantive damage to their life prospects, given various safety nets (i.e., concerned adults and access to high-quality treatment services). To examine this possibility, we returned to our high school Cohort I data, as older teens reflect more variability on such forms of behavioral deviance than middle school students do. Once again, our findings showed that youth at the socio-economic extremes were more similar than different (Luthar & Ansary, in press). In both settings, we found a distinct subgroup of teens who manifested multiple behavior problems—substance use, delinquency, poor interest in academics—and had school grades that were significantly lower than the average. Although the findings on urban adolescents were unsurprising in light of prior empirical evidence, the results on affluent youth were noteworthy in indicating that, despite the resources ostensibly available to them, nearly 1 of every 10 teenagers in this cohort exhibited high levels of behavior disturbances across multiple domains, and concurrently experienced significant risk for poor grades during the sophomore year of high school.

We also examined substance use among this subgroup of suburban sophomores annually through the remainder of high school (McMahon & Luthar, 2004). Twenty percent of these students showed persistently high substance use across time. Furthermore, across all three assessments, this group also showed relatively high levels of depression and physiologically manifest anxiety (e.g., nausea, difficulty breathing), as well as poor grades and negative teacher ratings. For as many as one in five of these affluent youth, therefore, high substance use, coexisting with depression, anxiety, and both behavioral and academic problems, was sustained up to the age of 18 years.

IMPLICATIONS FOR INTERVENTIONS

All is not necessarily well among children of the affluent. Across three suburban cohorts, a nontrivial proportion of youth reported diverse adjustment problems, and disconnectedness in families and pressured lifestyles constituted discernible challenges (for parallel evidence among adult samples, see Csikszentmihalyi, 1999; Kasser, 2002; Myers, 2000).

Why do affluent youth have these problems—despite all the mental health services ostensibly available? One possibility is that although high-income parents are generally willing to place overtly troubled youth in psychotherapy or on medication, they are less eager to delve into the less "conspicuous" problems in their children, in themselves, or in family processes more generally. Research has shown, for example, that parents in general tend to be aware when their children are depressed, but tend not to seek professional help unless symptoms include those that inconvenience adults, such as disobedience or asthma (Puura et al., 1998).

Upper-class parents can be particularly reluctant to seek help for the less visible problems because of privacy concerns, as well as embarrassment. Affluent adults are often very concerned about keeping family troubles private; this is not surprising, as misfortunes of the wealthy tend to evoke a malicious pleasure in people who are less well-off (a phenomenon called *schadenfreude*; see Feather & Sherman, 2002). Upper-class parents also can feel more compelled than most to maintain a veneer of well-being, feeling that "those at the top are supposed to be better able to handle their problems than those further down the scale" (Wolfe & Fodor, 1996, p. 80).

Then there are realities of everyday lives that impede change. In the subculture of affluent suburbia, overscheduled days are often the norm for young people, with high school students participating in numerous activities, which can then be logged on college applications. The careers of many parents, similarly, do in fact demand long work hours: Job sharing and flexible hours are not an option for chief executive officers or university presidents. At the same time, these careers do bring many personal rewards, including the gratification of mastering substantial professional challenges, and of providing well for stellar educations and leisure activities for the next generation. Few people would blithely repudiate such rewards.

Also relevant is practitioners' perseverance—or lack thereof—in pursuing nascent signs of trouble. School psychologists, for example, often hesitate to express concerns to high-income parents, anticipating resistance and sometimes even threats of lawsuits. Consequently (and paradoxically), wealthy youth can end up having less access to school-based counseling services than do students who are less well-off (Pollak & Schaffer, 1985). Clinicians may also minimize problems they see among the wealthy. The same symptoms are more often viewed as signs of mental illness among the poor than among the affluent; by corollary, the rich are more often dismissed as "not needing help" even when they report distress commensurate with that of others typically judged to be needing assistance (Luthar & Sexton, 2004).

Even if affluent youth do, in fact, receive high-quality psychiatric care, it should be emphasized that this is no substitute for strong attachments with parents. Decades of work on children's mental health policies have established that psychotherapy to address crystallized maladjustment is largely unproductive as long as the child's everyday life continues to present major challenges to adjustment (Knitzer, 2000).

In the future, an expedient first step toward addressing these issues would be to raise awareness of the potential costs of overscheduled, competitive lifestyles (Luthar & Sexton, 2004). This can be done effectively via books comprehensible to the lay public, such as those by Kasser (2002) and Myers (2000). Although obviously not panaceas, such dissemination efforts could begin to sensitize caregivers to risks in the context of affluence—risks that they (like developmental scientists) may have been only faintly aware of in the past.

Consideration of these issues is important not only for the families themselves, but also for society in general. Many children of highly educated, affluent parents will likely come to assume positions of influence in society, and their own equanimity of spirit may have far-reaching ramifications. Depression vastly impairs productivity. And people who are unhappy, with a fragile, meager sense of self, can be more acquisitive than philanthropic, focused more on gaining more for themselves than on improving the lot of others (Diener & Biswas-Diener, 2002).

CONCLUSIONS

Until the 1970s, developmental scientists had largely ignored children in poverty, and it is critical to correct the neglect of another group of youngsters heretofore invisible in psychological science: those in high-income families. Systematic research is needed on the generalizability of research results obtained thus far. Scientists need to establish, for instance, whether elevated distress or pressured lifestyles occur in wealthy metropolitan locations, and not just in suburban communities. It will also be important to determine whether these problems are discernible in nationally representative samples (assuming, of course, that high-income families are appropriately represented in them). Also critical are prospective studies that can indicate (a) whether problems such as depression or drug use generally represent temporary blips of adolescent angst among the wealthy or are early signs of continuing problems and, conversely, (b) if factors such as prolonged isolation and pressure within families do, in fact, set apart those teens who carry adolescent adjustment disturbances into adulthood. Finally, practitioners and parents must be alert to the risks potentially attached to wealth and status. The American dream spawns widespread beliefs that Ivy League educations and subsequently lucrative careers are critical for children's long-term happiness. In the sometimes single-minded pursuit of these goals, let us not lose sight of the possible costs to mental health and well-being of all concerned.

Recommended Reading

Csikszentmihalyi, M. (1999). (See References)
Kasser, T. (2002). (See References)
Luthar, S.S. (2003). The culture of affluence: Psychological costs of material wealth. *Child Development, 74,* 1581–1593.
Luthar, S.S., & Sexton, C. (2004). (See References)
Myers, D.G. (2000). (See References)

Acknowledgments—Preparation of this manuscript was supported by grants from the National Institutes of Health (RO1-DA10726, RO1-DA11498, RO1-DA14385), the William T. Grant Foundation, and the Spencer Foundation.

Notes

1. Address correspondence to Suniya S. Luthar, Teachers College, Columbia University, 525 West 120th St., Box 133, New York, NY 10027-6696.
2. We are currently examining effects of varying affluence across neighborhoods subsumed in wealthy townships.

References

Csikszentmihalyi, M. (1999). If we are so rich, why aren't we happy? *American Psychologist, 54,* 821–827.
Diener, E., & Biswas-Diener, R. (2002). Will money increase subjective well-being? *Social Indicators Research, 57,* 119–169.

Feather, N.T., & Sherman, R. (2002). Envy, resentment, Schadenfreude, and sympathy: Reactions to deserved and undeserved achievement and subsequent failure. *Personality and Social Psychology Bulletin, 28,* 953–961.

Kasser, T. (2002). *The high price of materialism.* Cambridge, MA: MIT Press.

Knitzer, J. (2000). Early childhood mental health services: A policy and systems development perspective. In J.P. Shonkoff & S.J. Meisels (Eds.), *Handbook of early childhood intervention* (2nd ed., pp. 416–438). New York: Cambridge University Press.

Luthar, S.S., & Ansary, N.S. (in press). Dimensions of adolescent rebellion: Risks for academic failure among high- and low-income youth. *Development and Psychopathology.*

Luthar, S.S., & Becker, B.E. (2002). Privileged but pressured: A study of affluent youth. *Child Development, 73,* 1593–1610.

Luthar, S.S., & D'Avanzo, K. (1999). Contextual factors in substance use: A study of suburban and inner-city adolescents. *Development and Psychopathology, 11,* 845–867.

Luthar, S.S., & Latendresse, S.J. (in press). Comparable "risks" at the SES extremes: Pre-adolescents' perceptions of parenting. *Development and Psychopathology.*

Luthar, S.S., & Sexton, C. (2004). The high price of affluence. In R.V. Kail (Ed.), *Advances in child development* (Vol. 32, pp. 126–162). San Diego, CA: Academic Press.

McMahon, T.J., & Luthar, S.S. (2004). *Substance use, psychopathology, and social competence: A longitudinal study of affluent, suburban, high school students.* Manuscript submitted for publication.

Myers, D.G. (2000). *The American paradox: Spiritual hunger in an age of plenty.* New Haven, CT: Yale University Press.

Pollak, J.M., & Schaffer, S. (1985). The mental health clinician in the affluent public school setting. *Clinical Social Work Journal, 13,* 341–355.

Puura, K., Almqvist, F., Tamminen, T., Piha, J., Kumpulainen, K., Raesaenen, E., Moilanen, I., & Koivisto, A.M. (1998). Children with symptoms of depression: What do adults see? *Journal of Child Psychology and Psychiatry and Allied Disciplines, 39,* 577–585.

Wolfe, J.L., & Fodor, I.G. (1996). The poverty of privilege: Therapy with women of the "upper classes." *Women & Therapy, 18,* 73–89.

This article has been reprinted as it originally appeared in *Current Directions in Psychological Science*. Citation information for this article as originally published appears above.

Siblings' Direct and Indirect Contributions to Child Development

Gene H. Brody[1]

Department of Child and Family Development and Center for Family Research, University of Georgia

Abstract

Since the early 1980s, a growing body of research has described the contributions of sibling relationships to child and adolescent development. Interactions with older siblings promote young children's language and cognitive development, their understanding of other people's emotions and perspectives, and, conversely, their development of antisocial behavior. Studies address the ways in which parents' experiences with older children contribute to their rearing of younger children, which in turn contributes to the younger children's development. Finally, by virtue of having a sibling, children may receive differential treatment from their parents. Under some conditions, differential treatment is associated with emotional and behavioral problems in children.

Keywords

siblings; interaction; development; differential treatment

The first studies of the contributions that older siblings make to their younger brothers' and sisters' development were conducted in Britain around the turn of the 20th century by Sir Francis Galton, a cousin of Charles Darwin. Sibling research, however, only recently has begun to address many of the issues that concern families. Parents, clinicians, and now researchers in developmental psychology recognize the significance of the sibling relationship as a contributor to family harmony or discord and to individual children's development. Since the early 1980s, a growing interest in the family has prompted research on those aspects of sibling relationships that contribute to children's cognitive, social, and emotional adjustment. These contributions can be direct, occurring as a result of siblings' encounters with one another, or indirect, occurring through a child's impact on parents that influences the care that other brothers and sisters receive. Differential treatment by parents is a third way in which having a sibling may contribute to child development. Children may be treated differently by their parents than their siblings are, or at least believe that they are treated differently. The development of this belief has implications for children's and adolescents' mental health. In this article, I present an overview of the ways in which siblings' direct and indirect influences and parental differential treatment contribute to child development.

SIBLINGS' DIRECT CONTRIBUTIONS TO DEVELOPMENT

Currently, research suggests that naturally occurring teaching and caregiving experiences benefit cognitive, language, and psychosocial development in both older and younger siblings. Studies conducted in children's homes and in laboratories show that older siblings in middle childhood can teach new cognitive concepts and language skills to their younger siblings in early childhood. Across the middle childhood years, older siblings become better teachers as they learn how to simplify tasks for their younger siblings. The ability to adjust their teaching behaviors to their younger siblings' capacities increases as older siblings develop the ability to take other people's perspectives (Maynard, 2002). Older siblings who assume teaching and caregiving roles earn higher reading and language achievement scores, gain a greater sense of competence in the caregiving role, and learn more quickly to balance their self-concerns with others' needs than do older siblings who do not assume these roles with their younger siblings (Zukow-Goldring, 1995). When caregiving demands on the older sibling become excessive, however, they may interfere with the older child's time spent on homework or involvement in school activities. Caregiving responsibilities during middle childhood and adolescence can compromise older siblings' school performance and behavioral adjustment (Marshall et al., 1997).

Children who are nurtured by their older siblings become sensitive to other people's feelings and beliefs (Dunn, 1988). As in all relationships, though, nurturance does not occur in isolation from conflict. Sibling relationships that are characterized by a balance of nurturance and conflict can provide a unique opportunity for children to develop the ability to understand other people's emotions and viewpoints, to learn to manage anger and resolve conflict, and to provide nurturance themselves. Indeed, younger siblings who experience a balance of nurturance and conflict in their sibling relationships have been found to be more socially skilled and have more positive peer relationships compared with children who lack this experience (Hetherington, 1988).

Sibling relationships also have the potential to affect children's development negatively. Younger siblings growing up with aggressive older siblings are at considerable risk for developing conduct problems, performing poorly in school, and having few positive experiences in their relationships with their peers (Bank, Patterson, & Reid, 1996). The links between older siblings' antisocial behavior and younger siblings' conduct problems are stronger for children living in disadvantaged neighborhoods characterized by high unemployment rates and pervasive poverty than for children living in more advantaged neighborhoods (Brody, Ge et al., 2003). Younger siblings who live in disadvantaged neighborhoods have more opportunities than do children living in more affluent areas to practice the problematic conduct that they learn during sibling interactions as they interact with peers who encourage antisocial behavior.

The importance of the sibling relationship is probably best demonstrated by older siblings' ability to buffer younger siblings from the negative effects of family turmoil. Younger siblings whose older siblings provide them with emotional support (caring, acceptance, and bolstering of self-esteem) during bouts of intense, angry interparental conflict show fewer signs of behavioral or emotional problems than do children whose older siblings are less supportive (Jenkins, 1992).

SIBLINGS' INDIRECT CONTRIBUTIONS

Conventional wisdom suggests that parents' experiences with older children influence their expectations of subsequent children and the child-rearing strategies that parents consider effective. Similarly, the experiences that other adults, particularly teachers, have with older siblings may influence their expectations and treatment of younger siblings. Research has confirmed the operation of these indirect effects on younger siblings' development. Whiteman and Buchanan (2002) found that experiences with earlier-born children contributed to parents' expectations about their younger children's likelihood of experiencing conduct problems, using drugs, displaying rebellious behavior, or being helpful and showing concern for others. Teachers are not immune from the predisposing effects of experiences with older siblings. As a result of having an older sibling in class or hearing about his or her accomplishments or escapades, teachers develop expectations regarding the younger sibling's academic ability and conduct even before the younger child becomes their student (Bronfenbrenner, 1977). Some parents and teachers translate these expectations into parenting and teaching practices they subsequently use with younger siblings that influence the younger children's beliefs about their academic abilities, interests, and choice of friends; children often choose friends whom they perceive to be similar to themselves.

Rather than viewing behavioral influence as flowing in one direction, from parents to children, developmental psychologists now recognize that these influences are reciprocal. The behaviors that children use during everyday interactions with their parents partially determine the behaviors that the parents direct toward their children. Children with active or emotionally intense personalities receive different, usually more negative, parenting than do children with calm and easygoing personalities. Some studies suggest that older siblings' individual characteristics may contribute indirectly to the quality of parenting that younger siblings receive. For example, East (1998) discovered that negative experiences with an earlier-born child lead parents to question their ability to provide good care for their younger children and to lower their expectations for their younger children's behavior.

In our research, my colleagues and I explored the specific ways in which older siblings' characteristics contribute to the quality of parenting that younger siblings receive, which in turn contributes to younger siblings' development of conduct problems and depressive symptoms. The premise of the study was simple. Rearing older siblings who are doing well in school and are well liked by other children provides parents with opportunities for basking in their children's achievements. (Basking is a phenomenon in which one's psychological well-being increases because of the accomplishments of persons to whom one is close.) Using a longitudinal research design in which we collected data from families for 4 years, we found that academically and socially competent older siblings contributed to an increase in their mothers' self-esteem and a decrease in their mothers' depressive symptoms. Positive changes in mothers' psychological functioning forecast their use of adjustment-promoting parenting practices with younger siblings. Over time, these practices forecast high levels of self-control and low levels of behavior problems and depressive symptoms in the younger siblings (Brody, Kim, Murry, & Brown, 2003). We expect future research to clarify further the indirect pathways through which siblings influence one another's development, including the processes by which children's negative characteristics affect their parents' child-rearing practices. A difficult-to-rear older sibling, for example, may contribute over time to decreases in his or her parents' psychological well-being, resulting in increased tension in the family. Under these circumstances, the parents' negativity and distraction decrease the likelihood that a younger sibling will experience parenting that promotes self-worth, academic achievement, and social skills.

PARENTAL DIFFERENTIAL TREATMENT

Any discussion of siblings' contributions to development would be incomplete without acknowledging parental differential treatment. Having a sibling creates a context in which parental behavior assumes symbolic value, as children use it as a barometer indicating the extent to which they are loved, rejected, included, or excluded by their parents. Children's and adolescents' beliefs that they receive less warmth and more negative treatment from their parents than do their siblings is associated with poor emotional and behavioral functioning (Reiss, Neiderhiser, Hetherington, & Plomin, 2000).

Not all children who perceive differential treatment develop these problems, however. Differential parental treatment is associated with poor adjustment in a child only when the quality of the child's individual relationship with his or her parents is distant and negative. The association between differential treatment and adjustment is weak for children whose parents treat them well, even when their siblings receive even warmer and more positive treatment (Feinberg & Hetherington, 2001). Children's perceptions of the legitimacy of differential treatment also help determine its contribution to their adjustment. Children who perceive their parents' differential behavior to be justified report fewer behavior problems than do children who consider it to be unjust, even under conditions of relatively high levels of differential treatment. Children and adolescents who perceive differential treatment as unfair experience low levels of self-worth and have high levels of behavior problems (Kowal, Kramer, Krull, & Crick, 2002). Children justify differential treatment by citing ways in which they and their siblings differ in age, personality, and special needs. Sensitive parenting entails treating children as their individual temperaments and developmental needs require. Nevertheless, it is important that children understand why parents treat siblings differently from one another so that they will be protected from interpreting the differences as evidence that they are not valued or worthy of love.

FUTURE DIRECTIONS

Considerable work is needed to provide a comprehensive understanding of the processes through which siblings influence one another's cognitive development, language development, psychological adjustment, and social skills. Current studies can best be considered "first generation" research. They describe associations between older and younger siblings' behaviors and characteristics. Some studies have demonstrated that the prediction of younger siblings' outcomes is more accurate if it is based on older siblings' characteristics plus parenting, rather than parenting alone (Brody, Kim et al., 2003). More research is needed to isolate influences other than parenting, such as shared genetics, shared environments, and social learning, before siblings' unique contributions to development can be specified. The next generation of research will address the ways in which sibling relationships contribute to children's self-images and personal identities, emotion regulation and coping skills, explanations of positive and negative events that occur in family and peer relationships, use of aggression, and involvement in high-risk behaviors.

Recommended Reading

Brody, G.H. (1998). Sibling relationship quality: Its causes and consequences. *Annual Review of Psychology, 49*, 1–24.
Feinberg, M., & Hetherington, E.M. (2001). (See References)
Kowal, A., Kramer, L., Krull, J.L., & Crick, N.R. (2002). (See References)
Maynard, A.E. (2002). (See References)
Whiteman, S.D., & Buchanan, C.M. (2002). (See References)

Acknowledgments—I would like to thank Eileen Neubaum-Carlan for helpful comments. Preparation of this article was partly supported by grants from the National Institute of Child Health and Human Development, the National Institute of Mental Health, and the National Institute on Alcohol Abuse and Alcoholism.

Note

1. Address correspondence to Gene H. Brody, University of Georgia, Center for Family Research, 1095 College Station Rd., Athens, GA 30602-4527.

References

Bank, L., Patterson, G.R., & Reid, J.B. (1996). Negative sibling interaction patterns as predictors of later adjustment problems in adolescent and young adult males. In G.H. Brody (Ed.), *Sibling relationships: Their causes and consequences* (pp. 197–229). Norwood, NJ: Ablex.
Brody, G.H., Ge, X., Kim, S.Y., Murry, V.M., Simons, R.L., Gibbons, F.X., Gerrard, M., & Conger, R. (2003). Neighborhood disadvantage moderates associations of parenting and older sibling problem attitudes and behavior with conduct disorders in African American children. *Journal of Consulting and Clinical Psychology, 71*, 211–222.
Brody, G.H., Kim, S., Murry, V.M., & Brown, A.C. (2003). Longitudinal direct and indirect pathways linking older sibling competence to the development of younger sibling competence. *Developmental Psychology, 39*, 618–628.
Bronfenbrenner, U. (1977). Toward an experimental ecology of human development. *American Psychologist, 32*, 513–531.
Dunn, J. (1988). Connections between relationships: Implications of research on mothers and siblings. In R.A. Hinde & J. Stevenson-Hinde (Eds.), *Relationships within families: Mutual influences* (pp. 168–180). New York: Oxford University Press.
East, P.L. (1998). Impact of adolescent childbearing on families and younger siblings: Effects that increase younger siblings' risk for early pregnancy. *Applied Developmental Science, 2*, 62–74.
Feinberg, M., & Hetherington, E.M. (2001). Differential parenting as a within-family variable. *Journal of Family Psychology, 15*, 22–37.
Hetherington, E.M. (1988). Parents, children, and siblings: Six years after divorce. In R.A. Hinde & J. Stevenson-Hinde (Eds.), *Relationships within families: Mutual influences* (pp. 311–331). New York: Oxford University Press.
Jenkins, J. (1992). Sibling relationships in disharmonious homes: Potential difficulties and protective effects. In F. Boer & J. Dunn (Eds.), *Children's sibling relationships: Developmental and clinical issues* (pp. 125–138). Hillsdale, NJ: Erlbaum.

Kowal, A., Kramer, L., Krull, J.L., & Crick, N.R. (2002). Children's perceptions of the fairness of parental preferential treatment and their socioemotional well-being. *Journal of Family Psychology, 16,* 297–306.

Marshall, N.L., Garcia-Coll, C., Marx, F., McCartney, K., Keefe, N., & Ruh, J. (1997). After-school time and children's behavioral adjustment. *Merrill-Palmer Quarterly, 43,* 497–514.

Maynard, A.E. (2002). Cultural teaching: The development of teaching skills in Maya sibling interactions. *Child Development, 73,* 969–982.

Reiss, D., Neiderhiser, J.M., Hetherington, E.M., & Plomin, R. (2000). *The relationship code: Deciphering genetic and social influences on adolescent development.* Cambridge, MA: Harvard University Press.

Whiteman, S.D., & Buchanan, C.M. (2002). Mothers' and children's expectations for adolescence: The impact of perceptions of an older sibling's experience. *Journal of Family Psychology, 16,* 157–171.

Zukow-Goldring, P.G. (1995). Sibling caregiving. In M.H. Bornstein (Ed.), *Handbook of parenting: Vol. 3. Status and social conditions of parenting* (pp. 177–208). Mahwah, NJ: Erlbaum.

This article has been reprinted as it originally appeared in *Current Directions in Psychological Science*. Citation information for this article as originally published appears above.

Understanding Popularity in the Peer System

Antonius H.N. Cillessen[1]
University of Connecticut

Amanda J. Rose
University of Missouri-Columbia

Abstract

Much research has focused on youth who are rejected by peers; who engage in negative behavior, including aggression; and who are at risk for adjustment problems. Recently, researchers have become increasingly interested in high-status youth. A distinction is made between two groups of high-status youth: those who are genuinely well liked by their peers and engage in predominantly prosocial behaviors and those who are seen as popular by their peers but are not necessarily well liked. The latter group of youth is well known, socially central, and emulated, but displays a mixed profile of prosocial as well as aggressive and manipulative behaviors. Research now needs to address the distinctive characteristics of these two groups and their developmental precursors and consequences. Of particular interest are high-status and socially powerful aggressors and their impact on their peers. The heterogeneity of high-status youth complicates the understanding of the social dynamics of the peer group, but will lead to new and important insights into the developmental significance of peer relationships.

Keywords

peer relations; popularity; social status

Developmental psychologists continue to be interested in the social structure and dynamics of the peer group in childhood and adolescence. Peer status is an important construct in their research. In the past, much of this research has been driven by a concern for children and adolescents with low social status, who operate at the fringe of the peer system and may be categorized as rejected. As a result, much has been learned about the origins of peer rejection and its effects on development (Asher & Coie, 1990). More recently, researchers have become increasingly interested in peer-group members with high social status. Interestingly, high-status children and adolescents do not form a uniform group.

For example, consider the profiles of two eighth graders, Tim and Jason. Tim is well liked by his peers. He is genuinely nice to others and helps out when needed. Tim is athletic but does not use his physical abilities to aggress against others. In fact, Tim tends to avoid even verbal confrontations when possible, preferring instead to find prosocial ways of solving conflicts. Compared with Tim, Jason is better known by his classmates but he is not necessarily well liked. Even peers who do not know him personally know who he is. Many of Jason's classmates imitate his style of dress and taste in music and would like to be better friends with him so they could be part of the in-crowd. Jason can be very nice to other kids but can also intimidate them when provoked or angry, or can manipulate social situations to his advantage.

Developmental psychologists know a fair amount about youth like Tim. Youth who are well liked by others are categorized by peer-relations researchers as *sociometrically popular*. Sociometrically popular youth generally display high levels of pro-social and cooperative behavior and low levels of aggression (Rubin, Bukowski, & Parker, 1998). But although developmentalists would refer to Tim as sociometrically popular, he is not the type of person most youth would consider one of their "popular" peers. They think of popular peers as those who, like Jason, are well known, socially central, and emulated (Adler & Adler, 1998). In recent years, developmentalists have begun to study more seriously youth like Jason, referring to them as *perceived popular*, rather than sociometrically popular. Although evidence suggests that perceived-popular youth have aggressive traits in addition to prosocial ones, youth aspire to be popular like Jason more than they aspire to be like Tim (Adler & Adler, 1998). Accordingly, it is important to consider seriously the meaning and function of these divergent forms of popularity.

In this article, we consider how perceived-popular youth are similar to and different from sociometrically popular youth. Specifically, we discuss: (a) the conceptualization and measurement of sociometric and perceived popularity, (b) the social behavior of sociometrically and perceived-popular youth, and (c) the adjustment outcomes for the two groups. We conclude by outlining important directions for future research.

SOCIOMETRIC VERSUS PERCEIVED POPULARITY

Traditionally, the study of peer relations has focused on sociometric status, how well liked (or rejected) youth are by their peers (Asher & Coie, 1990; Coie & Cillessen, 1993). Several decades of research have provided data on the behavioral and adjustment correlates of sociometric status (Kupersmidt & Dodge, 2004). This research provides a crucial foundation for understanding peer relations.

Recently, researchers have begun to examine perceived popularity as a unique but equally important dimension. Educational sociologists have long recognized the social power (influence over others) of perceived-popular youth as evidenced by qualitative descriptions of them by their peers (Adler & Adler, 1998; Eder, 1985). Only in the past 5 to 10 years have researchers begun to study perceived popularity with quantitative methods.

Sociometric popularity is usually assessed with a peer-nomination procedure, in which participants are asked to name the peers in their grade who they like most and like least. Nominations for each question are counted and adjusted for grade size so that the data are comparable across grades (Coie, Dodge, & Coppotelli, 1982). Sociometric popularity for each person is represented with a score on a continuous scale (social preference) calculated by using the number of liked-most nominations minus the number of liked-least nominations he or she received. Alternatively, rather than using such scores, researchers may employ a categorical approach and identify sociometrically popular youth as those with many liked-most and few liked-least nominations.

In early qualitative research, educational sociologists using ethnographic methods identified perceived-popular youth by simply observing which classmates were referred to as popular by their peers (Adler & Adler, 1998; Eder, 1985). In recent quantitative studies, however, perceived popularity has been derived from peer nominations (i.e., participants name who they see as most popular and who they see as least popular; Cillessen & Mayeux, 2004; LaFontana & Cillessen, 2002; Parkhurst & Hopmeyer, 1998; Rose, Swenson, & Waller, 2004). Scores on a continuous scale of perceived popularity have been derived from the number of most-popular nominations or the number of most-popular minus least-popular nominations. In other studies, researchers have taken a categorical approach and identified youth with high perceived popularity as those with many most-popular nominations and few least-popular nominations. Interestingly, in neither the original ethnographic research nor the recent quantitative studies did researchers provide participants with an a priori definition of popularity; rather, they relied on the participants' intuitive understanding of the concept. Recently, researchers have begun to map the meanings children and adolescents ascribe to "popularity," again without providing an a priori definition (e.g., LaFontana & Cillessen, 2002). Findings from these studies show that children and adolescents associate a mixture of prosocial and antisocial traits and behaviors with perceived popularity.

Although there is overlap between sociometric and perceived popularity, the constructs are not redundant (LaFontana & Cillessen, 2002; Rose et al., 2004). Consider one study that employed a categorical approach to identify sociometrically popular and perceived-popular youth (Parkhurst & Hopmeyer, 1998). Only 36% of sociometrically popular students were also perceived popular, and only 29% of perceived-popular students were also sociometrically popular. There is enough distinction between the two constructs to determine similarities as well as differences between the characteristics of sociometrically popular and perceived-popular youth.

BEHAVIORAL PROFILES

Research on the behavioral profiles of sociometrically and perceived-popular youth has revealed similarities and differences. Both kinds of youth are found to be prosocial and co-operative. However, whereas sociometrically popular youth score very low on aggression, perceived popularity is positively associated with aggression (see Rubin et al., 1998, for a review of the behavioral profiles of sociometrically popular youth).

In quantitative studies on how perceived popularity correlates with behavior, researchers have typically measured overt and relational aggression separately. Overt aggression refers to physical assaults and direct verbal abuse. Relational aggression is aimed at damaging relationships and includes behaviors such as ignoring or excluding a person and spreading rumors (Crick & Grotpeter, 1995). Both overt and relational aggression are related to perceived popularity. For example, Parkhurst and Hopmeyer (1998) found that youth who were perceived popular but not sociometrically popular were overtly aggressive. Rodkin, Farmer, Pearl, and Van Acker (2000) empirically discriminated a subgroup of "model" popular youth with high scores for affiliative (e.g., friendly) behaviors and low scores for overt aggression from a subgroup of "tough" popular youth with high scores for overt aggression and average scores for affiliative behavior. Studies in which both overt and relational aggression were assessed and in which perceived popularity was measured as a continuous variable demonstrated positive associations of both forms of aggression with perceived popularity (LaFontana & Cillessen, 2002; Rose et al., 2004).

Why would presumably aversive aggressive behaviors be associated with high status as indicated by perceived popularity? It may be that some children or adolescents use aggression in certain situations (e.g., when publicly provoked) or against certain people (e.g., competitors for social status) strategically to achieve or maintain perceived popularity. For example, perceived-popular youth may use overt or relational aggression to intimidate and deter competitors or other youth who in some way threaten their social standing. Consistent with this idea, a study by Vaillancourt, Hymel, and McDougall (2003) revealed an association between bullying and perceived popularity. Moreover, perceived-popular youth use a strategic combination of both aggressive and prosocial behaviors to manipulate peers in ways that result in high status (Hawley, 2003).

Recent longitudinal research supports the hypothesis that some youth deliberately act aggressively to enhance their perceived popularity. This research also suggests an especially important association between relational aggression and perceived popularity. In a 5-year longitudinal study (Cillessen & Mayeux, 2004), relational aggression was found to be more strongly related to later perceived popularity than was overt aggression. Similarly, another study (Rose et al., 2004) found that relational aggression was more strongly related to perceived popularity 6 months later than was overt aggression. Overt aggression may be related to perceived popularity because youth can display dominance through overtly aggressive acts. However, relational aggression may be especially effective for managing social power. For example, by selectively excluding others, youth may influence who is in the popular crowd and keep out those who threaten their social status. Engaging in other relationally aggressive behaviors, such as spreading rumors, affords one a degree of anonymity and therefore the opportunity to strategically hurt other people while hiding the appearance of being mean.

Research further indicates that the relation between aggression and perceived popularity may vary by age and gender. In our research, we found positive associations between overt and relational aggression and perceived popularity in 12- to 15-year-old adolescents (grades 6–9), but not in 9- to 11-year-old children (grades 3–5). This shift coincided with the transition from elementary school to middle school and may have been due to the fact that the social skills required to act aggressively in ways that lead to high status are complex and develop with age (LaFontana & Cillessen, 2002; Rose et al., 2004).

We also found that the link between relational aggression and perceived popularity was stronger for girls than for boys (Cillessen & Mayeux, 2004; Rose et al., 2004). Figure 1 illustrates this finding for data collected in eighth grade (Cillessen & Mayeux, 2004), but the pattern was similar across grades six through nine. As can be seen in Figure 1, relational aggression was positively associated with perceived popularity for both boys and girls but was a particularly strong predictor of high status for girls.

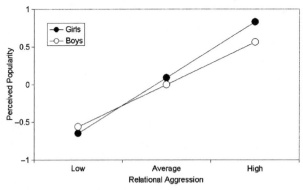

Fig. 1. Perceived popularity of girls and boys who exhibit low, average, and high levels of relational aggression (Cillessen & Mayeux, 2004).

ADJUSTMENT OUTCOMES

An important reason for studying peer relations is that experiences with peers may be predictive of personal adjustment. Accordingly, much research has addressed how sociometric status correlates with adjustment, and the research consistently indicates that sociometric popularity is predictive of positive adjustment both concurrently and in the future (Rubin et al., 1998). For example, sociometrically popular youth tend to be well adjusted emotionally and to have high-quality friendships.

Considerably less is known about the adjustment of perceived-popular youth. Previous research on status and behavior in the peer group leads to opposing expectations. On the one hand, because aggression is associated with behavior problems, one would expect similar behavior problems for popular youth who are aggressive. On the other hand, because high status in the peer group is associated with being well adjusted, one would expect that perceived popularity, even if achieved through aggressive means, is associated with positive adjustment. The limited evidence available at this time seems to favor the second expectation—that perceived popularity has immediate rewards (Hawley, 2003) without concurrent negative consequences (Rodkin et al., 2000). Hawley's (2003) research indicates that a mixture of prosocial behavior and coercive or aggressive behavior makes youth effective at getting what they want in social contexts. And the tough popular youth identified by Rodkin and his colleagues (2000) did not demonstrate elevated symptoms, such as depression or anxiety. The contradictory expectations may be reconciled if perceived-popular and aggressive youth experience benefits in the immediate social context of the adolescent peer group, but pay a price in terms of their long-term adjustment beyond adolescence.

Thus, we hypothesize that for perceived-popular youth, short-term advantages may be combined with long-term disadvantages. Establishing whether this is true will require long-term follow-up studies of such youth. Just as there are tough and model high-status subgroups (Rodkin et al., 2000), there may be two diverging developmental paths that popular youth follow into young adulthood. In one path, perceived-popular youth may continue to be influential and serve in leadership roles in later peer groups. In the other, they may no longer be socially central and successful when they move into new social contexts that have different reward structures and different criteria for social prominence. Which of these two pathways an individual follows may depend on whether he or she is able to strike the optimal, delicate balance between prosocial and Machiavellian behaviors, to gain both social preference as well as influence in new groups. Discovering how this balance may be achieved developmentally and how it may affect what pathway is followed in later life is an exciting avenue for future research.

CONCLUSIONS

Decades of research on sociometric popularity have produced consistent and important findings with potential practical application. Recent research suggests that the complex construct of perceived popularity needs to be incorporated into this research. Given all that is known about the negative developmental consequences of aggression, researchers need to learn why aggression sometimes leads to high status in the form of perceived popularity. Moreover, it will be important to learn whether aggressive perceived-popular youth are on a positive or negative developmental trajectory. Although they seem to benefit in the short term in the immediate social context of the peer group, the longer-term outcomes associated with their status and behavior are not yet known.

Researchers also must learn about the impact of perceived-popular aggressors on the development and adjustment of their peers. Of particular concern are youth who are victimized by them. The negative consequences of victimization may be exacerbated when the aggressor is socially central and powerful and therefore can easily engage other people in the victimization. Furthermore, perceived-popular youth may influence the development of antisocial behavior among their peers. Because perceived-popular youth are emulated, their antisocial or risky behaviors may disperse through the peer group especially quickly. Clearly, the function and impact of popularity in the peer context are complex; learning more about these processes will be challenging, but will yield important new insights into the social dynamics of peer groups across the life span.

Recommended Reading

Adler, P.A., & Adler, P. (1998). (See References)
Asher, S.R., & Coie, J.D. (1990). (See References)
Kupersmidt, J.B., & Dodge, K.A. (Eds.). (2004). (See References)

Note

1. Address correspondence to Antonius H.N. Cillessen, Department of Psychology, University of Connecticut, 406 Babbidge Rd., U-1020, Storrs, CT 06269-1020; e-mail: antonius.cillessen@uconn.edu.

References

Adler, P.A., & Adler, P. (1998). *Peer power: Preadolescent culture and identity.* New Brunswick, NJ: Rutgers University Press.
Asher, S.R., & Coie, J.D. (1990). *Peer rejection in childhood.* New York: Cambridge University Press.

Cillessen, A.H.N., & Mayeux, L. (2004). From censure to reinforcement: Developmental changes in the association between aggression and social status. *Child Development, 75*, 147–163.

Coie, J.D., & Cillessen, A.H.N. (1993). Peer rejection: Origins and effects on children's development. *Current Directions in Psychological Science, 2*, 89–92.

Coie, J.D., Dodge, K.A., & Coppotelli, H. (1982). Dimensions and types of social status: A cross-age perspective. *Developmental Psychology, 18*, 557–570.

Crick, N.R., & Grotpeter, J.K. (1995). Relational aggression, gender, and social-psychological adjustment. *Child Development, 66*, 710–722.

Eder, D. (1985). The cycle of popularity: Interpersonal relations among female adolescents. *Sociology of Education, 58*, 154–165.

Hawley, P.H. (2003). Prosocial and coercive configurations of resource control in early adolescence: A case for the well-adapted Machiavellian. *Merrill-Palmer Quarterly, 49*, 279–309.

Kupersmidt, J.B., & Dodge, K.A. (Eds.). (2004). *Children's peer relations: From development to intervention to policy.* Washington, DC: American Psychological Association.

LaFontana, K.M., & Cillessen, A.H.N. (2002). Children's stereotypes of popular and unpopular peers: A multi-method assessment. *Developmental Psychology, 38*, 635–647.

Parkhurst, J.T., & Hopmeyer, A.G. (1998). Sociometric popularity and peer-perceived popularity: Two distinct dimensions of peer status. *Journal of Early Adolescence, 18*, 125–144.

Rodkin, P.C., Farmer, T.W., Pearl, R., & Van Acker, R. (2000). Heterogeneity of popular boys: Antisocial and prosocial configurations. *Developmental Psychology, 36*, 14–24.

Rose, A.J., Swenson, L.P., & Waller, E.M. (2004). Overt and relational aggression and perceived popularity: Developmental differences in concurrent and prospective relations. *Developmental Psychology, 40*, 378–387.

Rubin, K.H., Bukowski, W.M., & Parker, J.G. (1998). Peer interactions, relationships, and groups. In W. Damon (Series Ed.) & N. Eisenberg (Vol. Ed.), *Handbook of child psychology: Vol. 3. Social, emotional, and personality development* (5th ed., pp. 619–700). New York: Wiley.

Vaillancourt, T., Hymel, S., & McDougall, P. (2003). Bullying is power: Implications for school-based intervention strategies. In M.J. Elias & J.E. Zins (Eds.), *Bullying, peer harassment, and victimization in the schools: The next generation of prevention* (pp. 157–176). New York: Haworth Press.

Section 1: Critical Thinking Questions

1. How do interactions with family members determine how one then interacts with others who are deemed different? What does this tell you about the impact of adult role models' behavior and attitudes on the behavior and attitudes of the children who look up to them?

2. How does attachment evolve throughout the lifespan? What sorts of relationships characterize the different points of development—infancy, childhood, and adolescence?

3. Describe the role of both "nature" and "nurture" during an individual's development. What kind of impact does each factor have on a person's growth and in defining who that person becomes as an adult?

4. Why is social interaction throughout the course of development so important? What functions and/or adaptive purposes does it serve?

This article has been reprinted as it originally appeared in *Current Directions in Psychological Science*. Citation information for this article as originally published appears above.

Section 2: Cognitive Neuroscience

In the late 1950s individuals from the academic fields of psychology and neuroscience began to work together to address questions aimed at understanding the neural underpinnings (neuroscience) of mental processes (cognition) and their behavioral manifestations (psychology). The papers presented in this section will underscore the unique and adaptive nature of the human brain, and how this contributes to the expansive and flexible nature of human behavior.

Amir Amedi (2005) and colleagues present fascinating data about the way in which the brains of blind individuals compensate for the lack of incoming visual information. The occipital cortex lies at the very back of the human brain, and is responsible for making use of the visual information received from the eyes. When individuals are born without functioning eyes, the portion of the brain that ordinarily helps with visual processing (the occipital cortex), takes up the responsibility of supplying extra support to other types of sensory information, specifically tactile reading and verbal language. In this paper the authors pose a critical question: does the part of the brain that "sees" reorganize in the context of visual deprivation or is this cortex flexible from birth; meaning that it innately has the capacity to process non-visual information? Amedi and colleagues contend that cortical development incorporates aspects of both processes. This complex interaction of neurophysiological processes is present not only in primary sensory parts of the brain, but also in portions of the brain known to support "higher" cognitive and emotional behaviors. Located behind the forehead, above the eyes, the human prefrontal cortex is believed to be the part of the brain that supports the behaviors that make us "human" including planning and executing ideas, abstract reasoning and decision-making, social interactions and many aspects of language. In human beings, the prefrontal cortex can be seen as a type of conductor of behavior, working closely with virtually every other part of the brain, and formulating, organizing, and overseeing human behavior. Naqvi, Shiv and Bechara (2006), discuss how a portion of the prefrontal cortex, the ventromedial prefrontal cortex (vmPFC), an area of the brain above the eye sockets, is critical for using emotional information to inform decision-making. Emotion is known to aid in a great deal of decision-making scenarios by creating a bodily state during the decision-making process that help to mark some options as advantageous, and some as disadvantageous. Once these associations have been made, the vmPFC is able to call on these previous experiences to inform present and future decisions. In humans, this system has evolved to help us make extremely rapid and socially-appropriate decisions based on what "feels right" (e.g. not hitting the person in front of us in line at the market when they are taking *forever* to pay for their purchase). Furthermore, it is thought that it is precisely this type of neural advancement in the connectivity and coordination of the prefrontal cortex that allows humans to make the moral and social decisions that make us human. Naqvi, Shiv and Bechara also underscore the importance of the amygdala in creating the body state that is remembered. The amygdala can be thought of the brain's "burglar alarm" in that it checks all incoming (and abstractly generated) stimuli and determines whether or not a response needs to be generated, and if necessary "sounds the alarm" and initiates a behavioral response. This process is most typically known as the "fight or flight" response, but the amygdala has also been shown to be essential for emotional learning. The next paper in the section, by Kevin LeBar (2007) provides a much richer description of how the human amygdala contributes to emotional memory. While a great deal of evidence has demonstrated the amygdala's critical role in the creation of emotional memories, little has been made of its function during memory retrieval. LeBar argues that the amygdala is comparably active when emotional memories are retrieved from memory, and that this emotional enhancement serves to better instantiate the memory for future recall. It is also thought that the amygdala may use information about arousal and body state to assist in searching for old memories, and that this may in turn facilitate the retrieval of information related to the specific memory from other brain regions. This process recruits increased neural participation during the re-experiencing of the memory, and as a result adds to the vividness and permanence of the specific memory. Although this ability in human beings is remarkable, and incredibly useful to guiding behavior and social interactions, it is also fundamentally flawed. Due to the fact that humans can generate their own abstract stimuli (e.g. you are able to mentally envision a pink chicken despite—hopefully—never having actually seen such an animal), we are able to modify, and even entirely create our own memories. Elizabeth Loftus (2004) details how the very functions that make human memory so effective, leave it very vulnerable to "suggestion" meaning that if a story is offered to an individual with enough emotion, repetition and insistence, they will likely begin to believe that aspects of it (although entirely fabricated) are true. The most common way in which this takes place is a technique called guided imagination, where an individual is asked to imagine an event (or a pink chicken) and details and emotions are added until the memory begins to feel real. Remember from the work of LeBar just described, that every time we re-experience a memory it makes it stronger. An important perspective to consider, however, is that the memory need not be true, this is the focus of Loftus's work. While the idea of believing that one has seen a pink chicken as a child might be amusing, false memories in the context of a courtroom can be lethal. In this way the work of Loftus is critical, reminding us that like so many other facets of human cognition, memory evolved primarily as a process to help create and maintain social bonds, not to keep an exact record of daily events. The evolutionary importance of social bonds is emphasized in the final article in this section. Shelly Taylor (2006) describes the neurocognitive mechanisms that have evolved to help human beings (particularly females) deal with stress. As mentioned above, the "fight or flight" response has been the dominant theory about how humans respond to stress or threat. Taylor draws on the extensive cognitive neuroscience literature describing an affiliative response to stress among humans. It is thought that the drive to seek out social contact and support is much like many other drives known to relieve stress, such as those that exist to respond to hunger, thirst, and sexual longing. In neurphysiological terms, the "tend and befriend" response is believed to rely heavily on the hormone oxytocin, as well as the dopaminergic and opiod systems. These neurochemical systems are all essential for creating and maintaining social relationships. Given all that is known about the critical importance of social relationships in human beings (for basic protection as well as abstract relief from abstract worries), it is not surprising to find complex and efficient neurocircuitry devoted to this critical drive.

As a group the articles of this section shine an important light on the importance of examining the multiple levels at which human behavior can be described. As we learn more about the brain we are able to add understanding to human behavior. Critically though, the study of human behavior is essential to understanding the ways in which our brains, and minds, come to be. It is through this reciprocal understanding that we are able to appreciate the intricacy, adaptability and resiliency of the human animal.

The Occipital Cortex in the Blind: Lessons About Plasticity and Vision

Amir Amedi,[1] Lotfi B. Merabet, Felix Bermpohl and Alvaro Pascual-Leone

Department of Neurology, Harvard Medical School, Beth Israel Deaconess Medical Center

Abstract

Studying the brains of blind individuals provides a unique opportunity to investigate how the brain changes and adapts in response to afferent (input) and efferent (output) demands. We discuss evidence suggesting that regions of the brain normally associated with the processing of visual information undergo remarkable dynamic change in response to blindness. These neuroplastic changes implicate not only processing carried out by the remaining senses but also higher cognitive functions such as language and memory. A strong emphasis is placed on evidence obtained from advanced neuroimaging techniques that allow researchers to identify areas of human brain activity, as well as from lesion approaches (both reversible and irreversible) to address the functional relevance and role of these activated areas. A possible mechanism and conceptual framework for these physiological and behavioral changes is proposed.

Keywords

plasticity; visual cortex; blindness; Braille reading; verbal memory

Conventional wisdom in neuroscience dictates that the brain possesses only limited capacity to reorganize itself following damage (e.g. from sensory loss or brain injury). However, more recent evidence demonstrates that the brain is capable of remarkable dynamic change and adaptation throughout the lifespan. Studying individuals who are peripherally blind (e.g., from eye disease or injury) or using experimental visual deprivation (e.g., prolonged blindfolding) allow researchers to investigate adaptive brain changes and behavioral consequences in response to changes in sensory input. Lessons learned from how the brain adapts to blindness are likely to apply to other situations (e.g., damage to the inner ear) and will provide novel insights for the development of rehabilitative and educational strategies and the advance of sensory substitution and restoration devices (Merabet, Rizzo, Amedi, Somers, & Pascual-Leone, 2005).

ADJUSTMENT TO BLINDNESS AND COMPENSATORY PLASTICITY

Blind individuals have to make major adjustments in order to interact effectively with their environment. One might imagine that blind individuals develop superior abilities in the use of their remaining senses in order to compensate for their loss of sight. The accounts of remarkable accomplishments of blind musicians and artists could be taken as anecdotal support for this view. However, blindness has the potential to disrupt brain development and knowledge acquisition, thus ultimately leading to more general problems. For example, because of the strong reliance on vision for the acquisition and construction of spatial and form representations, the loss of sight may have detrimental repercussions on the processing of spatial information that is gathered through the remaining senses. Contradicting the latter view is evidence that blind individuals (as compared with sighted controls) show superior skills in tasks involving touch and hearing (Gougoux, Zatorre, Lassonde, Voss, & Lepore, 2005; Pascual-Leone, Amedi, Fregni, & Merabet, 2005; Rauschecker, 1995; Roder, & Neville, 2003).

The process of seeing is as follows: Focused light landing on the retina causes neuronal signals to leave the eye through the optic nerve; those signals are sent via the lateral geniculate nucleus of the thalamus to the occipital cortex, where the majority of visual processing actually takes place. Sighted people read through visual recognition of words, involving a complex network of language-processing areas intimately related with spatial information processed by the visual system. In contrast, a blind Braille reader relies on touch. Using the pad of the index finger (or multiple fingers for some proficient Braille readers), arrays of raised dots are scanned and spatial information is extracted and interpreted into meaningful patterns that encode semantic and lexical properties. Furthermore, a blind subject also learns to rely on verbal descriptions and verbal memory, in place of visual perception as employed by sighted subjects. This dependence on language and memory may also be accompanied by the development of superior capabilities for these functions (Amedi, Raz, Pianka, Malach, & Zohary, 2003). This raises the question: Does the part of the brain used by a sighted person to recognize objects or read visually (in other words, to see) play a role in a blind person reading through touch and relying heavily on verbal language? Growing experimental evidence suggests that it does.

THE OCCIPITAL CORTEX IN THE BLIND: TOUCHING THE DOTS

The development of functional neuroimaging techniques (such as functional magnetic resonance imagery, fMRI, and positron emission tomography, PET) allows researchers to observe with unprecedented detail brain activity as a function of behavior. Several groups have used these techniques to study activation in the occipital cortex during nonvisual sensory tasks. Sadato et al. (1996) demonstrated activation on both sides of the "visual" cortex, including the primary visual cortex, while early-blind subjects (usually defined as those blinded from birth up to the age when learning to read Braille begins, between 4 and 6 years) performed a Braille-reading task (Fig. 1a). Activation of the primary visual cortex was also evident (though to a lesser extent) in non-Braille tactile-discrimination tasks such as angle discriminations (judging the angles of tactile lines created from Braille dots), but the passive sweeping of the fingers over a homogeneous pattern of Braille dots did not lead to such activation. Subsequent investigators have further refined and extended these early findings, addressing the role of imagery, the differences between people who are early blind and those who are

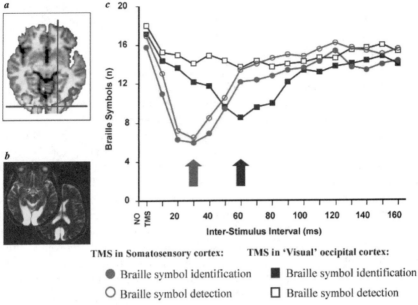

Fig. 1. Brain image (a) showing activation in the occipital lobe during Braille reading in an early-blind subject (modified from Sadato et al., 1996); brain scan (b) of a congenitally blind woman who was rendered unable to read Braille following a bilateral occipital stroke (area shaded in gray indicates area of highly damaged tissue within the occipital cortex on both sides; modified from Hamilton et al., 2000); and effects of temporary disruption of the somatosensory cortex or of the "visual" occipital cortex using single-pulse transcranial magnetic stimulation (TMS) on tactile recognition of Braille characters in congenitally blind subjects (c). The TMS pulse was delivered at different times (interstimulus interval) after presenting a tactile stimulus to the pad of the index finger. The graph displays the number of tactile stimuli detected (open circles/squares) and correctly identified (filled circles/squares). Disruption of the somatosensory cortex led to a decrease in the number of detected and identified letters at an interstimulus interval of 30 ms (red arrow). Disruption of the occipital cortex led to a decrease in the number of identified letters only at an interstimulus interval of approximately 60 ms (blue arrow; modified from Hamilton, Keenan, Catala, & Pascual-Leone, 2000).

late blind (i.e., subjects blinded after the age of 6 years, usually after acquiring reading abilities), and the role of tactile versus verbal or linguistic aspects of the task (for reviews see Burton, 2003; Pascual-Leone, Amedi, Fregni, & Merabet, 2005; Roder, & Neville, 2003). Cross-modal plasticity (i.e., brain changes in the processing and representation of different senses) in the occipital cortex of the blind has also been reported in the auditory domain, suggesting that such plasticity in cases of early sensory loss might be a general principle (e.g. Gougoux, Zatorre, Lassonde, Voss, & Lepore, 2005; Roder, & Neville, 2003).

It is important to realize that patterns of activation revealed by functional neuroimaging establish an association between activity in a given region or network and the performance of tasks, rather than proving a causal link (e.g., activation of the occipital cortex might be due to irregularities in blood flow in the blind rather than to the area's contributing to Braille reading). To establish a causal link, neuro-scientists have classically relied on studying patients with localized brain damage. Indeed, a serendipitous clinical case of an early-blind woman, once highly proficient at reading Braille but later rendered unable to do so following a bilateral occipital stroke, supports the notion of a causal link between the ability to read Braille and occipital function (Hamilton, Keenan, Catala, & Pascual-Leone, 2000; Fig. 1b).

In an experimental setting, transcranial magnetic stimulation (TMS) can be used as a means to recreate the behavioral deficits observed following damage to specific areas of the cortex. Briefly, a TMS device generates a rapidly alternating electromagnetic pulse that travels through the scalp and can temporarily disrupt cortical activity. Thus, in essence, TMS represents a method of creating a "virtual lesion" in a focal, reversible, and noninvasive manner (Pascual-Leone, Walsh, & Rothwell, 2000). Cohen and colleagues used TMS to study early-blind subjects performing a Braille-identification task (for review, see Pascual-Leone et al., 2005). When TMS was delivered to the occipital cortex, tactile identification of Braille letters was impaired. In contrast, TMS of the occipital cortex in sighted controls did not impair their ability to identify embossed Roman letters by touch. Interestingly, during occipital TMS, blind subjects also reported distorted tactile perceptions and, occasionally, feeling additional ("phantom") Braille dots.

The functional significance of the occipital activation during Braille reading was further evaluated using single-pulse TMS, allowing assessment of the timing of information processing (Pascual-Leone, Walsh, & Rothwell, 2000). A disrup-tive TMS pulse was applied at varying time intervals following the presentation of a Braille symbol to the subject's index finger (Hamilton & Pascual-Leone, 1998). In sighted and blind subjects, TMS delivered to the somatosensory cortex (the part of the brain, located in the anterior parietal cortex, involved in the percep-tion of touch) interfered with the detection of a tactile stimulus presented 20 to 40 milliseconds earlier to the pad of the index finger (Fig. 1c; only the early-blind group data is shown), while occipital stimulation had no effect on detection. However, TMS to the occipital cortex disrupted processing of Braille symbols only in congenitally blind subjects and when intervals between pulses were 50 to 80 milliseconds (Fig. 1c). Contrary to the findings after sensorimotor TMS, fol-lowing occipital TMS blind subjects generally knew whether a peripheral stimu-lus had been presented. However, they were unable to tell what Braille symbol it was. These results suggest that in early-blind subjects, tactile information reaches the cortex by the somatosensory cortex, which is engaged in detection, while the occipital cortex contributes later to the perception of tactile stimuli.

INSIGHTS FROM STUDIES IN BLINDFOLDED SUBJECTS

Complete but temporary visual deprivation in sighted subjects (i.e., 5 days of blindfolding) seems to be sufficient to lead to recruitment of the primary visual cortex for tactile and auditory processing (i.e. activation of visual areas by Braille-letter identification, touch, and hearing; see Pascual-Leone, Amedi, Fregni, & Merabet, 2005 for review). The speed of these functional changes in sighted individuals is such that it is highly improbable that new cortical connections are established. Therefore, somatosensory and auditory connections to the occipital cortex must already be present and are presumably "unmasked" under these experimental conditions. Nevertheless, these findings in the tactile domain, comparable to previous findings in the blind, do not show that the mechanisms in blindfolded subjects are identical to those in blindness (i.e., a similar result of higher primary visual cortex processing in the two groups could be mediated by release from inhibition during blindfolding or via establishing new connections in blind subjects). Thus, more studies are needed to address this important issue.

BEYOND TACTILE PROCESSING: OCCIPITAL ACTIVATION IN HIGH-LEVEL COGNITIVE TASKS

Recent neuroimaging studies in the blind have demonstrated occipital cortex activation during tasks requiring auditory-verb generation, during semantic-judgment tasks, and during speech processing (see Burton, 2003; Pascual-Leone, Amedi, Fregni, & Merabet, 2005; Roder, Stock, Bien, Neville, & Rosler, 2002). In one study, Burton and colleagues reported differences in brain activity between early-blind and late-blind subjects. The researchers used a verb-generation task, in which subjects were instructed to generate a verb in response to a noun cue (e.g., for "cake" the subject would have to generate "bake") presented in Braille or via hearing. Activation in the occipital cortex was evident in both groups (showing some left-hemisphere dominance, especially in the auditory version), but it was more prominent in subjects who were early blind (Burton, 2003). The sighted control group showed activation in typical language-related areas (e.g., Broca's area, in the prefrontal cortex) but no occipital activation.

Amedi and colleagues found similar results for auditory-verb generation in congenitally blind subjects. They also reported strong activation of the occipital cortex on the left side—including along the calcarine sulcus (an area corresponding to the primary visual cortex in sighted people)—to a verbal-memory task requiring the retrieval of abstract words from long-term memory (Amedi, Raz, Pianka, Malach, & Zohary, 2003), suggesting that the primary visual cortex can be activated without introducing any sensory input. Notably, blind subjects showed superior verbal-memory capabilities when compared to age-matched sighted controls and to reported standardized population averages. Furthermore, in the blind group alone, a strong positive correlation was found between the magnitude of primary visual cortex activation and individual subjects' verbal-memory capabilities (Fig. 2).

The functional relevance of these findings was demonstrated by showing that TMS of the left primary visual cortex or left occipito-temporal cortex led to a disruption in performance (increase in the error rate) in a verb-generation task (Amedi, Floel, Knecht, Zohary, & Cohen, 2004). The most common error produced by the TMS was semantic (e.g., "apple" would lead to the verb "jump"), while phonological errors and interference with motor execution or articulation (stuttering and slurring of responses) were rare. These results suggest that language and memory processing in blind people incorporate a widespread network that encompasses "visual" brain areas.

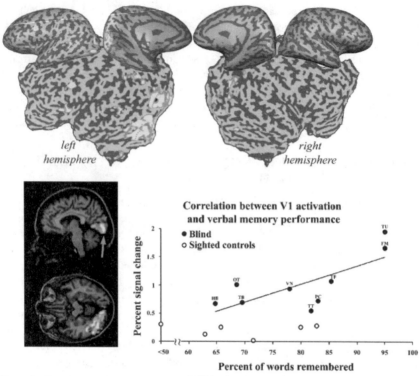

Fig. 2. Brain activation in congenitally blind subjects during a verbal-memory task (involving no sensory stimulation) and correlation between activation and verbal-memory performance for both blind subjects and sighted controls. Yellow/orange areas in upper and lower-left panels show activation. Verbal-memory activation can be seen across the entire cortex of blind subjects; and only in blind subjects was activation also found in visual areas, mainly in the left hemisphere (compare the activation patterns in the left and right brain reconstructions; areas corresponding to the primary visual cortex and adjacent visual areas in sighted people are denoted by continuous and dashed cyan lines respectively). Subjects were tested on the percent of words they remembered 6 months after the scan; in general, blind subjects remembered more words and showed greater activation of the primary visual cortex (V1; activation is measured as percent signal change) than the sighted controls did. Only blind subjects also showed significant correlation between brain activity and performance in this task and general verbal-memory abilities. Modified from Amedi et al. (2003).

PROPOSED CONCEPTUAL FRAMEWORK AND POSSIBLE IMPLICATIONS

It seems reasonable to presume that in the context of visual deprivation, the brain reorganizes to exploit the sensory inputs at its disposal. In this context, the functional and structural identity of the occipital cortex may switch from processing visual information to the processing of information from other senses. Alternatively, it is possible that the occipital cortex inherently possesses the computational machinery necessary for the processing of nonvisual information.

According to this hypothesis, the occipital cortex might be viewed as an "operator" of a given function based on the best-suited input available. When sight is present, visual input may be deemed as ideal for the operation of the occipital cortex, to the point of suppressing or masking inputs from other senses. In the absence of visual input, the occipital cortex may employ nonvisual inputs for its operation (Pascual-Leone & Hamilton, 2001).

Thus, two possible mechanisms may account for the reviewed changes in occipital function. The first represents de novo cross-modal plasticity, in which new sensory associations and connectivity patterns are created in response to visual deprivation (Burton, 2003). A second mechanism represents expression of normal physiology, in which functions that are normally inhibited or masked in the sighted are revealed by visual loss. We suggest here that these two mechanisms are inextricably linked. The unmasking of pre-existing connections and shifts in connectivity are rapid, early-occurring plastic changes, which can lead, if sustained and reinforced, to slower-developing, but more permanent, structural changes, such as the establishment of new neural connections. This can account for the rapid recruitment of occipital cortex function observed in blindfolded subjects and the difference in the magnitude of the reorganization between early- and late-blind subjects. This hypothesis also results in the prediction that careful task choice and experimental design will reveal nonvisual roles of the occipital cortex in sighted subjects. Indeed, such nonvisual roles can be demonstrated for object recognition (Amedi et al., 2001), processing of orientation (Zangaladze et al., 1999), and judging of distance between Braille dots (Merabet et al., 2004; for review, see Amedi, Von Kriegstein, Van Atteveldt, Beauchamp, & Naumer, 2005). Therefore, the occipital cortex is not "simply" visual, but rather participates in tactile, auditory, and perhaps even linguistic tasks.

This set of results might also have important implications regarding teaching, learning, and rehabilitation strategies in persons with developmental disabilities and in stroke and accident victims. The results from late-blind and blindfold studies support the notion that the adult brain is capable of undergoing considerable plastic change throughout the lifespan (Kaas, 1991; Pascual-Leone, Amedi, Fregni, & Merabet, 2005). Fundamental principles underlying neural plasticity in response to visual deprivation may be applicable across neural systems (Pascual-Leone, Amedi, Fregni, & Merabet, 2005; Bavelier & Neville, 2002). However, it is important to remember that plasticity is an intrinsic property of the human nervous system and plastic changes may not necessarily lead to a behavioral gain. Plasticity is the mechanism that underlies development and learning, but it is also a potential cause of pathology. Our challenge is to modulate neural plasticity for each individual's optimal behavioral gain. This might be possible, for example, through behavioral modification or brain-stimulation techniques. In this respect, the results from the week-long blindfold study suggest that release from inhibition might facilitate increased participation of the visual cortex in auditory and tactile tasks and enhance functional gain. The mechanisms and conditions that promote recruitment of the visual cortex for high-level cognitive functions and the resulting superior verbal-memory capabilities in the early blind remain unclear. Strategies to promote such plastic changes are important to aid blind individuals to compensate for their disabilities.

Recommended Reading

Amedi, A., Raz, N., Pianka, P., Malach, R., & Zohary, E. (2003). (See References)
Burton, H. (2003). (See References)
Hamilton, R.H., Pascual-Leone, A. (1998). (See References)
Merabet, L., Rizzo, J.F., Amedi, A., Somers, D., & Pascual-Leone, A. (2005). What blindness can tell us about seeing again: Merging neuroplasticity and neuroprostheses. *Nature Reviews Neuroscience, 6,* 71–77.
Pascual-Leone, A., & Hamilton, R. (2001). (See References)

Acknowledgments—The work on this article was supported by National Institutes of Health Grants RO1EY12091, K24 RR018875, RO1NS47754, RO1-NS 20068 and NCRR MO1 RR01032 to APL and by the Human Frontiers Science Program to AA.

Note

1. Address correspondence to Alvaro Pascual-Leone or Amir Amedi, Center for Noninvasive Brain Stimulation, Department of Neurology, Harvard Medical School, Beth Israel Deaconess Medical Center, 330 Brookline Avenue KS-452, Boston, MA 02215; e-mail: apleone@bidmc.harvard.edu or aamedi@bidmc.harvard.edu.

References

Amedi, A., Floel, A., Knecht, S., Zohary, E., & Cohen, L.G. (2004). Transcranial magnetic stimulation of the occipital pole interferes with verbal processing in blind subjects. *Nature Neuroscience, 7,* 1266–1270.

Amedi, A., Raz, N., Pianka, P., Malach, R., & Zohary, E. (2003). Early 'visual' cortex activation correlates with superior verbal-memory performance in the blind. *Nature Neuroscience, 6,* 758–766.

Amedi, A., Von Kriegstein, K., Van Atteveldt, N., Beauchamp, M.S., & Naumer, M.J. (2005). Functional imaging of human crossmodal identification and object recognition. *Experimental Brain Research, 166,* 559–571.

Bavelier, D., & Neville, H. (2002). Cross-modal plasticity: Where and how? *Nature Reviews Neuroscience, 3,* 443–452.

Burton, H. (2003). Visual cortex activity in early and late blind people. *Journal of Neuroscience, 23,* 4005–4011.

Gougoux, F., Zatorre, R.J., Lassonde, M., Voss, P., & Lepore, F. (2005). A functional neuroimaging study of sound localization: Visual cortex activity predicts performance in early-blind individuals. *PloS Biology, 3,* 324–333.

Hamilton, R.H., Keenan, J.P., Catala, M.D., & Pascual-Leone, A. (2000). Alexia for Braille following bilateral occipital stroke in an early blind woman. *Neuroreport, 7,* 237–240.

Hamilton, R.H., & Pascual-Leone, A. (1998). Cortical plasticity associated with Braille learning. *Trends in Cognitive Science, 2,* 168–174.

Kaas, J.H. (1991). Plasticity of sensory and motor maps in adult mammals. *Annual Reviews of Neuroscience, 14,* 137–167.

Pascual-Leone, A., Amedi, A., Fregni, F., & Merabet, L.B. (2005). The plastic human brain cortex. *Annual Reviews of Neuroscience, 28,* 377–401.

Pascual-Leone, A., & Hamilton, R. (2001). The metamodal organization of the brain. In C. Casanova & M. Ptito (Eds.), *Vision: From neurons to cognition,* Progress in Brain Research, Vol. 134 (pp. 427–445). Amsterdam: Elsevier.

Pascual-Leone, A., Walsh, V., & Rothwell, J. (2000). Transcranial magnetic stimulation in cognitive neuroscience—virtual lesion, chronometry, and functional connectivity. *Current Opinion in Neurobiology, 10,* 232–237.

Rauschecker, J.P. (1995). Compensatory plasticity and sensory substitution in the cerebral cortex. *Trends in Neuroscience, 18,* 36–43.

Roder, B., & Neville, H. (2003). Developmental functional plasticity. In S. Grafman & I.H. Robertson (Eds.), *Handbook of neuropsychology* (2nd ed. Vol. 9, pp. 231–270). Amsterdam: Elsevier.

Roder, B., Stock, O., Bien, S., Neville, H., & Rosler, F. (2002). Speech processing activates visual cortex in congenitally blind humans. *European Journal of Neuroscience, 16*, 930–936.

Sadato, N., Pascual-Leone, A., Grafman, J., Ibanez, V., Deiber, M.P., Dold, G., & Hallett, M. (1996). Activation of the primary visual cortex by Braille reading in blind subjects. *Nature, 11*, 526–528.

This article has been reprinted as it originally appeared in *Current Directions in Psychological Science*. Citation information for this article as originally published appears above.

The Role of Emotion in Decision Making: A Cognitive Neuroscience Perspective

Nasir Naqvi

Division of Cognitive Neuroscience, Department of Neurology, University of Iowa College of Medicine

Baba Shiv

Graduate School of Business, Stanford University

Antoine Bechara[1]

Brain and Creativity Institute, and Department of Psychology, University of Southern California

Abstract

Decision making often occurs in the face of uncertainty about whether one's choices will lead to benefit or harm. The somatic-marker hypothesis is a neurobiological theory of how decisions are made in the face of uncertain outcome. This theory holds that such decisions are aided by emotions, in the form of bodily states, that are elicited during the deliberation of future consequences and that mark different options for behavior as being advantageous or disadvantageous. This process involves an interplay between neural systems that elicit emotional/bodily states and neural systems that map these emotional/bodily states.

Keywords

decision making; frontal lobes; neuropsychology; neuroeconomics; emotion

Decision making precedes many of life's most important events: choosing whom to marry, which house to buy, which stock to invest in, whether to have just one more drink before hitting the road, whether to have surgery, and whether to quit smoking, to name a few examples. Properly executed decision making gives rise to some of the most elevated human abilities, such as ethics, politics, and financial reasoning. Derangements of decision making underlie some of the more tragic consequences of psychiatric illnesses such as drug addiction, eating disorders, obsessive-compulsive disorder, schizophrenia, mania, and personality disorders (Rahman, Sahakian, Cardinal, Rogers, & Robbins, 2001).

The field of economics, which is concerned with formalizing the rules that govern human decision making, has begun to focus increasingly on forms of decision making that go beyond simple cost–benefit analysis. Traditional economic theory assumed that most decision making involves rational Bayesian maximization of expected utility, as if humans were equipped with unlimited knowledge, time, and information-processing power. The prevalent assumption of this view was that a direct link exists between knowledge and the implementation of behavioral decisions—that is, that one does what one actually knows. In the 1970s and 1980s, decision-making researchers identified phenomena that systematically violated such normative principles of economic behavior (see

Kahneman & Tversky, 1979). In the 1990s, they began to show that many forms of decision making, especially those that involve a high level of risk and uncertainty, involve biases and emotions that act at an implicit level (see Hastie & Dawes, 2001).

In recent years, decision making has become a subject of neuroscience research. Neuroscientists applying diverse methods, including the lesion method (using brain damage that occurs as a result of stroke, etc., to examine how different brain areas contribute to various mental functions), functional imaging, and other physiological techniques, have begun to elucidate the neural process underlying the execution of successful and unsuccessful decisions. This effort has converged with the field of behavioral economics in showing that decision making involves not only the cold-hearted calculation of expected utility based upon explicit knowledge of outcomes but also more subtle and sometimes covert processes that depend critically upon emotion. Here, we focus on a particular neurobiological theory of decision making, termed the somatic-marker hypothesis, in which emotions, in the form of bodily states, bias decision making toward choices that maximize reward and minimize punishment.

INSIGHTS FROM PATIENTS WITH FOCAL BRAIN DAMAGE

The modern era of the neuroscience of decision making began with the observation by Antonio Damasio that patients with damage in the ventromedial prefrontal cortex (vmPFC), an area of the brain located above the eye sockets, often engaged in behaviors that were detrimental to their well-being. The actions that these patients elected to pursue led to diverse kinds of losses including financial losses, losses in social standing, and losses of family and friends. These patients seemed unable to learn from previous mistakes, as reflected by repeated engagement in decisions that led to negative consequences. In striking contrast to this real-life decision-making impairment, these patients' intellect and problem-solving abilities were largely normal; their decision-making deficits could not be explained by impairments in the retrieval of semantic knowledge pertinent to the situation, language comprehension or expression, attention, working memory, or long-term memory (Damasio, 1994).

An important insight into the nature of the impairments resulting from vmPFC damage came from the observation that, in addition to their inability to make advantageous decisions in real life, patients with damage to the vmPFC evinced a generally flat affect, and their ability to react to emotional situations was somewhat impaired. This led Damasio to hypothesize that the primary dysfunction of patients with vmPFC damage was an inability to use emotions to aid in decision making, particularly decision making in the personal, financial, and moral realms. This was the fundamental tenet of the somatic-marker hypothesis: that emotions play a role in guiding decisions, especially in situations in which the outcome of one's choices, in terms of reward and punishment, are uncertain.

Testing the somatic-marker hypothesis required first devising a task that simulated the demands of real-life decision making by factoring in uncertain reward and punishment. This led one of us (Antoine Bechara) to develop what is now known as the Iowa Gambling Task (the details of this task and the results from lesion studies using it are reviewed in Bechara & Damasio, 2005). In this task, subjects choose from four decks of cards that provide varying levels of reward and punishment (winning and losing play money). Two of the decks provide low reward, but also a low level of punishment. Choosing consistently from these decks eventually leads to a net gain of money; they are designated as "advantageous" decks. The other two decks provide a high reward, but also a high punishment. Choosing consistently from these decks eventually leads to a net loss of money; they are designated as "disadvantageous" decks.

In the Iowa Gambling Task, normal individuals initially sampled the advantageous and disadvantageous decks equally, but, after experiencing the high punishments from the disadvantageous decks, they shifted their choices to the advantageous decks. In contrast, subjects with vmPFC damage tended to continue choosing from the disadvantageous decks, seemingly insensitive to the negative consequences of this choice. This strategy mimicked the real-life impairments of these subjects.

The next step in testing the somatic-marker hypothesis was to address the role of emotions in decision making. According to the theory, emotions are constituted by changes in the body. These bodily states are elicited during the decision-making process and function to "mark" certain options as advantageous and other options as disadvantageous. To test this hypothesis, Bechara and colleagues coupled their gambling task with the measurement of skin-conductance response (SCR), an autonomic index of emotional arousal. In a series of experiments, it was shown that normal subjects elicited SCRs that were larger before choosing from the disadvantageous decks than before choosing from the advantageous decks. Furthermore, it was found that this anticipatory emotional response preceded explicit knowledge of the correct strategy. Patients with vmPFC damage, in contrast, did not show such anticipatory emotional responses. Importantly, vmPFC-damaged subjects had intact SCRs to receiving rewards and punishments, suggesting that the vmPFC is not necessary for registering the emotional impact of rewards and punishments after they are delivered. Rather, this region is necessary for anticipating the emotional impact of future rewards and punishment.

Further experiments showed that subjects with lesions in the amygdala, a medial-temporal-lobe region that is also known to be involved in emotion, also had impaired performance on the gambling task. Like patients with vmPFC damage, patients with amygdala damage also tended to choose more often from the disadvantageous decks. Also like patients with vmPFC damage, those with amygdala damage did not have anticipatory SCRs before choosing from the disadvantageous decks. However, unlike vmPFC-damaged subjects, these subjects also had impaired SCRs to receiving rewards and punishments. This suggested that subjects with amygdala damage had an impairment in registering the emotional impact of rewards and punishments caused by specific behaviors, a function necessary for being able to anticipate the rewarding and punishing consequences of these behaviors in the future.

This set of results gave rise to a model of decision making in which the amygdala and vmPFC play distinct but related roles (Fig. 1). The amygdala triggers emotional/bodily states in response to receiving rewards and punishments that are caused by specific behaviors. Through a learning process, these emotional/bodily

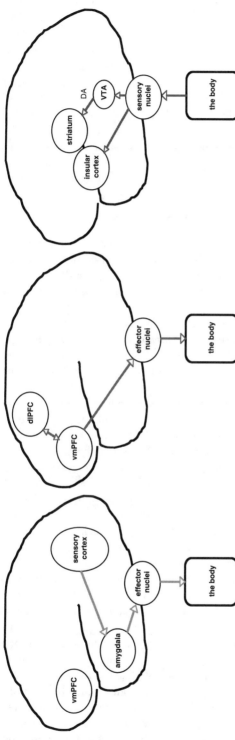

Fig. 1. Schematic model of somatic-state activation during reward-related decision making. First, sensory properties of rewards and punishments drive the amygdala to elicit emotional/bodily responses. This occurs through connections from higher-order cortices that represent the sensory properties of rewards (sensory cortex) to the amygdala to effector nuclei in the brain stem, which control bodily processes such as autonomic responses (left diagram). These responses become linked to internal representations in the ventromedial prefrontal cortex (vmPFC) of the specific behavioral choices that brought them about. During decision making, the vmPFC re-enacts these emotional/bodily states as the same behavioral choices are contemplated as options for the future. This occurs through connections between the dorsolateral prefrontal cortex (dlPFC), which is involved in holding mental representations of specific behaviors in mind, and the vmPFC (middle diagram). Emotional/bodily states elicited during decision making are then mapped within sensory systems (right diagram). The mapping of body states within the insular cortex gives rise to conscious "gut feelings" of desire or aversion that are attributed to specific behavioral options. Emotional/bodily states can also be mapped within the mesolimbic dopamine system, which includes the dopamine (DA) neurons within the ventral tegmental area (VTA) and their targets within the striatum. This latter process can bias decision making towards the advantageous choice in a nonconscious fashion.

states become linked to mental representations of the specific behaviors that brought them about. During decision making, the subject deliberates these behaviors as options for the future. As each option is brought to mind, the somatic state that was triggered by that behavior in the past is reenacted by the vmPFC. After the emotional/bodily states are elicited in the body during decision making, they are represented in the brain through a sensory process. This can occur in two ways. The mapping of bodily/emotional states at the cortical level, such as within the insular cortex, gives rise to conscious "gut feelings" of desire or aversion that are attributed to specific behavioral options. The mapping of bodily states at the subcortical level, such as within the mesolimbic dopamine system, occurs in a non-conscious fashion, such that subjects choose the advantageous option without feeling specific feelings of desire for that option or aversion to the disadvantageous option.

EVIDENCE FROM PHYSIOLOGICAL STUDIES

At around the same time that Damasio and his colleagues were using lesion studies to address the role of the vmPFC in decision making, Edmund Rolls and his colleagues were exploring the reward-related functions of the vmPFC by recording the electrical activity of single neurons within this region (this work is reviewed in Rolls, 2004). They found that vmPFC neurons respond to the receipt of various primary reinforcers, such as palatable foods. Furthermore, they found that responses to specific primary reinforcers were reduced by manipulations that diminished their value, such as feeding someone a palatable food to satiety. In addition, they found that vmPFC neurons respond to conditioned stimuli that predict the delivery of primary reinforcers.

Functional imaging studies have extended these findings to humans. A functional magnetic resonance imagery (fMRI) study by Gottfried, O'Doherty, & Dolan (2003) found that the responses of the vmPFC to conditioned stimuli that predict primary reinforcers are reduced by devaluation of the specific primary reinforcer that they predict. This suggests that the vmPFC plays a role in predicting the future rewarding consequences of different behaviors by accessing information about their specific rewarding consequences in the past. Combined lesion and physiological studies in rodents by Schoenbaum, Setlow, Saddoris, and Gallagher (2003) have shown that this ability of the vmPFC to encode "predictive reward value" requires an intact amygdala. This is consistent with findings from human lesion studies, described earlier.

Recent functional imaging studies have also shown that the insular cortex is engaged by certain kinds of decision making. An fMRI study by Paulus, Rogalsky, Simmons, Feinstein, and Stein (2003) has shown that activity in the insular cortex is greater during high-risk decisions than it is during low-risk decisions. Furthermore, this study showed that the level of activity within the insular cortex predicted the probability of selecting a safe response following a punished response. An fMRI study by Sanfey and colleagues (Sanfey, Rilling, Aronson, Nystrom, & Cohen, 2003) found that the insular cortex is activated when subjects evaluate the fairness of offers of money from another subject, which can be considered as an emotional process. This study found that the level of activity in the insular cortex predicts the likelihood of rejecting an unfair offer. The results of these studies suggest that the insular cortex plays a role in assessing risk and guiding behavior based upon the anticipation of emotional consequences, especially negative emotional consequences. The somatic-marker hypothesis attributes this function to the mapping of visceral states within the insular cortex, which gives rise to gut feelings of desire or aversion.

The mesolimbic dopamine system, which is hypothesized by the somatic-marker hypothesis to play a role in the unconscious biasing of action, has increasingly become a focus of attention as an area that plays a role in reward processing and decision making. Schultz, Montague, and colleagues have shown that the activity of single neurons within the mesolimbic dopamine system is increased by primary reinforcers (e.g., palatable foods), but only when these are delivered in an unpredictable fashion. Furthermore, they have found that these neurons also respond to stimuli that predict primary reinforcers and that these responses shift in time from occurring during the receipt of primary reinforcers to occurring at the onset of the predictive cues. Using sophisticated computational-modeling techniques, they have shown that activity within the mesolimbic dopamine system signals an error between actual and predicted reward and that such a signal can bias behavior in the direction of behaviors that are likely to lead to rewards in the future (this work is reviewed in Schultz, Dayan, & Montague, 1997). This is consistent with the role of the mesolimbic dopamine system proposed by the somatic-marker hypothesis.

APPLICATIONS OF THE SOMATIC-MARKER HYPOTHESIS

Increasingly, the principles that were originally established by observing the decision-making deficits of patients with focal lesions are being applied to understanding a diverse range of human decision-making behaviors in which emotions play a critical role. For example, Greene and his colleagues (Greene, Sommerville, Nystrom, Darley, & Cohen, 2001) have used fMRI to examine the neural systems that enable moral decision making. They found that reasoning about a variety of moral dilemmas, compared to reasoning about nonmoral dilemmas, activates a network of structures that include the vmPFC. Furthermore, this activation is greater when the moral decision involves negative consequence for another person, compared to when it involves no negative consequence for another person. This finding suggests that moral decisions, compared to non-moral decisions, engage emotions, especially when one is required to consider the consequences of one's actions for another's well-being.

The somatic-marker framework has also been applied to understanding the decision-making impairments that are associated with drug addiction. Substance abusers show real-life decision-making impairments that are similar to those of patients with vmPFC damage. Studies by Bechara et al. (reviewed in Bechara, 2005) have shown that the performance of substance abusers on the Iowa Gambling Task is similar to that of patients with vmPFC damage. This suggests that drug addiction may be promoted in part by a dysfunction of the vmPFC whereby information about the negative emotional consequences of drug abuse cannot be used to motivate quitting. Such studies may provide important insights into how to treat substance dependence.

FUTURE DIRECTIONS

Much of the work on the neuroscience of decision making has lent support to the neuroanatomical framework originally put forth in the somatic-marker hypothesis. However, some components of this framework still remain to be addressed. For example, it will be important to examine the extent to which the sensory feedback of emotional/bodily states within regions such as the mesolimbic dopamine system and the insular cortex influences both conscious gut feelings and nonconscious biasing of behavior. It will also be important to see how the areas implicated in this theory work together to facilitate decision making. This may be aided by computational models of decision making (e.g., Yechiam, Busemeyer, Stout, & Bechara, 2005) that generate predictions about how these areas will be activated under different conditions of reward, uncertainty, and risk, and how lesions in these regions will affect different components of the decision-making process. A further question regards the role of neurotransmitter systems, such as the mesolimbic dopamine system, in decision making (see Robbins, 2000, for a review of work on pharmacologic manipulations of decision making). These studies may shed light on how drug therapies can be used to treat the decision-making impairments associated with certain mental illnesses.

In general terms, the somatic-marker hypothesis provides a basis for understanding how the most elevated of human abilities—the capacity to make decisions in the moral, social, and financial realms—are related to basic motivational and homeostatic processes that are shared among all mammalian species. The theory serves as a launching point for understanding not only decision making but also a variety of goal-directed processes in which affect and motivation are integrated with the planning of complex action.

Recommended Reading

Damasio, A.R. (1994). (See References)
Glimcher, P. (2003). *Decisions, uncertainty, and the brain: The science of neuroeconomics.* Cambridge, MA: Bradford Books.
Hastie, R., & Dawes, R.M. (2001). (See References)
Senior, C., Russell, T., & Gazzaniga, M. (Eds.). (in press). *Methods in mind: The study of human cognition.* MIT Press: Cambridge, MA.

Acknowledgments—The decision-neuroscience research of Antoine Bechara is supported by National Institute on Drug Abuse Grants DA11779-02, DA12487-03, DA16708, and by National Institute of Neurological Disorders and Stroke Grant NS19632-23, and that of Baba Shiv is supported by National Science Foundation Grant SES 03-50984.

Note

1. Address correspondence to Antoine Bechara, Hedco Neuroscience Building, University of Southern California, Los Angeles, CA 90089-2520; e-mail: bechara@usc.edu.

References

Bechara, A. (2005). Decision making, impulse control and loss of willpower to resist drugs: A neurocognitive perspective. *Nature Neuroscience, 8,* 1458–1463.

Bechara, A., & Damasio, A. (2005). The somatic marker hypothesis: A neural theory of economic decision-making. *Games and Economic Behavior, 52,* 336–372.

Damasio, A.R. (1994). *Descartes' error: Emotion, reason and the human brain.* New York: Putnam and Sons.

Gottfried, J.A., O'Doherty, J., & Dolan, R.J. (2003). Encoding predictive reward value in human amygdala and orbitofrontal cortex. *Science, 301,* 1104–1107.

Greene, J.D., Sommerville, R.B., Nystrom, L.E., Darley, J.M., & Cohen, J.D. (2001). An fMRI investigation of emotional engagement in moral judgment. *Science, 293,* 2105–2108.

Hastie, R., & Dawes, R.M. (2001). *Rational choice in an uncertain world.* Thousand Oaks, CA: Sage Publications.

Kahneman, D., & Tversky, A. (1979). Prospect theory: An analysis of decision under risk. *Econometrica, 47,* 263–291.

Paulus, M.P., Rogalsky, C., Simmons, A., Feinstein, J.S., & Stein, M.B. (2003). Increased activation in the right insula during risk-taking decision making is related to harm avoidance and neuroticism. *Neuroimage, 19,* 1439–1448.

Rahman, S., Sahakian, B.J., Cardinal, R.N., Rogers, R.D., & Robbins, T.W. (2001). Decision making and neuropsychiatry. *Trends in Cognitive Science, 5,* 271–277.

Robbins, T.W. (2000). Chemical neuromodulation of frontal-executive functions in humans and other animals. *Experimental Brain Research, 133,* 130–138.

Rolls, E.T. (2004). The functions of the orbitofrontal cortex. *Brain and Cognition, 55,* 11–29.

Sanfey, A.G., Rilling, J.K., Aronson, J.A., Nystrom, L.E., & Cohen, J.D. (2003). The neural basis of economic decision-making in the ultimatum game. *Science, 300,* 1755–1758.

Schoenbaum, G., Setlow, B., Saddoris, M.P., & Gallagher, M. (2003). Encoding predicted outcome and acquired value in orbitofrontal cortex during cue sampling depends upon input from basolateral amygdala. *Neuron, 39,* 855–867.

Schultz, W., Dayan, P., & Montague, P.R. (1997). A neural substrate of prediction and reward. *Science, 275,* 1593–1599.

Yechiam, E., Busemeyer, J.R., Stout, J.C., & Bechara, A. (2005). Using cognitive models to map relations between neuropsychological disorders and human decision-making deficits. *Psychological Science, 16,* 973–978.

This article has been reprinted as it originally appeared in *Current Directions in Psychological Science*. Citation information for this article as originally published appears above.

Beyond Fear: Emotional Memory Mechanisms in the Human Brain

Kevin S. LaBar[1]
Duke University

Abstract

Neurobiological accounts of emotional memory have been derived largely from animal models investigating the encoding and retention of memories for events that signal threat. This literature has implicated the amygdala, a structure in the brain's temporal lobe, in the learning and consolidation of fear memories. Its role in fear conditioning has been confirmed, but the human amygdala also interacts with cortical regions to mediate other aspects of emotional memory. These include the encoding and consolidation of pleasant and unpleasant arousing events into long-term memory, the narrowing of focus on central emotional information, the retrieval of prior emotional events and contexts, and the subjective experience of recollection and emotional intensity during retrieval. Along with other mechanisms that do not involve the amygdala, these functions ensure that significant life events leave a lasting impression in memory.

Keywords

affect; anxiety; traumatic memory; medial temporal lobe; fear conditioning

How we remember emotional episodes from the past has captivated scholarly interest for centuries, from philosophical accounts of the relationship between the passions and mental faculties to psychoanalytic views on the emotional unconscious. When recalling events from one's personal history, not only do emotions figure prominently in the content of the memory, but one also feels differently during the act of emotional recollection than during the recall of a mundane fact. Emotions therefore contribute to both the selective retention and the subjective experience of memory. Rapaport (1950) argued that "memory laws based on logical 'meaning' and 'organization' of the memory material refer only to special cases of memory organization; the more general theory of memory is the theory based on 'emotional organization' of memories" (p. 268). In other words, theorizing how cognitive processes influence memory in the absence of emotion is to consider only a limited set of circumstances in which memory is normally engaged. A current major goal is to understand the psychological and neural mechanisms by which emotions exert their influence over learning and memory processes in the brain.

Animal studies have used training procedures based on classical conditioning principles to elucidate how the brain forms and retains memories for cues and contexts that predict aversive or rewarding outcomes. For example, when presented with a tone that reliably predicts the delivery of a foot shock, rats will readily acquire fear responses to the tone and other features of the environment. Fear-conditioning models have emphasized a key role of the amygdala, a subcortical structure in the medial temporal lobe of the brain. The amygdala integrates sensory information about threats across subcortical and cortical routes of processing and orchestrates integrated defensive reactions by controlling autonomic

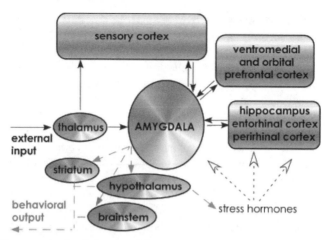

Fig. 1. The central role of the amygdala in emotional learning and memory as initially derived from animal models of fear conditioning. The amygdala integrates sensory information from subcortical and cortical processing pathways (solid black arrows) and orchestrates coordinated emotional responses to salient events (dashed grey arrows). Inputs from the frontal and temporal lobes (right side) exert contextual control over emotional behavior. Many of the input projections from the cortex are reciprocal, which provides a means for amygdala-dependent emotional processing to influence memory and other cognitive functions. In parallel, activation of stress-hormone systems facilitates storage of newly acquired information via feedback mechanisms from the periphery onto central receptor sites. Subcortical structures are indicated with ovals; cortical structures are indicated with boxes.

and motor output centers (Fig. 1). The amygdala's internal processing and its interactions with the frontal lobes and hippocampus, another structure in the temporal lobe, are important in the acquisition and subsequent suppression (extinction) of fear associations to cues and environmental contexts, and these findings have been confirmed in humans (LaBar and LeDoux, 2006).

There are lingering questions over whether the neural circuitry revealed by conditioning studies extends to the domain of human emotion beyond situations involving imminent primary reinforcers. What can such an evolutionarily old structure like the amygdala contribute to emotional forms of human memory? Surprising answers to this question continue to emerge as more functions of the amygdala and its cortical interactions are revealed by neuroimaging and by neuropsychological and pharmacological research.

AROUSAL-MEDIATED MEMORY CONSOLIDATION

McGaugh's (2004) *memory modulation hypothesis* posits that, following an emotionally arousing experience, the amygdala engages adrenergic and cortisol stress-hormone systems that interact to promote memory storage in the cortex. Accumulating evidence supports this hypothesis in studies of human emotional memory. For example, people with amygdala damage are impaired in remembering details of the emotionally arousing portion of a story learned several weeks earlier, despite having normal memory for the nonemotional portions of the story

(Cahill, Babinsky, Markowitsch, & McGaugh, 1995). When healthy adults are administered a drug (propranolol) that antagonizes the adrenergic system prior to learning the story, they exhibit the same selective emotional-memory deficits as the amygdaladamaged patients (Cahill, Prins, Weber, & McGaugh, 1994), implicating a converging mechanism. Although these findings are typically interpreted as reflecting enhanced memory consolidation by emotional arousal, alternative interpretations—such as effects on attention at encoding that enhance both short- and long-term memory—are possible. In order to specifically implicate consolidation, the emotion effects must be augmented after a delay, as consolidation is defined as a time-dependent selective transfer of new information into long-term storage.

Phelps et al. (1998) presented a list of emotionally arousing and neutral words to amygdala-damaged patients, and recall was tested immediately and following a 1-hour delay. Control subjects showed different forgetting curves for the material over the delay interval, with a decline in memory for the neutral words but a relative increase in memory for the arousing words over time. In contrast, the patients forgot both classes of words at the same rate. Because the effect of emotion on memory was boosted over the delay in control subjects and the patient deficit was exacerbated following this delay, the results specifically implicate a role for the amygdala in arousal-mediated memory consolidation.

But how does the amygdala influence memory circuits in the brain to achieve this retention boost? Dolcos, LaBar, and Cabeza (2004) showed participants pleasant, unpleasant, and neutral pictures while they underwent functional magnetic resonance imaging (fMRI), and participants recalled the pictures after scanning was completed. For each participant, brain activity during encoding was segregated into responses to pictures that were subsequently remembered versus those that were forgotten. Comparison of these activation patterns yields a neural marker for the successful encoding of items into long-term memory: the *Difference in memory* (Dm) *effect*. The Dm effect in the amygdala and other temporal lobe structures was larger for the emotionally arousing pictures than for the neutral pictures. In addition, the emotional Dm effects were highly correlated across different regions of the temporal lobe, indicating that the amygdala and other temporal lobe structures are functionally coupled during the successful encoding of emotional memories. What makes these fMRI analyses so intriguing is that they provide a glimpse into the momentary neural interactions that predict whether an item a participant is currently viewing will be remembered or forgotten on a subsequent memory test. Whether this fMRI activity is subject to pharmacological alterations that affect stress-hormone systems is an active topic of inquiry.

FOCUSING OF EMOTIONAL MEMORIES

One account of the emotional-story findings discussed earlier is that the amygdala (and adrenergic engagement) normally focuses attention on material presented during the emotional segments of the story, which in turn foregrounds in memory this central thematic information (called *gist*) at the expense of background peripheral details. Adolphs, Tranel, and Buchanan (2005) tested this hypothesis by presenting amygdala-damaged patients with target items embedded in a series

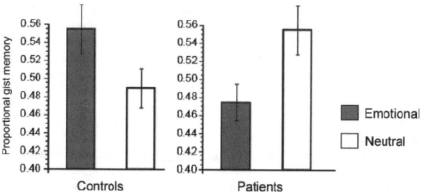

Fig. 2. Emotional focusing on central (gist) information in memory in normal controls as compared with patients with amygdala damage. Participants viewed target pictures embedded in neutral or emotional audiovisual story contexts. Recognition memory for central (gist) information and peripheral details in the target pictures was assessed after a 24-hour delay. (Memory for gist information is depicted as a proportion of the total memory score.) When target pictures were embedded in emotional contexts, control subjects (left) recognized more central than peripheral information, but patients with amygdala damage (right) recognized more peripheral than central information. The opposite pattern was found for target pictures embedded in neutral contexts. Adapted from "Amygdala Damage Impairs Emotional Memory for Gist But Not Details of Complex Stimuli," by R. Adolphs, D. Tranel, & T.W. Buchanan, 2005, *Nature Neuroscience, 8*, p. 514. Copyright 2005, Nature Publishing Group. Adapted with permission.

of either emotional or neutral pictures (Fig. 2). Gist and peripheral-detail memory were then tested for the targets as a function of the emotional-encoding manipulation. A narrowing of memory focus on gist information was found for the emotional-encoding condition in the control subjects but not in the patients. It is not yet clear whether central focusing occurs during the initial learning of the material or is a consequence of consolidation or retrieval, since the brain damage could have affected any one of these memory stages.

Focusing of memory on central information during emotional situations occurs in various real-world scenarios. In eyewitness testimony, memory is often focused on the weapons present at a crime scene at the expense of peripheral information such as the clothing worn by accomplices. In posttraumatic stress disorder (PTSD), patients sometimes report tunnel vision in their traumatic flashbacks, such that the memory contains a central event (e.g., detonating of a bomb) without contextual details. It will be important to characterize with neuroimaging techniques the brain regions that focus memory under these circumstances.

BEYOND THE MEMORY MODULATION HYPOTHESIS: RETRIEVAL OF EMOTIONAL EXPERIENCES

McGaugh's memory modulation hypothesis concerns consolidation mechanisms and does not postulate a critical role for the amygdala during the retrieval of emotional experiences. However, recent fMRI studies in humans suggest that this classic view of amygdala function may be incomplete. Smith, Henson, Dolan, and Rugg (2004) found greater activation in the amygdala and other structures when individuals accurately recognized neutral objects that were previously encoded in emotional picture contexts (both pleasant and unpleasant) relative to those encoded in neutral picture contexts. This pattern occurred despite the fact that only the neutral objects were presented during the recognition test. Thus, the amygdala participates in reinstating emotional contextual information during retrieval and/or links emotional changes signaled by other brain regions to specific retrieval cues.

Dolcos, LaBar, and Cabeza (2005) conducted an fMRI study of recognition memory 1 year after participants had been exposed to positive, negative or neutral pictures. For each participant, brain activity was segregated into responses to pictures that were accurately remembered versus those that were forgotten. Comparison of these activation patterns serves as a neural marker for the successful retrieval of items from long-term memory. In the amygdala and other temporal lobe regions, activity was enhanced for the successful retrieval of the emotional pictures (both positive and negative) relative to the neutral ones (Fig. 3). This activity was correlated more strongly across the temporal lobe regions for the emotional pictures than it was for the neutral ones, implicating a tighter functional connectivity during successful emotional item retrieval than during neutral item retrieval.

fMRI studies of autobiographical memory confirm the engagement of similar brain areas during retrieval. For instance, Greenberg et al. (2005) showed that the retrieval of pleasant autobiographical memories in response to personally tailored cue words elicited activation of the amygdala, hippocampus, and frontal lobes. Activity in these regions was also more highly correlated during autobiographical retrieval than during the retrieval of general semantic knowledge. The findings indicate that the amygdala was functionally incorporated into a frontotemporal memory network but only when experiences from the personal past were being retrieved.

An issue that is commonly raised with retrieval studies is whether the activation patterns reflect retrieval processes per se or whether instead they reflect the formation of new memories for the retrieval episodes. Although retrieval of prior events recapitulates activity in some brain areas that were active during the initial encoding of the events, the brain regions discussed here may make unique contributions to encoding and retrieval. For instance, amygdala activity signals successful retrieval of both emotional items and contexts, but during encoding its activity more strongly predicts emotional item memory (Kensinger & Schacter, 2006). Moreover, in the Dolcos et al. (2004, 2005) studies, the temporal lobe regions exhibited some hemispheric asymmetry as a function of memory stage within participants: Whereas the encoding effects were localized mainly in the left hemisphere, the retrieval effects were localized mainly in the right hemisphere. As discussed further below, the amygdala and hippocampus make selective contributions to some retrieval processes but not others, which would not be predicted according to an encoding-of-retrieval account.

Nonetheless, important questions regarding the amygdala's contribution to retrieval processes remain. For instance, does the amygdala engage neurohormonal

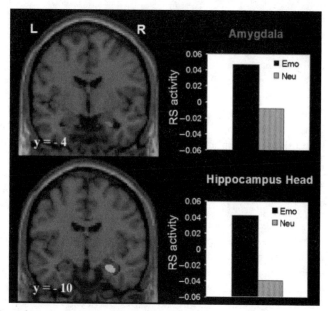

Fig. 3. Contribution of the amygdala and hippocampus to successful retrieval of emotionally arousing pictures 1 year after encoding. Retrieval success (RS) is defined as a difference in blood-oxygen-level-dependent signal change for pictures that were successfully remembered versus those that were forgotten. In the right amygdala and head (forward) region of the hippocampus, RS activity was larger for emotional (Emo) compared to neutral (Neu) pictures. L = left hemisphere, R = right hemisphere. Reproduced from "Remembering One Year Later: Role of the Amygdala and the Medial Temporal Lobe Memory System in Retrieving Emotional Memories," by F. Dolcos, K.S. LaBar, & R. Cabeza, 2005, *Proceedings of the National Academy of Sciences, USA, 102*, p. 2629. Copyright 2005, National Academy of Sciences. Reproduced with permission.

systems to reconsolidate emotional events in memory when they are retrieved? The issue of memory reconsolidation is currently receiving intense scrutiny. If memories are always reconsolidated upon retrieval, then interventions that block the reconsolidation process may reduce the details available in subsequent retrievals of the same memory, including their emotional salience. For the treatment of PTSD and other affective disorders, blocking reconsolidation of specific memories would have immense clinical value but, at the same time, would raise ethical concerns.

THE SUBJECTIVE EXPERIENCE OF EMOTIONAL REMEMBERING

Most studies attempt to reveal how emotional content alters the strength of memory traces. However, emotional memories are also distinctive in their phenomenological characteristics, including their vividness, one's sense of traveling back in time to re-experience the contextual details of the memory (called *recollection*), and their physiologic changes that generate feeling states. Researchers have begun to explore how brain activity during retrieval relates to the subjective aspects of emotional remembering in ways that go beyond mere alterations in memory strength. For instance, amygdala and hippocampal activity during auto-biographical memory retrieval correlates with subjective ratings of emotional intensity provided by the participants, even when the potentially confounding influence of event recency is controlled (Addis, Moscovitch, Crawley, & McAndrews, 2004; Daselaar et al., in press). When participants attempt to retrieve personal memories from generic cue words (e.g., *picnic*), fMRI activity in the amygdala begins before they have a fully-formed memory in mind (as indicted by a voluntary button press), and this activity predicts subsequent emotional-intensity ratings provided by the participants (Daselaar et al., in press). Therefore, the amygdala may use arousal information based on incomplete memory representations to help select memories during search attempts and to facilitate the retrieval of associated contextual information from other brain regions—which, in turn, leads to greater vividness and reliving as the memory unfolds in the mind.

Several experiments have contrasted the sense of recollection with the sense of *familiarity*, a form of retrieval in which the memory trace has little supporting contextual information. As a commonplace example, feelings of familiarity often occur when individuals are encountered outside of their typical social context. Emotionally arousing events are more likely to be retrieved with a sense of recollection than with a sense of familiarity, and the selective retention advantage for recollected memories has been linked to activity in the amygdala and hippocampus during the retrieval of emotional items and contexts (e.g., Dolcos et al., 2005). This line of work is catapulting the neurobiology of emotional memory into the realm of subjective aspects of recall, promising to unveil how the feelings that arise during personal life reflections are mediated neurally.

OTHER EMOTIONAL MEMORY MECHANISMS

The cortical interactions and hormonal engagement by the amygdala are not the only means by which emotional experiences are remembered. Kensinger and Corkin (2004) found that another region of the frontal lobes interacts with the hippocampus to boost memory for less-arousing emotional stimuli and that this effect bypasses the amygdala. Valence-based effects in the absence of high arousal are thought to reflect semantic relatedness and other organizational benefits of emotion. For example, words that share emotional valence tend to be more semantically related than a random selection of neutral words, and this shared valence yields retention advantages. Amygdala-damaged patients can use semantic knowledge and other organizational strategies to improve memory for emotional material under some circumstances—an important compensatory avenue in the face of impaired amygdala function.

CONCLUSIONS AND FUTURE DIRECTIONS

More than just the brain's watchdog for detecting impending threat, the amygdala is now known to regulate various aspects of emotional learning and memory by interacting, both directly and indirectly, with memory-related regions of the frontal and temporal lobes. The effects of emotion appear at multiple stages of memory processing, and the same brain regions may make unique contributions at each of these stages. Traditional accounts of amygdala function as a facilitator of memory consolidation are being extended by contemporary approaches to include aspects of memory retrieval and the subjective experiences that occur during autobiographical recollection. Although this review highlighted emotional influences on long-term declarative memory, other memory systems are receiving increased attention, including working memory and procedural learning. Individual differences in emotional memory are being investigated at multiple levels of analysis—from the study of age and sex differences in brain activation to genetic variation of neurotransmitter receptors expressed in the relevant neural circuitry. Finally, while beneficial in many respects, emotion can impair memory under some conditions, including prolonged or intense stress, task-irrelevant emotional distraction, and anxiety and mood disorders. Studying these adverse consequences and identifying how emotion-regulation strategies and pharmacologic interventions ameliorate them will promote a fuller understanding of the emotional organization of memory.

Recommended Reading

LaBar, K.S., & Cabeza, R. (2006). Cognitive neuroscience of emotional memory. *Nature Reviews Neuroscience, 7,* 54–64.

Acknowledgments—This work was supported by National Science Foundation CAREER award 0239614 and National Institutes of Health Grants R01 DA14094, R01 AG023123, and P01 NS041328. The author wishes to thank Joseph LeDoux, Elizabeth Phelps, Roberto Cabeza, and David Rubin for their contributions to the ideas and studies presented in this review.

Note

1. Address correspondence to Kevin S. LaBar, Center for Cognitive Neuroscience, Box 90999, Duke University, Durham, NC 27708-0999; e-mail: klabar@duke.edu.

References

Addis, D.R., Moscovitch, M., Crawley, A.P., & McAndrews, M.P. (2004). Recollective qualities modulate hippocampal activation during autobiographical memory retrieval. *Hippocampus, 14,* 752–762.

Adolphs, R., Tranel, D., & Buchanan, T.W. (2005). Amygdala damage impairs emotional memory for gist but not details of complex stimuli. *Nature Neuroscience, 8,* 512–518.

Cahill, L., Babinsky, R., Markowitsch, H.J., & McGaugh, J.L. (1995). The amygdala and emotional memory. *Nature, 377,* 295–296.

Cahill, L., Prins, B., Weber, M., & McGaugh, J.L. (1994). Beta-adrenergic activation and memory for emotional events. *Nature, 371,* 702–704.

Daselaar, S., Rice, H.J., Greenberg, D.L., Cabeza, R., LaBar, K.S., & Rubin, D.C. (in press). Spatiotemporal dynamics of autobiographical memory: Neural correlates of recall, emotional intensity and reliving. *Cerebral Cortex.*

Dolcos, F., LaBar, K.S., & Cabeza, R. (2004). Interaction between the amygdala and the medial temporal lobe memory system predicts better memory for emotional events. *Neuron, 42,* 855–863.

Dolcos, F., LaBar, K.S., & Cabeza, R. (2005). Remembering one year later: Role of the amygdala and the medial temporal lobe memory system in retrieving emotional memories. *Proceedings of the National Academy of Sciences, USA, 102,* 2626–2631.

Greenberg, D.L., Rice, H.J., Cooper, J.J., Cabeza, R., Rubin, D.C., & LaBar, K.S. (2005). Co-activation of the amygdala, hippocampus and inferior frontal gyrus during autobiographical memory retrieval. *Neuropsychologia, 43,* 659–674.

Kensinger, E.A., & Corkin, S. (2004). Two routes to emotional memory: Distinct neural processes for valence and arousal. *Proceedings of the National Academy of Sciences, USA, 101,* 3310–3315.

Kensinger, E.A., & Schacter, D.L. (2006). Amygdala activity is associated with the successful encoding of item, but not source, information for positive and negative stimuli. *Journal of Neuroscience, 26,* 2564–2570.

LaBar, K.S., & LeDoux, J.E. (2006). Fear and anxiety pathways. In S. Moldin & J.L. Rubenstein (Eds.), *Understanding Autism: From Basic Neuroscience to Treatment* (pp. 133–154). Boca Raton, FL: CRC Press.

McGaugh, J.L. (2004). The amygdala modulates the consolidation of memories of emotionally arousing experiences. *Annual Review of Neuroscience, 27,* 1–28.

Phelps, E.A., LaBar, K.S., Anderson, A.K., O'Connor, K.J., Fulbright, R.K., & Spencer, D.D. (1998). Specifying the contributions of the human amygdala to emotional memory: A case study. *Neurocase, 4,* 527–540.

Rapaport, D. (1950). *Emotions and Memory* (2nd ed.). New York: International Universities Press.

Smith, A.P., Henson, R.N., Dolan, R.J., & Rugg, M.D. (2004). fMRI correlates of the episodic retrieval of emotional contexts. *Neuroimage, 22,* 868–878.

This article has been reprinted as it originally appeared in *Current Directions in Psychological Science*. Citation information for this article as originally published appears above.

Tend and Befriend: Biobehavioral Bases of Affiliation Under Stress

Shelley E. Taylor[1]
University of California, Los Angeles

Abstract

In addition to fight-or-flight, humans demonstrate tending and befriending responses to stress—responses underpinned by the hormone oxytocin, by opioids, and by dopaminergic pathways. A working model of affiliation under stress suggests that oxytocin may be a biomarker of social distress that accompanies gaps or problems with social relationships and that may provide an impetus for affiliation. Oxytocin is implicated in the seeking of affiliative contact in response to stress, and, in conjunction with opioids, it also modulates stress responses. Specifically, in conjunction with positive affiliative contacts, oxytocin attenuates psychological and biological stress responses, but in conjunction with hostile and unsupportive contacts, oxytocin may exacerbate psychological and biological stress responses. Although significant paradoxes remain to be resolved, a mechanism that may underlie oxytocin's relation to the health benefits of social support may be in view.

Keywords

oxytocin; opioids; tending; befriending; affiliation

The dominant conception of biobehavioral responses to stress has been the fight-or-flight response. In response to threat, humans or animals can become aggressive and confront a stressor or flee either literally or metaphorically, as through avoidant coping. Fight-or-flight responses depend on two interacting stress systems, the sympathetic nervous system (SNS) and the hypothalamic-pituitary-adrenocortical (HPA) axis, which mobilize the organism for concerted efforts to combat or escape from threat. In important respects, fight-or-flight provides a good characterization of responses to stress. However, from the standpoint of human beings, this analysis is incomplete. One of the most striking aspects of the human stress response is the tendency to affiliate—that is, to come together in groups to provide and receive joint protection in threatening times (Baumeister & Leary, 1995; Taylor, 2002).

Our laboratory has explored a biobehavioral model that characterizes these affiliative behaviors. From animal studies and our own data, we infer that there is an affiliative neurocircuitry that prompts affiliation, especially in response to stress. We suggest that this system regulates social-approach behavior and does so in much the same way as occurs for other appetitive needs. That is, just as people have basic needs such as hunger, thirst, sexual drives, and other appetites, they also need to maintain an adequate level of protective and rewarding social relationships.

As occurs for these other appetites, we suggest there is a biological signaling system that comes into play if one's affiliations fall below an adequate level (see Fig. 1). Once signaled, the appetitive need is met through purposeful social behavior. If social contacts are hostile or unsupportive, then psychological and biological stress

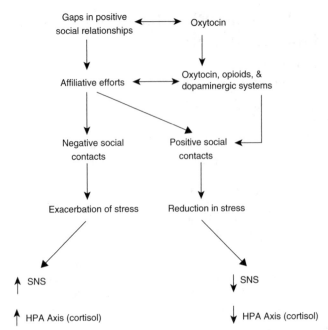

Fig. 1. A model of affiliative responses to stress. Elevations in plasma oxytocin accompany gaps in positive social relationships and are believed to prompt affiliative efforts aimed at restoring positive social contacts; engagement of opioid and dopaminergic systems coupled with oxytocin may lead to a reduction in stress responses, including those of the sympathetic nervous system (SNS) and the hypothalamic-pituitary-adrenocortical (HPA) axis. However, negative social contacts exacerbate stress, leading to an increase in these same biological stress responses.

responses are heightened. If social contacts are supportive and comforting, stress responses decline. Positive contacts, in turn, lead to a decline in the need and, in the context of stress, a decline in stress responses. The fact that affiliation may look like other appetitive needs is not coincidental. Because biological neurocircuitries tend to be efficient, the dopamine and opioid systems that are recruited for other reward-based systems may well be recruited for the satisfaction of affiliative needs as well (see Depue & Morrone-Strupinksy, 2005).

In characterizing these social responses to stress we have used the metaphor "tend and befriend" (Taylor, 2002; Taylor et al., 2000). Our position is that under conditions of stress, tending to offspring and affiliating with others ("befriending") are at least as common responses to stress in humans as fight-or-flight. In building our model, we have focused heavily on the hormone oxytocin (see Fig. 1). We maintain that oxytocin is released in response to (at least some) stressors, especially those that may trigger affiliative needs; oxytocin prompts affiliative behavior in response to stress, in conjunction with dopaminergic and opioid systems. This affiliative activity may serve tending needs, including protective responses toward offspring, and/or it may take the form of befriending, namely seeking social contact for one's own protection and solace. Oxytocin, in conjunction with positive social contacts, attenuates biological stress responses (SNS, HPA axis) that can arise in response to social threats. In the sections that follow, we detail the elements in Figure 1, which is used as an organizational as well as a conceptual device.

It is important to note that oxytocin has been implicated in a broad array of social relationships and social activities, including peer bonding, sexual activity, and affiliative preferences under nonstressful circumstances (Carter, 1998; Insel, 1997). Thus, the model to be characterized in the subsequent sections primarily elucidates social behavior under stress and does not address larger issues concerning how oxytocin may be implicated in social activity in nonstressful times.

RELATIONSHIP GAPS AND SEPARATION DISTRESS

Affiliation is vital to the survival of human beings; accordingly, there are likely to be biobehavioral mechanisms that are sensitive to social threats or loss of social contact. Evidence for such an assertion comes from research on separation distress. When young are separated from their mothers, separation distress in offspring can result, leading to distress vocalizations that may prompt the return of the caregiver. This system appears to be dependent, in part, on oxytocin and brain opioids. Evidence consistent with the existence of such a system includes the facts that brain opioids reduce separation distress and that drugs such as morphine reduce distress vocalizations in animals (Panksepp, 1998).

Adults experience separation distress as well, but until recently the biological underpinnings of adult relationship gaps were not explored. To address this issue, we examined the relation of plasma oxytocin levels to reports of relationship distress in adult women (Taylor et al., 2006). We found that women who were experiencing gaps in their social relationships had elevated levels of oxytocin. Specifically, women with high levels of oxytocin were more likely to report reduced contact with their mothers, their best friends, their pets, and social groups to which they belonged. In addition, those with significant others were more likely to report that their partners were not supportive, did not understand the way they felt about things, and did not care for them. Poor quality of the marital relationship and infrequent display of affection by the partner were also associated with higher levels of plasma oxytocin. Thus, oxytocin appears to signal relationship distress, at least in women.

Plasma oxytocin was not related to general psychological distress, only to gaps or problems in positive relationships; and whereas oxytocin appeared to signal gaps in relationships, levels of the stress hormone cortisol were not similarly elevated. These points suggest that oxytocin may be distinctively related to relationship distress. Similar findings have been reported by Turner, Altemus, Enos, Cooper, and McGuinness (1999), who found that elevated plasma oxytocin was associated with anxiety over relationships, perceived coldness or intrusiveness in relationships, and not being in a primary romantic relationship. Thus, the relation of oxytocin to relationship distress has been confirmed in two independent laboratories.

RELATION OF OXYTOCIN TO AFFILIATION

If oxytocin is related to social distress, then as an affiliative hormone, oxytocin may provide an impetus for social contact to ameliorate stress. There is manifold evidence that oxytocin, indeed, promotes affiliation, most of which has come from animal studies (e.g., Panksepp, Nelson, & Bekkedal, 1999; see Insel, 1997, for a review). Exogenously administered oxytocin has been related to increases in physical proximity, increased maternal behavior, grooming, and preferences for conspecifics in whose presence elevated oxytocin was experienced (see Panksepp, 1998; Taylor, 2002, for reviews). Oxytocin is also thought to underlie affiliative activities in humans as well, including maternal behavior and social bonding more generally (e.g., Carter, 1998; Carter, Lederhendler, & Kirkpatrick, 1999; Taylor, 2002). Thus, it appears that a fairly broad array of affiliative behaviors may be subserved by oxytocin.

RELATIONSHIP OF OXYTOCIN TO STRESS RESPONSES

The next link in the model relates oxytocin to stress responses. Animal studies have shown that exogenous administration of oxytocin or stimulation of oxytocin secretion decreases sympathetic reactivity, blood pressure, pain sensitivity, and corticosteroid levels, among other findings suggestive of a reduced stress response (e.g., Carter, 1998; Insel, 1997). A more modest literature in humans suggests similar effects. For example, among breastfeeding women who have high levels of oxytocin (Light et al., 2000), among women reporting more frequent hugs from partners (Light, Grewen, & Amico, 2005), and among men receiving exogenous oxytocin (Heinrichs, Baumgartner, Kirshbaum, & Ehlert, 2003), psychological and biological stress responses are lower. Overall, the evidence that high levels of or exogenously administrated oxytocin attenuate stress responses is strong in animals and suggestive in human studies.

As our model maintains, however, if affiliative efforts are unrequited or negative, heightened stress responses may occur. In a study consistent with this point (Taylor et al., 2006), women participated in a socially threatening laboratory challenge task and their responses were assessed. Those with low levels of plasma oxytocin showed an increase in cortisol in response to the social threat and a decrease during recovery. By contrast, women with initially high plasma oxytocin levels had significantly higher cortisol levels initially, which decreased early on in the laboratory procedures but then again became elevated during the threat tasks. These findings suggest that women with high levels of oxytocin may be especially attuned to social features of the environment and that their levels of stress may be especially exacerbated by unsupportive social contacts. Thus, quality of social contacts during stressful times may be a pivotal variable for understanding the relation of oxytocin to stress responses.

The fact that high levels of oxytocin can be associated both with relationship distress and with reduced stress responses appears inconsistent. One hypothesis is that bursts of oxytocin, as may occur in response to anticipated or actual social contact or exogenous administration of oxytocin, reduce stress responses but that elevated oxytocin in plasma, which likely represents trace evidence of some preceding process, is associated with relationship distress (Turner et al., 1999; but see Grewen, Girdler, Amico, & Light, 2005). Another possible resolution stems from the fact that most studies documenting the stress-reducing qualities of oxytocin have not disentangled the effects of oxytocin from affiliation itself or its anticipation. Oxytocin increases the sensitivity of brain opioid systems, and at least some of the stress-reducing properties of oxytocin appear to be mediated by an opioid pathway and also, as noted earlier, by dopaminergic pathways. It is possible that a need for social contact that is unrequited does not implicate these downstream stress-reducing effects of oxytocin that appear to occur in the context of actual or anticipated affiliative contact.

BENEFITS OF TENDING UNDER STRESS

Why would humans (and some animals) have a biologically regulated affiliative system? Looking at the affiliative system from the standpoint of evolutionary theory suggests that there would be clear survival benefits of a biobehavioral mechanism that signals gaps in social support and prompts affiliation for beneficial communal responses to stress. Tending to offspring in times of stress would be vital to ensuring the survival of the species. Oxytocin may be at the core of such tending responses in threatening circumstances. Evidence from a broad array of animal studies shows that central administration of oxytocin enhances maternal behavior (see Taylor et al., 2000, for a review; Taylor, 2002). Such tending also has a wide array of immediate benefits—for example, reducing HPA and SNS activity in both mother and offspring.[2]

Evidence concerning the biological bases and consequences of maternal–infant contact in humans is more limited. Oxytocin is believed to be implicated initially in bonding between mother and infant. Oxytocin is at high levels in the mother following giving birth and may promote bonding; however, mother–infant attachment may soon become independent of its hormonal bases, maintained instead by neuromechanisms in the brain that underlie attachment (Taylor, 2002).

BENEFITS OF BEFRIENDING UNDER STRESS

A large social-support literature documents that "befriending" leads to substantial mental and physical health benefits in times of stress. Social isolation is tied to a significantly enhanced risk of mortality, whereas social support is tied to a broad array of beneficial health outcomes, including reduced risk of mortality (see Taylor, 2007, for a current review). Whether oxytocin is implicated in these processes has been unknown. However, in one study (Detillion, Craft, Glasper, Prendergast, & DeVries, 2004), Siberian hamsters received a skin wound and were then exposed to immobilization stress. The stressor increased cortisol concentrations and impaired wound healing, but only in socially isolated animals and not in socially housed ones. Thus, social housing acted as a stress buffer. Removing cortisol via adrenalectomy (removal of the adrenal glands) eliminated the impact of the stressor on wound healing, thereby implicating the HPA axis in the healing process. Of particular relevance to the current arguments, treating the isolated hamsters with oxytocin eliminated the stress-induced increases in cortisol and facilitated wound healing; treating socially housed hamsters with an oxytocin antagonist delayed wound healing. These data strongly imply that social contacts can protect against the adverse effects of stress through a mechanism that implicates oxytocin-induced suppression of the HPA axis. Thus, there appear to be discernible clinical consequences of oxytocin suppression of the HPA axis.

GENDER DIFFERENCES IN THE RELATION OF OXYTOCIN TO TENDING AND BEFRIENDING

The effects of oxytocin on social behavior have been heavily studied in estrogen-treated female animals and in women. The evidence that oxytocin plays an important role in male social relationships is less plentiful. Heinrichs et al. (2003) found that oxytocin had anti-stress effects in men. However, their paradigm used exogenous administration of oxytocin and therefore showed that oxytocin can have such effects in men, but not necessarily that it typically does.

There are several reasons to believe that oxytocin may play a more important role in influencing women's social behavior than men's, especially under stress. At the time when human stress responses evolved, work was largely sex segregated, with women more responsible for childcare. Thus, selection pressures for responses to threat that benefit both self and offspring may have been greater for females than for males—favoring social responses to stress in women especially (Taylor, 2002). Women's consistently stronger affiliative responses to stress compared to those of men (Tamres, Janicki, & Helgeson, 2002; Taylor, 2002) is consistent with this point. Estrogen strongly enhances the effects of oxytocin, which is also consistent with a greater role for oxytocin in women's behavior than in men's. At present, there appears to be a stronger basis for making inferences about the relation of oxytocin to social behavior in females than in males.

CONCLUSIONS

A large animal literature and a small human literature have tied oxytocin to separation distress, maternal tending, befriending responses to stress, and reduced psychological and biological stress responses. Exactly how oxytocin is implicated in these processes and how this may differ for males and females is not yet clear. Moreover, significant paradoxes remain, most especially the relation of oxytocin to both relationship distress and to reduced stress responses. Despite these gaps in knowledge, the mechanisms underlying oxytocin's relation to the reduction of stress and the beneficial effects of social responses to stress on health appears to be in view.

Clarifying the role of oxytocin in relationship processes—those implicated in both stressful and nonstressful times—will be valuable for scientific yield regarding the biological underpinnings of social bonds. Such knowledge will also help to clarify oxytocin's potential role in social dysfunction and disease processes. For example, the centrality of social deficits to mental disorders such as depression and autism suggests that with greater understanding of the oxytocin system, these disorders might become better understood as well.

Basic research issues for the future include resolution of significant methodological issues regarding oxytocin-based underpinnings of social relationships, especially the differences between experimental findings manipulating oxytocin and findings relating plasma oxytocin and social processes. More broadly, whether affiliation is best characterized as an appetitive need with dynamics approximating those in Figure 1 remains to be seen. The model proposed here hopefully provides a heuristic for further examination of these processes.

Recommended Reading

Carter, C.S., Lederhendler, I.I., & Kirkpatrick, B., eds. (1999). (See References)
Taylor, S.E. (2002). (See References)

Acknowledgments—Preparation of this article was supported by National Science Foundation Grant SES-0525713.

Notes

1. Address correspondence to Shelley E. Taylor, UCLA Department of Psychology, 1282A Franz Hall, Los Angeles, CA 90095; taylors@psych.ucla.edu.
2. All the animal data are based on responses of mothers, not those of fathers.

References

Baumeister, R.F., & Leary, M.R. (1995). The need to belong: Desire for interpersonal attachments as a fundamental human motivation. *Psychological Bulletin, 117*, 497–529.

Carter, C.S. (1998). Neuroendocrine perspectives on social attachment and love. *Psychoneuroendocrinology, 23*, 779–818.

Carter, C.S., Lederhendler, I.I., & Kirkpatrick, B. (Eds.). (1999). *The integrative neurobiology of affiliation.* Cambridge, MA: MIT Press.

Depue, R.A., & Morrone-Strupinsky, J.V. (2005). A neurobiobehavioral model of affiliative bonding: Implications for conceptualizing a human trait of affiliation. *Behavioral and Brain Sciences, 28*, 313–395.

Detillion, C.E., Craft, T.K., Glasper, E.R., Prendergast, B.J., & DeVries, C. (2004). Social facilitation of wound healing. *Psychoneuroendocrinology, 29*, 1004–1011.

Grewen, K.M., Girdler, S.S., Amico, J., & Light, K.C. (2005). Effects of partner support on resting oxytocin, cortisol, norepinephrine, and blood pressure before and after warm partner contact. *Psychosomatic Medicine, 67*, 531–538.

Heinrichs, M., Baumgartner, T., Kirshbaum, C., & Ehlert, U. (2003). Social support and oxytocin interact to suppress cortisol and subjective responses to psychological stress. *Biological Psychiatry, 54*, 1389–1398.

Insel, T.R. (1997). A neurobiological basis of social attachment. *American Journal of Psychiatry, 154*, 726–735.

Light, K., Grewen, K., & Amico, J.(2005).More frequent partnerhugs and higher oxytocin levels are linked to lower blood pressure and heart rate in premenopausal women. *Biological Psychiatry, 69*, 5–21.

Light, K.C., Smith, T.E., Johns, J.M., Brownley, K.A., Hofheimer, J.A., & Amico, J.A. (2000). Oxytocin responsivity in mothers of infants: A preliminary study of relationships with blood pressure during laboratory stress and normal ambulatory activity. *Health Psychology, 19*, 560–567.

Panksepp, J. (1998). *Affective neuroscience.* London: Oxford University Press.

Panksepp, J., Nelson, E., & Bekkedal, M. (1999). Brain systems for the mediation of social separation distress and social-reward: Evolutionary antecedents and neuropeptide intermediaries. In C.S. Carter, I.I. Lederhendler, & B. Kirkpatrick (Eds.), *The integrative neurobiology of affiliation* (pp. 221–244). Cambridge, MA: MIT Press.

Tamres, L., Janicki, D., & Helgeson, V.S. (2002). Sex differences in coping behavior: A meta-analytic review. *Personality and Social Psychology Review, 6*, 2–30.

Taylor, S.E. (2002). *The tending instinct: How nurturing is essential to who we are and how we live.* New York: Holt.

Taylor, S.E. (2007). Social support. In H.S. Friedman & R.C. Silver (Eds.), *Foundations of health psychology* (pp. 145–171). New York: Oxford University Press.

Taylor, S.E., Gonzaga, G., Klein, L.C., Hu, P., Greendale, G.A., & Seeman S. E. (2006). Relation of oxytocin to psychological and biological stress responses in older women. *Psychosomatic Medicine, 68*, 238–245.

Taylor, S.E., Klein, L.C., Lewis, B.P., Gruenewald, T.L., Gurung, R.A.R., & Updegraff, J.A. (2000). Biobehavioral responses to stress in females: Tend-and-befriend, not fight-or-flight. *Psychological Review, 107*, 411–429.

Turner, R.A., Altemus, M., Enos, T., Cooper, B., & McGuinness, T. (1999). Preliminary research on plasma oxytocin in normal cycling women: Investigating emotion and interpersonal distress. *Psychiatry, 62*, 97–113.

This article has been reprinted as it originally appeared in *Current Directions in Psychological Science*. Citation information for this article as originally published appears above.

Memories of Things Unseen

Elizabeth F. Loftus[1]
University of California, Irvine

Abstract

New findings reveal more about the malleability of memory. Not only is it possible to change details of memories for previously experienced events, but one can sometimes also plant entirely false memories into the minds of unsuspecting individuals, even if the events would be highly implausible or even impossible. False memories might differ statistically from true ones, in terms of certain characteristics such as confidence or vividness, but some false memories are held with a great degree of confidence and expressed with much emotion. Moreover, false memories can have consequences for later thoughts and behaviors, sometimes rather serious ones.

Keywords

memory; false memory; suggestibility

Faulty memory has led to more than its share of heartbreak. The cases of individuals who have been released from prison after DNA evidence revealed their innocence make compelling examples. Larry Mayes of Indiana had the dubious distinction of being the 100th such person to be freed in the United States. He was convicted of raping a gas station cashier after the victim positively identified him in court. Apparently it did not matter that she had failed to identify him in two earlier lineups and did so in court only after she was hypnotized by the police. Mayes spent 21 years in prison for a crime he did not commit. Attorney Thomas Vanes had prosecuted Mayes, believing at the time that Mayes was guilty. But two decades later, after Vanes saw the result of old evidence being subjected to new DNA testing, he changed his mind. "He was right, and I was wrong," wrote Vanes (2003), in a newspaper op-ed piece arguing for the DNA testing of another individual who was awaiting execution for an ugly robbery-murder of an elderly couple. For Vanes, it was a "sobering lesson."

The DNA exonerations have taught all of us a sobering lesson, namely, that faulty memory is the major cause of wrongful convictions. Concerns about justice are but one reason why the study of memory is so important.

MEMORY DISTORTION: FROM CHANGING DETAILS TO PLANTING FALSE MEMORIES

Pick up any textbook in the field of memory or cognition, and you will invariably find mention of faulty memory. That has been true for decades. But lately, the study of memory distortion has been thriving. In the 1970s through 1990s, hundreds of studies showed the power of new information to contaminate memory reports. Stop signs became yield signs, hammers turned into screwdrivers, and broken glass got "added" to memories for accidents. The inaccuracies in memory caused by erroneous information provided after the event became known as the "misinformation effect."

In the mid 1990s, memory investigators went further. It was one thing to change a detail in memory for a previously experienced event, but quite another thing to plant an entirely false memory into the mind. Using fairly strong suggestions, investigators succeeded in getting people to incorrectly believe that when they were children, they had been lost in a shopping mall for an extended time, hospitalized overnight, or involved in an unfortunate accident at a family wedding (see Loftus, 1997). The "strong suggestion" involved enlisting the help of family members to construct scenarios describing true and false experiences and feeding these scenarios to the subjects as if they were all true. The method was later dubbed the "familial-informant false-narrative procedure" (Lindsay, Hagen, Read, Wade, & Garry, 2004), but it is easier to call it the "lost in the mall" procedure. After being fed suggestive information that ostensibly came from their relatives, a significant minority of subjects came to accept all or part of the suggestion and claimed it as their own experience.

Would people also fall sway to suggestion if the to-be-planted event was particularly horrible? The answer is yes, as revealed in one study that convinced one third of subjects that when they were children they had nearly drowned and had to be rescued by a lifeguard (Heaps & Nash, 2001). Another research group convinced about half of their subjects that they had had particularly awful experiences as children, such as being a victim of a vicious animal attack (Porter, Yuille, & Lehman, 1999).

The suggestion used in these lost-in-the-mall studies was strong. In the real world, some forms of suggestion that are used are far more subtle. Perhaps their persuasive powers would be weaker. Take *guided imagination*, a technique in which individuals are led to imagine that they have had experiences (like breaking a window) that they have previously denied. Even a minute's worth of such imagination can increase people's confidence that in the past they had an experience like the imagined one—a phenomenon called *imagination inflation*. (See Garry & Polaschek, 2000, for an excellent review.) Imagining another person engaged in an event can also increase your confidence that it happened to you. Finally, some individuals, such as those who tend to have lapses in memory and attention, are more susceptible to imagination inflation than others. The clinical implications are evident—many therapy techniques involve imagination-based interventions; their capacity for distorting autobiography (an unexpected side effect?) needs to be appreciated.

PLANTING FALSE MEMORIES OR EXTRACTING TRUE MEMORIES?

When people claim, after suggestion, that they were lost in a mall, or attacked by an animal, perhaps the suggestive manipulation has extracted true memories rather than planting false ones. This quite-legitimate challenge has been met with research efforts to plant memories of events that would be highly implausible or even impossible.

In one such study, subjects evaluated advertisements under a pretense. One of the ads was for Disneyland and featured Bugs Bunny by the magic castle. The text made reference to meeting Bugs—the perfect end to the perfect day. After evaluating this ad, or a control ad, subjects were asked about their own childhood experiences at Disneyland (Braun, Ellis, & Loftus, 2002). About 16% of those who had been exposed to the fake Bugs ad later said they had personally met Bugs Bunny at Disneyland. Later studies showed that with multiple exposures to fake Disney ads that mentioned Bugs Bunny, the percentages rose even higher. Many of those subjects who fell sway to the suggestion remembered the impossible encounter in quite a bit of detail (e.g., they hugged Bugs or touched his ear). Of course, this memory is impossible because Bugs Bunny is a Warner Bros. character and would not be found at a Disney theme park. But the study shows that suggestive methods are indeed capable of leading to false beliefs or memories.

Other efforts to plant impossible or implausible memories show just how far one can go in tampering with people's autobiographies. In one case, people were led to believe that they had witnessed a person being demonically possessed as a child (Mazzoni, Loftus, & Kirsch, 2001). In the most powerful of these studies, subjects read articles that described demonic possession and were designed to increase its plausibility. One article was a testimonial from a prominent individual describing his own childhood experience with witnessing a possession. Subjects also received false feedback about causes of certain fears; they were told that witnessing a possession probably led to their particular childhood fears. Finally, they answered questions about their own childhood experiences. Relative to control subjects, those who had received the suggestion were more confident that they had witnessed possession as a child.

In yet another study, subjects were led to remember an event that never occurs in the country in which they lived, namely, "having a nurse remove a skin sample from my little finger" before age 6 (Mazzoni & Memon, 2003, p. 187). The most powerful method of suggestion in this study involved having subjects imagine that they had had the experience.

Perhaps you are thinking that these events are not sufficiently implausible— that Bugs might not be at Disneyland but other rabbits are, that demonic possession may not have been witnessed but other bizarre behavior was. Such critiques have encouraged researchers to come up with new pseudoevents that are less susceptible to these charges. Some researchers have also tried to make the false event so specific that it is unlikely to have happened to large numbers of people. So, in another study, subjects were persuaded that they had gotten in trouble with a friend for putting Slime (a brightly colored gelatinous substance manufactured as a toy) in their teacher's desk when in the first or second grade (Lindsay et al., 2004). The pseudoevent was chosen to be distinctive and memorable, and neither entirely implausible nor likely actually to have occurred. What was surprising about the findings was the sheer number of people who were led to believe that they had "Slimed" their teacher. The most powerful method of suggestion in this study involved the combination of a narrative and a photo ostensibly provided by the subject's parents. The narrative for the pseudoevent was customized for each subject by inserting the subject's name and the teacher's name into it:

I remember when Jane was in Grade 1, and like all kids back then, Jane had one of those revolting Slime toys that kids used to play with. I remember her telling me one day that she had taken the Slime to school and slid it into the teacher's desk before she arrived.

Jane claimed it wasn't her idea and that her friend decided they should do it. I think the teacher, Mrs. Smollett, wasn't very happy and made Jane and her friend sit with their arms folded and legs crossed, facing a wall for the next half hour. (Lindsay et al., 2004, p. 150)

The photo provided was the subject's actual class photo for Grade 1 or 2.

Using a fairly strict criterion for classifying a response as a pseudomemory, Lindsay and his colleagues found that when subjects returned to the lab for a second interview, more than 65% of subjects had developed such memories. Moreover, when debriefed and told their memories were false, some individuals expressed great surprise, as revealed in their verbalizations: "You mean that didn't happen to me?" and "No way! I remember it! That is so weird!" (Lindsay et al., 2004, pp. 152–153).

So (almost certainly), false memories do get planted by suggestion. Some methods are more powerful than others, leading to very high rates of false-memory reports. In the Slime study, the suggestion included a suggestive narrative ostensibly provided by an authoritative figure, namely, the subject's parent. Moreover, the class photo may have added to the authoritativeness of the suggestive narrative and increased the subject's confidence that the Slime event happened. The photo may have further encouraged speculation about the details of the pseudoevent. So, for example, a subject looking at the photo might have mused over who the co-perpetrator might have been in the Slime prank and even picked out a likely candidate. Finally, these studies indicate that rather unlikely events can be planted in the mind, and they counter the criticism that the events planted in such studies revive true memories.

CHARACTERISTICS OF FALSE MEMORIES

Can we tell the difference between true memories and false ones? Many studies show that there are some statistical differences, that true memories are held with more confidence or seem more vivid than false ones. But other studies do not demonstrate such differences. In the Slime study, for example, subjects rated their memories on a number of scales, including scales indicating their confidence that the event actually took place and the extent to which they felt their memory experience resembled reliving the event. False memories were as compelling as true memories, at least on these dimensions.

Are false memories felt with as much emotion as true ones? One answer to this question comes from research on individuals who presumably have false memories of events not planted experimentally. In a study of people who have memories of abduction by space aliens (McNally et al., 2004), physiological measures (e.g., heart rate and electrical conductance of the skin) were taken while abductees listened to tape-recorded accounts of their reported alien encounters. The abductees showed greater reactivity to their abduction scripts than to other scripts (positive and neutral). Moreover, this effect was more pronounced among the abductees than among control subjects who did not have abduction memories and listened to the same accounts. Assuming no one was actually abducted, these results suggest that false memories of abduction can produce very strong physiological responses. Thus, a memory report accompanied by strong emotion is not good evidence that the memory report reflects a genuine experience (see also McNally, 2003).

CONSEQUENCES OF FALSE MEMORIES

Changing beliefs or memories can influence what people think or do later. In one study, people who were led by a fake advertisement to believe that they met Bugs at Disneyland were later asked to say how associated various pairs of characters were in their minds (e.g., How associated are Mickey Mouse and Minnie Mouse? How associated are Bugs Bunny and Mickey Mouse?). Those who fell for the fake ad and believed that they had met Bugs later on claimed that Bugs Bunny was more highly related to various Disney characters than did people who were not exposed to the fake ad. This suggests that the thought processes of ad-exposed individuals can be influenced (see Loftus, 2003, for other examples).

There are also real-world examples showing how false memories can have repercussions. Recall the Heaven's Gate cult, a group whose members had been led to believe they were in telepathic contact with aliens. Apparently the cult members had taken out an insurance policy, to insure against being abducted, impregnated, or killed by aliens. The group paid $1,000 a year for this coverage. So clearly their (presumably false) beliefs had economic consequences (Siepel, 1997). Thirty-nine members of the cult participated in the ultimate act of consequence: They partook in a mass suicide in 1997, killing themselves under the belief that to do so would free their souls.

FINAL REMARKS

There is now ample evidence that people can be led to believe that they experienced things that never happened. In some instances, these beliefs are wrapped in a fair amount of sensory detail and give the impression of being genuine recollections. Some researchers have suggested that implausible or unlikely events will be hard to plant into the minds of adults or children, but in fact people can be led to believe in experiences that are highly unlikely to be true (e.g., witnessing demonic possession, being abducted by aliens, being hugged by Bugs Bunny at Disneyland). In one recent study of false memories in children, the children came up with elaborate stories for such unlikely events as helping a woman find her lost monkey and helping a person who injured her ankle after spilling Play-Doh (Scullin, Kanaya, & Ceci, 2002). These "rich" false memories can have repercussions down the line, affecting later thoughts and behaviors.

A half century ago, Frederic C. Bartlett, the psychologist from Cambridge, England, shared his important insights about memory. He posited that remembering is "imaginative reconstruction, or construction," and "it is thus hardly ever exact" (Bartlett, 1932, p. 213). His insights link up directly with contemporary research on memory distortion, although even he might have been surprised to find out just how inexact memory can be. He might have also relished the contemporary research, which has brought us quite a ways toward understanding what it is like for people when they experience "imaginative construction" in both experimental and real-world settings. Bartlett died in 1969, just missing the beginning of a vast effort to investigate the memory processes that he so intelligently foreshadowed, and that show unequivocally how humans are the authors or creators of their own memories. They can also be the authors or creators of someone else's memory.

Recommended Reading

Lindsay, D.S., Hagen, L., Read, J.D., Wade, K.A., & Garry, M. (2004). (See References)
Loftus, E.F. (2002). Memory faults and fixes. *Issues in Science and Technology, 18,* 41–50.
Loftus, E.F. (2003). (See References)
McNally, R.J. (2003). (See References)

Note

1. Address correspondence to Elizabeth F. Loftus, 2393 Social Ecology II, University of California, Irvine, CA 92697-7085; e-mail: eloftus@uci.edu.

References

Bartlett, F.C. (1932). *Remembering: A study in experimental and social psychology.* Cambridge, England: Cambridge University Press.
Braun, K.A., Ellis, R., & Loftus, E.F. (2002). Make my memory: How advertising can change our memories of the past. *Psychology and Marketing, 19,* 1–23.
Garry, M., & Polaschek, D.L.L. (2000). Imagination and memory. *Current Directions in Psychological Science, 9,* 6–10.
Heaps, C.M., & Nash, M. (2001). Comparing recollective experience in true and false autobiographical memories. *Journal of Experimental Psychology: Learning, Memory, and Cognition, 27,* 920–930.
Lindsay, D.S., Hagen, L., Read, J.D., Wade, K.A., & Garry, M. (2004). True photographs and false memories. *Psychological Science, 15,* 149–154.
Loftus, E.F. (1997). Creating false memories. *Scientific American, 277*(3), 70–75.
Loftus, E.F. (2003). Make-believe memories. *American Psychologist, 58,* 864–873.
Mazzoni, G., & Memon, A. (2003). Imagination can create false autobiographical memories. *Psychological Science, 14,* 186–188.
Mazzoni, G.A.L., Loftus, E.F., & Kirsch, I. (2001). Changing beliefs about implausible autobiographical events. *Journal of Experimental Psychology: Applied, 7,* 51–59.
McNally, R.J. (2003). *Remembering trauma.* Cambridge, MA: Harvard University Press.
McNally, R.J., Lasko, N.B., Clancy, S.A., Macklin, M.L., Pitman, R.K., & Orr, S.P. (2004). Psychophysiological responding during script-driven imagery in people reporting abduction by space aliens. *Psychological Science, 15,* 493–497.
Porter, S., Yuille, J.C., & Lehman, D.R. (1999). The nature of real, implanted, and fabricated memories for emotional childhood events: Implications for the recovered memory debate. *Law and Human Behavior, 23,* 517–537.
Scullin, M.H., Kanaya, T., & Ceci, S.J. (2002). Measurement of individual differences in children's suggestibility across situations. *Journal of Experimental Psychology: Applied, 8,* 233–246.
Siepel, T. (1997, March 31). Leader's health tied to deaths. *San Jose Mercury News.* Retrieved June 24, 2003, from http://www.sacred-texts.com/ufo/39dead16.htm
Vanes, T. (2003, July 28). Let DNA close door on doubt in murder cases. *Los Angeles Times,* p. B11.

Session 2: Critical Thinking Questions

1. Why is it adaptive that memory not serve as an exact tape-recorder of events? What sorts of implications does the study of memory's shortcomings have? What does the imperfect nature of memory mean for the clinical setting? For the setting of the courtroom?

2. How do the various parts of the brain cooperate to produce optimal functioning? What would you expect to happen to the brain's overall functioning if one
specific part of the brain is injured or is unable to operate fully and properly?
Why?

3. What adaptive purpose do emotions serve? How might one use emotions for
survival? How are emotions used when forming memories? When making
decisions?

This article has been reprinted as it originally appeared in *Current
Directions in Psychological Science*. Citation information for this
article as originally published appears above.

Section 3: Health Psychology: Body and Brain

Health psychology is a field in which practitioners identify individual and environmental factors that contribute to or promote health, or prevent illness. Health psychologists work in hospitals, rehabilitation centers, university research settings, or community settings in which the health and wellbeing of a population is of particular concern. Additionally, public health initiatives often help inform us about how our behavior can affect our health or longevity. Practitioners of health psychology have many interests. What is the relationship between the body and the brain? Can one's emotional well-being influence one's physical well-being? Are there psychological steps people can take to prevent or treat physical illness? Alternatively, are there physical changes we can make to help improve our emotional health? In this section, you will read about some of the most recent and provocative research in health psychology.

In the first paper, Barbara Sherwin discusses how estrogen, a critical hormone in women, affects memory. Natural brain aging affects crucial neural functions like working memory. However, natural brain aging in women is compounded by the effects of the depletion of estrogen, which drops precipitously after menopause. Estrogen receptors are found throughout the brain but are particularly dense in areas implicated in working memory like the hippocampus and the prefrontal cortex. These areas are also negatively affected by natural cognitive aging, and over time, undergo drastic pruning and cell death simply as an artifact of progressing age. Although there is a voluminous body of research investigating the effects of estrogen on cognition, there is little agreement about how estrogen therapy (administration of artificial estrogen to women) affects cognitive functions. Whereas some studies find that estrogen therapy can protect women from developing problems in working memory, others find that estrogen therapy has either no effect or actually accelerates cognitive decline. In an attempt to disentangle conflicting results on the efficacy of estrogen therapy, Sherwin offers the "critical period hypothesis." The critical period hypothesis proposes that the success of estrogen therapy is largely dependent upon the time at which it is administered. In sum, women who received estrogen after surgical removal of their ovaries in their 40's showed protective effects of estrogen whereas women who were given estrogen years after menopause, in their 70's, showed no such benefit. Sherwin tackles a literature rich in disagreement and methodological problems and offers both an explanation for disparate findings and practical suggestions for future research.

Next, Sheldon Cohen and Sarah Pressman review the literature investigating the relationship between positive emotions and longevity. In the health psychology literature, emotions are thought to be the link between psychological stress and physical disease. Most research has focused on negative emotions and their role in health and illness. According to Cohen and Pressman, positive affect includes feelings "that reflect a level of pleasurable engagement with the environment", including happiness, joy, enthusiasm, excitement and contentment. The authors stress the importance of investigating both categories of emotions independently. To illustrate, if one wishes to determine the role of emotion in resistance to illness, one must determine whether it is a) the presence of high positive emotions or b) the absence of negative emotions that actually affect physical health. As presently understood, the relationship between emotions and longevity appears to be very complicated. In terms of survival from serious illness, positive affect may work differently depending upon the diagnosis of the patient. For example, for patients who have diseases with a decent chance for long-term survival, positive affect may actually be a benefit. However, for patients with diseases with a comparably poor prognosis, positive affect might result in symptom under-reporting, or treatment non-compliance and effectively decreased longevity. Like the Sherwin paper investigating the role of estrogen on memory function, Cohen and Pressman illuminate confounds to interpretation of existing research and offer compelling hypotheses to explain confusing conflicting results and guide future research.

In the third paper in this section, Nancy Frasure-Smith and François Lespérance address the complex relationship between depression and coronary heart disease. Both major depressive disorder and coronary heart disease (CHD) are among the most common causes of disability and death in industrialized countries. Although on first glance, these two syndromes appear quite different, they often co-occur. Depression causes significant physical problems for many sufferers by affecting the function of nearly all bodily systems. For patients with CHD, depressive symptoms may go unrecognized as it can be difficult to determine if problems in energy, mood, or concentration are due to depression or complications of CHD. Unfortunately, depression is associated with a worse prognosis in CHD patients. This forces the question, is major depression a risk factor for CHD? Attempts to disentangle the relationship between CHD and depression have revealed that there is an independent relationship between CHD and MDD. The authors review the data delineating common causes for CHD and depression and speculate about potential shared etiological pathways. Understanding how these diseases develop and how they affect one another can have significant impact on the health and well-being of thousands of people.

Finally, in a provocative paper by Paul Ekman and his colleagues, the Buddhist and Western views of emotion are compared and promising avenues for research are provided. Our understanding of emotion has evolved along with advances in neuroscience. We now appreciate that emotion and cognition are closely intertwined, in experience and similarly, in our neuro-circuitry. This is a fundamental principle of Buddhism, which acknowledges that emotions affect all areas of well-being. As a result, one goal of Buddhist practice is to obtain Sukha, a trait-like quality of enduring happiness and peace. The Buddhists believe that one can attain Sukha through practice and ultimately change one's emotions and personality. This provides a crucial departure from Western psychological theories that typically assert that temperament is largely determined at birth. The differences between western psychological and Buddhist approaches to emotion provide many compelling questions for researchers. Are practicing Buddhists better predictors of their own emotions? Are they more accurate judges of affect in others? Whereas the Buddhists provide a model for changing emotion in mentally healthy individuals, Western psychologists focus only on modifying affect that arises as a function of psychopathology. Ekman and his colleagues suggest that there might be much to learn about normal human emotion from a close examination of Buddhist theory and practice.

Taken together, the papers in this section provide a contemporary and progressive approach to psychological science. Creative methodology coupled with integration of seemingly disparate areas of behavior make health psychology interesting and relevant to all, regardless of their level of psychological expertise.

Does Estrogen Protect Against Cognitive Aging in Women?

Barbara B. Sherwin[1]

McGill University, Montreal, Quebec, Canada

Abstract

Although there is evidence from randomized controlled trials that estrogen therapy protects against aspects of cognitive decline that occur with normal aging in women, findings from the Women's Health Initiative Memory Study and from some cross-sectional and longitudinal studies failed to find neuroprotective effects of estrogen in older women. There is growing empirical support for the critical-period hypothesis, formulated in the attempt to resolve these discrepancies. It holds that estrogen therapy has protective effects on verbal memory and on working memory only when it is initiated closely in time to menopause, whereas starting treatment many years following menopause does not protect and may even be harmful. Supporting evidence for this hypothesis from basic neuroscience and from animal and human studies is evaluated for its ability to explain the inconsistencies and to describe the conditions under which estrogen may protect cognitive function in aging women.

Keywords

estrogen; cognition; aging; postmenopausal women

The intense interest in the causes and prevention of degenerative diseases common in older age can be attributed to a variety of factors. First, there has been a dramatic increase in life expectancy in industrialized countries during the past century due, in part, to the decrease in maternal and childhood mortality, the availability of vaccines to control many infectious diseases, the development of antibiotics and other drugs to treat chronic illnesses, and improvements in the standard of living. These medical and social advances mean that, on average, people in industrialized countries are living well into their eighth decade of life. Unfortunately, however, this increase in life expectancy has not been paralleled by a decrease in the rate of disability before death, so that more people are living longer but with a disability toward the end of life that causes considerable suffering for them and their families and a heavy financial and social burden for society. Prominent among the degenerative diseases of older age are those that affect cognitive functioning. In this article I evaluate the degree to which estrogen, whose production declines drastically at midlife, is implicated in cognitive aging in women and address possible reasons for the inconsistencies in this literature.

NORMAL COGNITIVE AGING

There is now a considerable amount of evidence to suggest that age-related changes in cognition occur with normal aging. Declines in cognitive function occur in several cognitive domains including memory, processing speed, and reasoning (Salthouse, 2004). Although cognitive decline begins in early adulthood, it accelerates after age 50. Moreover, the integrity of some brain areas is more vulnerable to some aging processes than that of others. Changes tend to occur most profoundly in the hippocampus and prefrontal cortex (PFC), the same brain areas that subserve the specific cognitive functions that decline with normal aging, including verbal memory and working memory, respectively (Esiri, 2007). While pathological cognitive decline is related to the loss of synapses, neurons, neurotransmitters, and neural networks, neuronal loss may not be an inevitable feature of normal brain aging. Indeed, neurogenesis, the synthesis of new neurons, continues throughout life, including in old age.

ESTROGEN AND COGNITIVE FUNCTIONING

After age 40, the ovaries become less and less efficient as a result of the gradual depletion of ovarian follicles along with age-related changes in the hypothalamic-pituitary-ovarian axis (the feedback system that controls the production of estrogen). The perimenopausal period, when the ovarian production of estrogen is decreasing, encompasses several years leading up to the spontaneous or natural menopause, the cessation of menstrual cycles, which occurs at an average age of 51.8 years in industrialized countries. A surgical menopause occurs whenever the ovaries are surgically removed from premenopausal women and is associated with an abrupt decrease in estrogen levels. Both types of menopause can give rise to symptoms such as hot flashes, cold sweats, disturbances in memory, and mood changes. Although estrogen therapy (ET) is effective in relieving some of these symptoms, naturally menopausal women are required to take progesterone along with estrogen in order to protect the uterus against estrogen's stimulatory effects, whereas women who have had their uteri surgically removed can receive estrogen alone.

Many investigators have sought to determine whether post-menopausal ET might protect against the decline in aspects of cognition that occur with normal aging. To provide a rationale for these clinical trials, it is important to first establish that estrogen actually influences aspects of brain anatomy and physiology that are important for cognitive functions. In fact, estrogen receptors are found in the hippocampus and in the PFC, and estrogen can affect neurons in these areas directly by interacting with receptors in the nucleus of a neuron or, indirectly, by interacting with nonnuclear receptors (Lee & McEwen, 2001). Through these mechanisms, estrogen is able to enhance neurotransmission by increasing the number of possible connections between neurons in the hippocampus, by indirectly increasing the production of the neurotransmitter acetylcholine that is critically important for memory, and by its numerous mechanisms that enhance the growth and survival of neurons (Lee & McEwen, 2001). Neuroimaging studies show that ET is associated with different patterns of activation in some regions of the brain that subserve memory and other cognitive functions and that estrogen seems to attenuate the decline in hippocampal volume that occurs with aging (Resnick, Pham, Kraut, Zonderman & Davatzikos, 2003).

Animal studies also provide evidence that estrogen influences learning and memory in a task-dependent fashion, suggesting that the hormone differentially affects specific brain regions. When estrogen was administered to young and

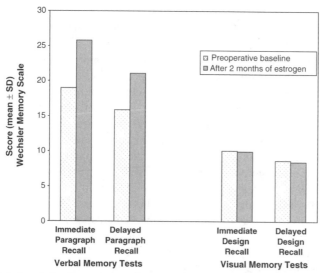

Fig. 1. Verbal and visual memory performance (as measured by the Wechsler Memory Scale) before and after 2 months of estrogen treatment in surgically menopausal women. Data from Phillips & Sherwin (1992).

aged female rats whose ovaries had been surgically removed, performance on hippocampally dependent spatial-memory tasks was enhanced (Gibbs & Gabor, 2003). Similarly, when aged monkeys whose ovaries had been removed were exposed to alternating treatments with estradiol, the most potent estrogen, and a placebo, only estradiol improved performance on a spatial-memory task (Lacreuse, Wilson, & Herndon, 2002). No treatment effects were observed on a delayed-response task, which assesses visuospatial working memory and is associated with PFC function. Therefore, in both rats and nonhuman primates, estrogen specifically protects memory functions that are dependent on the hippocampus.

There is now a voluminous body of literature on the putative protective effect of ET on aspects of cognitive functioning in women. While I will not undertake a comprehensive account of the findings here, I will attempt to summarize and interpret this body of knowledge. Prospective, randomized controlled trials (RCTs) of healthy, surgically menopausal women (mean age, 44 years) were the first to show the specificity of the beneficial effects of ET on verbal memory (Phillips & Sherwin, 1992; Fig. 1) and, more recently, on working memory (Grigorova, Sherwin, & Tulandi, 2006). Whereas these findings were supported by some other RCTs of naturally menopausal women, not all cross-sectional and longitudinal studies have provided confirmation (Sherwin, 2003). Although numerous critical analyses of this literature have attempted to account for the inconsistencies between studies, disagreement remains.

The inconsistencies regarding whether estrogen protected, failed to protect, or even caused harm with regard to cognitive decline in postmenopausal women were compounded when the findings from the Women's Health Initiative Memory Study (WHIMS), the largest RCT ever undertaken, were published in 2004 (Espeland et al., 2004). Approximately 3,000 naturally menopausal women randomly received conjugated equine estrogen (CEE) plus medroxyprogesterone acetate (MPA) or a placebo, and 4,500 surgically menopausal women received treatment with CEE alone or a placebo for 5 years. All participants were tested annually with the modified Mini Mental State Examination (3MSE), a measure of global cognitive function. Contrary to expectations, the risk for mild cognitive impairment and for probable all-cause dementia were nonsignificantly higher in the groups that received CEE alone or CEE plus MPA compared with the placebo (Espeland et al., 2004). Although the magnitude of the differences in 3MSE scores between the hormone- and placebo-treated groups was too small to be clinically meaningful, these findings failed to support the idea that estrogen protected against cognitive deterioration in women.

A second ancillary study to the Women's Health Initiative (WHI), the WHI Study of Cognitive Aging (WHISCA) was begun 3 years following randomization of women to CEE plus MPA or a placebo; it longitudinally evaluated specific cognitive functions in naturally postmenopausal women whose mean age was 73.7 years at the time of their recruitment from the WHI (Resnick et al., 2006). After an average of 1.35 years of follow-up, scores of women taking CEE plus MPA had declined significantly on a test of verbal learning and memory and had increased significantly on a test of short-term visual memory compared to the women on the placebo. The absence of pretreatment scores, the low 2-year adherence rate in the CEE plus MPA group (47.4%), and the fact that MPA was coadministered with CEE suggests that these findings should be interpreted cautiously.

THE CRITICAL-PERIOD HYPOTHESIS

Why did ET not only fail to protect against cognitive decline but possibly even cause harm to the postmenopausal women in WHIMS, whereas neuroprotective effects had been apparent in other, smaller RCTs and in some cross-sectional and longitudinal studies? An examination of some differences between the study populations and treatments administered in the WHIMS compared to those of the smaller RCTs that found beneficial effects of estrogen may help to understand these discrepancies. Perhaps the most striking observation is that the studies finding a protective effect of estrogen on cognitive aging came from the smaller RCTs in which premenopausal women in their forties had received estradiol alone or a placebo immediately following surgical removal of their uteri and ovaries (Sherwin, 2003), whereas the average age of the women in the WHIMS was 72 years at baseline.

Recently, the critical-period hypothesis was formulated in the attempt to resolve the inconsistencies in the estrogen-and-cognition literature (Resnick & Henderson, 2002). It holds that ET optimally protects against cognitive decline when treatment is begun close in time to menopause whereas starting treatment decades afterward is not beneficial and may even cause harm. Indeed, there is a growing body of evidence from basic neuroscience and from rodent, nonhuman primate, and human studies supporting the idea that ET protects against a deterioration in memory performance when treatment is started shortly following removal of the ovaries but not when estrogen is administered after a considerable

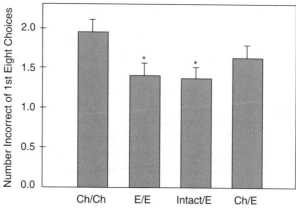

Fig. 2. Working memory performance (as mean number of incorrect choices in the first eight visits to a maze averaged over 24 training days) in four groups of rats subjected to ovary removal and cholesterol and/or estradiol treatment. Three groups were ovariectomized at 12 months of age and received cholesterol treatment 5 months before and during training in a radial arm maze (Ch/Ch), estradiol treatment 5 months before and during training (E/E), or cholesterol treatment for 5 months followed by estradiol treatment beginning 1 week before training (Ch/E). The fourth group underwent sham surgery at 12 months of age and was ovariectomized and treated with estradiol 1 week before training at 17 months of age (Intact/E). Reprinted from "Estradiol Replacement Enhances Working Memory in Middle-Aged Rats When Initiated Immediately After Ovariectomy But Not After a Long-Term Period of Ovarian Hormone Deprivation," by J.M. Daniel, J.L. Hulst, & J.L. Berbling, 2006, *Endocrinology, 147*, p. 610. Copyright 2006, The Endocrine Society. Reproduced with permission.

delay or when it is given to very old individuals (Sherwin, 2005). Similarly, there is evidence that ET protects against memory decline in women when started soon after a natural or surgical menopause but not when treatment is delayed for many years (Sherwin, 2005).

Why might ET be neuroprotective when administered to women shortly following menopause but not when it is initiated decades later? One way to understand these findings is to consider that brain aging results in a decrease in brain volume and neuron size and a 46% reduction in dendritic spine numbers in humans over the age of 50 (Esiri, 2007). Therefore, ET given to the 72-year-old women in the WHIMS was administered against the background of two decades of accrued brain aging, whereas the neuroprotective influences of ET in the 44-year-old surgically menopausal women (Sherwin, 2003) were not confounded by brain aging. Indeed, findings that estradiol increased hippocampal spine density in young, but not in aged, rats (Gibbs & Gabor, 2003) and enhanced working memory in middle-aged animals when given immediately after ovary removal, but not when administered after a prolonged period of estrogen deprivation (Daniel, Hulst, & Berbling, 2006; Fig. 2), support the idea that brain aging modulates responses to the hormone, although other, unknown factors may also be operative.

The results of recent reanalyses of the WHI data that examined risk for adverse events in other organ systems as a function of age at the time of the trial also accord with the critical-period hypothesis. Although the risks for both coronary heart disease and stroke were significantly elevated in the 60- to 79-year-old hormone-treated women, the risks for coronary heart disease and for total mortality were reduced by hormone therapy in the 50- to 59-year-old hormone-treated women, compared to those receiving a placebo (Rossouw et al., 2007). Of more direct relevance is the preliminary reanalysis of the WHIMS data, which found that women who took ET before the age of 65 (prior to their enrollment in the WHI) were 50% less likely to develop Alzheimer's disease and all-cause dementia (Henderson, Espeland, Hogan, Rapp, & Stefanick, 2007) compared to nonusers. Both reanalyses support the notion that ET has protective effects in younger, healthier women and may cause harm when given to older women.

Because of the considerable controversy concerning ET and breast cancer risk, it is important to consider yet another WHI data reanalysis, which found nonsignificant reductions in the risk for breast cancer for women who took CEE alone compared to placebo after 7 years of treatment, although the risk was elevated in naturally menopausal women given CEE plus MPA (Stefanick et al., 2006). Whether other synthetic progestins or natural progesterone may have a more benign effect when co-administered with estrogen is currently unknown.

SUMMARY AND CONCLUSIONS

Taken as a whole, the literature on estrogen and cognitive aging in women is marked by disagreement that needs to be resolved for both theoretical and clinical reasons. Results from basic neuroscience and from animal and human studies provide substantial empirical support for the critical-period hypothesis. This evidence suggests, but does not prove, that estrogen alone is neuroprotective when treatment is begun close in time to menopause in healthy women and is administered for a few years and that it is potentially harmful when administered to women over the age of 65. Moreover, recent reanalyses of the WHI data support the critical-period hypothesis and suggest that it may be generalizable to organ systems other than the brain.

OTHER MODULATORS OF THE ESTROGEN–COGNITION RELATIONSHIP

An analysis of the estrogen–cognition literature reveals that several variables modulate this hormone–behavior relationship and require careful consideration in designing future studies. First, because normal brain aging and the risk for the development of neuropathology increases in older women, it would be important for future RCTs to recruit same-aged women in individual investigations to eliminate the confound of aging. Second, in view of the specificity of the estrogenic effects on aspects of cognition, future studies need to administer valid and reliable measures of specific cognitive domains rather than tests that measure only global cognitive function such as the 3MSE. Third it is important to consider the effects of estrogen and progesterone (or synthetic progestins) separately on cognitive function in women; although the effects on the brain of the numerous available chemical formulations of progestins are poorly described, it is clear that progestins affect the brain in ways that, in some cases, are opposite to estrogen (Lee & McEwen, 2001). Therefore, a future priority is to establish the distinctive effects of each sex hormone on cognitive functions before dealing with the possible influence on the brain of administering them together.

Finally, in view of the potential benefits of ET in younger menopausal women, it is important to acknowledge that its efficacy most likely lies in its ability to delay cognitive decline and the clinical manifestations of Alzheimer's disease. That is, there is currently no reason to believe that this hormone would have direct effects on the actual causal factors that underlie cognitive decline and Alzheimer's disease, which are currently unknown. However, in view of the continuing increase in life expectancy in industrialized countries, the implementation of strategies that could delay cognitive decline would result in enormous personal and societal benefits with regard to maintaining the quality of life for our elderly populations.

Recommended Reading

Hogervorst, E., Yaffe, K., Richards, M., & Huppert, F. (2002). Hormone replacement therapy for cognitive functioning in postmenopausal women. *Cochrane Database of Systematic Reviews*, Issue 2, Art. No. CD003122. DOI:10.1002/14651858.
Lee, S.J., & McEwen, B.S. (2001). (See References)
Sherwin, B.B. (2003). (See References)
Sherwin, B.B. (2006). Estrogen and cognitive aging in women. *Neuroscience, 138,* 1021–1026.

Acknowledgments—The preparation of this manuscript was supported by a grant from the Canadian Institutes of Health Research (#MOP-77773) awarded to B.B. Sherwin.

Note

1. Address correspondence to Barbara B. Sherwin, McGill University, Department of Psychology, 1205 Dr. Penfield Ave., Montreal, Quebec, Canada H3A 1B1; e-mail: barbara.sherwin@mcgill.ca.

References

Daniel, J.M., Hulst, J.L., & Berbling, J.L. (2006). Estradiol replacement enhances working memory in middle-aged rats when initiated immediately after ovariectomy but not after a long-term period of ovarian hormone deprivation. *Endocrinology, 147,* 607–614.
Esiri, M.M. (2007). Aging and the brain. *Journal of Pathology, 211,* 181–187.
Espeland, M.A., Rapp, S.R., Shumaker, S.A., Brunne, E., Manson, J.E., Sherwin, B.B., et al. (2004). The effect of conjugated equine estrogens on global cognitive function in postmenopausal women: Women's Health Initiative Memory Study. *JAMA: Journal of the American Medical Association, 291,* 2959–2968.
Gibbs, R.B., & Gabor, R. (2003). Estrogen and cognition: Applying preclinical findings to clinical perspectives. *Journal of Neuroscience Research, 74,* 637–643.
Grigorova, M., Sherwin, B.B., & Tulandi, T. (2006). Effects of treatment with leuprolide acetate depot on working memory and executive functions in young premenopausal women. *Psychoneuroendocrinology, 31,* 935–947.
Henderson, V.W., Espeland, M.A., Hogan, P.E., Rapp, S.R., & Stefanick, M.L. (2007). Prior use of hormone therapy and incident Alzheimer's disease in the Women's Health Initiative Study. *Neurology, 68*(Suppl. 1), A205.

Lacreuse, A., Wilson, M.E., & Herndon, J.G. (2002). Estradiol, but not raloxifene, improves aspects of spatial working memory in aged ovariectomized rhesus monkeys. *Neurobiology of Aging, 23,* 589–600.

Lee, S.J., & McEwen, B.S. (2001). Neurotrophic and neuroprotective actions of estrogens and their therapeutic implications. *Annual Review of Pharmacology & Pharmacological Toxicology, 41,* 569–591.

Phillips, S.M., & Sherwin, B.B. (1992). Effects of estrogen on memory function in surgically menopausal women. *Psychoneuroendocrinology, 17,* 485–495.

Resnick, S.M., & Henderson, V.W. (2002). Hormone therapy and risk of Alzheimer's disease: A critical time. *JAMA: The Journal of the American Medical Association, 288,* 2170–2172.

Resnick, S.M., Maki, P.M., Rapp, S.R., Espeland, M.A., Brunner, R., Coker, L.H., et al. (2006). Effects of combined estrogen plus progestin hormone treatment on cognition and affect. *Journal of Clinical Endocrinology and Metabolism, 91,* 1802–1810.

Resnick, S.M., Pham, D.L., Kraut, M.A., Zonderman, A.B., & Davatzikos, C. (2003). Longitudinal magnetic resonance imaging studies of older adults: A shrinking brain. *Journal of Neuroscience, 23,* 3295–3301.

Rossouw, J.E., Prentice, R.L., Manson, J.E., Wu, L., Barnabei, V.M., Ko, M., et al. (2007). Post-menopausal hormone therapy and risk of cardiovascular disease by age and years since menopause. *JAMA: The Journal of the American Medical Association, 297,* 1465–1477.

Salthouse, T.A. (2004). What and when of cognitive aging. *Current Directions in Psychological Science, 13,* 140–144.

Sherwin, B.B. (2003). Estrogen and cognition in women. *Endocrine Reviews, 24,* 133–151.

Sherwin, B.B. (2005). Estrogen and memory in women: How can we reconcile the findings? *Hormones and Behavior, 47,* 371–375.

Stefanick, M.L., Anderson, G.L., Margolis, K.L., Rodaborough, R.J., Paskett, E.D., Lane, D.S., & Hubbell, F.A. (2006). Effects of conjugated equine estrogens on breast cancer and mammography screening in postmenopausal women with hysterectomy. *JAMA: The Journal of the American Medical Association, 295,* 1647–1657.

This article has been reprinted as it originally appeared in *Current Directions in Psychological Science*. Citation information for this article as originally published appears above.

Positive Affect and Health

Sheldon Cohen[1] and Sarah D. Pressman
Carnegie Mellon University

Abstract

Negative affective styles such as anxiety, depression, and hostility have long been accepted as predictors of increased risk for illness and mortality. In contrast, positive affective styles have been relatively ignored in the health literature. Here we highlight consistent patterns of research associating trait positive affect (PA) and physical health. The evidence we review suggests an association of trait PA and lower morbidity and decreased symptoms and pain. PA is also associated with increased longevity among community-dwelling elderly. The association of PA and survival among those with serious illness is less clear and suggests the possibility that PA may be harmful in some situations. We conclude by raising conceptual and methodological reservations about this literature and suggesting directions for future research.

Keywords

positive emotion; positive affect; morbidity; mortality; health; symptoms

The role of emotions in physical health has been a central topic in health psychology for some time. Emotions are thought to represent the principal pathway linking psychological stress to disease, and enduring affective styles such as anxiety and depression have been found to be associated with greater morbidity and mortality. However, when health psychologists have referred to the roles of emotions and affect in health, they have typically meant negative emotions such as anger, depression, and anxiety. Only recently has there been any serious discussion of the potential effect of positive affect (PA).

One challenge in making sense of the literature on PA and health is that there is little agreement on what is meant by PA. We define positive emotion or affect as feelings that reflect a level of pleasurable engagement with the environment, such as happiness, joy, excitement, enthusiasm, and contentment (Clark, Watson, & Leeka, 1989). These can be brief, longer lasting, or more stable trait-like feelings. Importantly, the lack of positive engagement does not necessarily imply negative affect such as anger, anxiety, and depression.

REVIEW

The strongest links between positive emotions and health are found in studies that examine trait affective style, which reflects a person's typical emotional experience, rather than state affect, which reflects momentary responses to events. Here we provide short descriptions of the associations between trait PA and mortality (longevity), morbidity (illness onset), survival from life-threatening disease, and reports of symptoms and pain. (For a comprehensive review of this literature see Pressman & Cohen, 2005). The studies we review use prospective designs that help to eliminate the explanation that being sick resulted in lower PA. This is done by measuring PA and health at study onset (base-line) and assessing whether PA predicts changes in health over the follow-up period. Because the measure of PA is given before the change in health, it cannot have been caused by that change. Many, but not all, of the studies also include controls for spurious (third) factors such as age, sex, socioeconomic status, and race/ethnicity. Overall, the literature reviewed here is provocative, although it suffers from a range of methodological and conceptual limitations. It does however allow us to highlight both consistencies in results as well as the issues that need to be addressed to ultimately determine if a positive affective style is an important predictor of good health.

Mortality

A study that has received considerable attention evaluated PA by coding autobiographical writing samples collected from a group of nuns when they were in their early twenties (Danner, Snowdon, & Friesen, 2001). The greater the number of positive emotion words and sentences, the greater was the probability (adjusting for age and education) of being alive 60 years later. In contrast, the number of negative emotions reported was not associated with mortality.

However, the overall evidence on PA and mortality is more complex. Most (seven) of these studies have been done in elderly persons (average age over 60) living either on their own or with their families. These studies are virtually unanimous in linking positive emotional dispositions to longer life. But positive emotions are not generally associated with increased longevity in studies of other populations. For example, two studies suggest that institutionalized elderly with high PA are at increased risk of mortality (Janoff-Bulman & Marshall, 1982; Stones, Dornan, & Kozma, 1989) and an analysis of a sample of gifted children found that PA during childhood was associated with greater risk for death 65 years later (Friedman et al., 1993).

Illness Onset

In a study from our own laboratory (Cohen, Doyle, Turner, Alper, & Skoner, 2003), 334 adult volunteers were phone interviewed seven times over a 3-week period. For each interview, participants rated how accurately each of nine positive and nine negative adjectives described how they felt over the last day. Examples of PA items included *lively, energetic, happy, cheerful, at ease*, and *calm*. Examples of negative-affect (NA) items included *sad, depressed, nervous*, and *hostile*. Daily mood scores were calculated and averaged across the 7 days to create summary measures of trait PA and NA. Subsequently, subjects were exposed to one of two viruses that cause a common cold and were monitored for 5 days for the development of clinical illness. Colds were defined by objective markers of illness, including infection, mucus production (assessed by weighing tissues), and congestion (assessed by the amount of time it took for a dye put into the nostrils to reach the back of the throat). Those with high levels of PA were less likely to develop a cold when exposed to a virus (see Fig. 1). This relationship remained after controlling for age, sex, immunity (baseline antibody to the experimental virus), education, and NA.

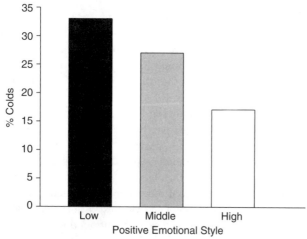

Fig. 1. The association between trait positive emotional style and the incidence of the common cold as diagnosed through objectively assessed markers of disease (infection, mucus weights, and congestion). Adapted from data reported in Cohen, Doyle, Turner, Alper, & Skoner (2003).

In other morbidity studies, trait PA has been associated with lower rates of stroke among noninstitutionalized elderly (Ostir, Markides, Peek, & Goodwin, 2001), lower rates of rehospitalization for coronary problems (Middleton & Byrd, 1996), fewer injuries (e.g., Koivumaa-Honkanen et al., 2000) and improved pregnancy outcomes among women undergoing assisted fertilization (Klonoff-Cohen, Chu, Natarajan, & Sieber, 2001). These studies are often limited by a lack of control for factors such as NA, optimism, and personal control that may influence both PA and disease susceptibility, and many do not rule out the possibility that PA itself (e.g., endorsing of items such as *energetic, full-of-pep*, and *vigorous*) is merely a marker of subclinical disease processes.

Survival

A popular hypothesis is that trait PA increases longevity of persons suffering from life-threatening disease. However, comparatively few studies have examined whether PA predicts survival among people with chronic diseases, and available findings are at best mixed. A pattern of results does however suggest a hypothesis. Individuals with diseases that have decent prospects for long-term survival, such as early-stage breast cancer, coronary heart disease, and AIDS, may benefit from PA. However, high levels of trait PA may be detrimental to the health of individuals who have advanced diseases with poor and short-term prognoses—e.g., patients with melanoma, metastatic breast cancer, and end-stage renal disease—possibly as a consequence of underreporting of symptoms resulting in inadequate care, or of a lack of adherence to treatment (Pressman & Cohen, 2005).

Symptoms and Pain

There is considerable evidence linking PA to reports of fewer symptoms, less pain, and better health. These outcomes have practical importance, but there is reason to think that this association may be driven primarily by PA influences on how people perceive their bodies rather than by affect-elicited changes in physiological processes (e.g., Pennebaker, 1983).

For example, a study from our own lab suggests that trait PA is associated with less symptom reporting when objective disease is held constant (Cohen et al., 2003). As described earlier, PA and NA were assessed by averaging responses across seven nightly interviews. Volunteers were then exposed to a virus that causes the common cold and monitored for objective signs of illness. To test whether trait affect could influence symptom reporting, we predicted self-reported cold symptoms (collected for 5 days following viral exposure) from trait affect, controlling for the objective markers of disease mentioned earlier. When objective signs of illness were held constant, those higher in trait PA reported less severe symptoms, and those higher in trait NA reported more severe ones. Figure 2 presents the residual scores derived from the PA analysis. These scores represent the extent to which one reports more (+ scores) or fewer (− scores) symptoms than would be predicted from the objective markers of disease. Interestingly, when both PA and NA were entered in the same regression equation, only PA continued to predict symptom reporting, suggesting that low PA (not high NA) may be the driving force in the reporting of unfound symptoms.

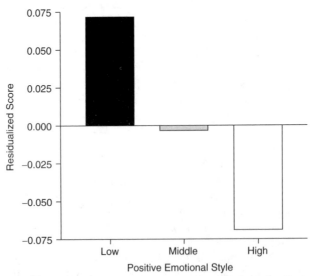

Fig. 2. The association between trait positive emotional style and self-reported symptoms, controlling for objective markers of disease (infection, mucus weights, and congestion). Residualized score represents the extent to which one reports more or fewer symptoms than is predicted by objective signs of illness. Scores above 0 indicate more symptoms than expected and those below 0 indicate fewer symptoms than expected. Adapted from data reported in Cohen, Doyle, Turner, Alper, & Skoner (2003).

Other prospective evidence also reveals that trait PA predicts better self-reported health, fewer symptoms in the elderly, and less pain among rheumatoid arthritis and fibromyalgia patients. Interestingly, experimental evidence suggests that inducing state PA in both healthy and mildly ill individuals results in more favorable self-evaluations of health as compared to individuals induced to feel NA and a neutral control condition (e.g., Salovey & Birnbaum, 1989).

Although these data are provocative, many of these studies also found that NA was associated with greater symptom reporting and poorer self-reported health, begging the question of whether NA or PA is responsible for the effects found. However, there are several studies, like the one described at the beginning of this section, that provide evidence that PA effects on self-reported health are independent of, and often stronger than, those of NA.

LIMITATIONS OF THE EXISTING LITERATURE

Overall, there is provocative evidence that trait PA may influence health and well-being. Strong inferences are not yet possible, however. One problem in interpreting this literature is that in many cases it is difficult to distinguish between the effects of positive and negative emotions. For example, do community-residing elderly live longer because they are happy or because they are not sad? Interestingly, people's experiences of positive and negative emotions are partly independent in some circumstances (e.g., Diener & Emmons, 1985). For instance, in looking back over the last year of one's life (a typical trait PA measure), one can reasonably report having been both happy and sad. A definitive answer to whether positive or negative emotions are making independent contributions to a health outcome can only come from studies that measure both types of emotions separately. Surprisingly, studies that have focused on the effects of negative emotions on health have similarly failed to control for positive emotions. Consequently, it is difficult to conclude from the existing literature whether sadness results in a less healthy, shorter life or whether happiness leads to a healthier and longer one.

There is also concern that some measures of positive emotions may themselves be markers of associated cognitive and social dispositions such as extraversion, self-esteem, personal control, and optimism. In general, these factors have moderate associations with trait PA, but few existing studies control for the possibility that they, and not PA, are responsible for any associations with health that are found. A further issue with PA measurement is that some types of PA may themselves be direct indicators of physical health. For example, endorsing adjectives such as *energetic, full-of-pep*, and *vigorous* may reflect a positive mood, but may also reflect how healthy one feels. Self-rated health has been found to predict illness and longevity above and beyond objective health measures such as physician ratings. Consequently, it is important for future work to include standard measures of self-rated health to help exclude the possibility that we are merely predicting good objective health from good perceived health masquerading as positive emotions.

Another issue is the potential importance of differentiating activated (e.g., enthusiastic, joyful) and nonactivated (e.g., calm, content) affect. Health researchers consider physiological arousal to be a primary pathway through which emotions may influence health. It is thus likely that the arousing nature of an emotion, not only its valence, plays into its potential influences on health outcomes. This is especially relevant given that most measures of PA assess primarily activated emotions.

It is also unclear whether it is important to distinguish among the various subcomponents of PA, such as happiness, elation, and joy, or whether these affects cluster together in experience or in the manner by which they influence health. Few studies explicitly compare different positive emotions or compare individual emotions to a PA aggregate. Finally, there is evidence that the expression of PA varies across cultures, even Western cultures. Consequently, it is difficult to know to what extent this work would apply outside of the United States.

HOW COULD PA IMPROVE HEALTH?

Higher trait PA has been associated with better health practices such as improved sleep quality, more exercise, and more intake of dietary zinc, as well as with lower levels of the stress hormones epinephrine, norepinephrine, and cortisol (Pressman & Cohen, 2005). PA has also been hypothesized to be associated with other health-relevant hormones, including increases in oxytocin and growth hormone and secretion of endogenous opioids. Induced PA in the laboratory has been shown to alter various aspects of immune function, although the direction of changes are not entirely consistent and seem to be dependent on details of the manipulation and the degree of arousal produced via the induction (see Pressman & Cohen, 2005). PA may also influence health by altering social interactions. Persons who report more PA socialize more often and maintain more and higher-quality social ties. PA may result in more and closer social contacts because it facilitates approach behavior and because others are drawn to form attachments with pleasant individuals. More diverse and closer social ties have been associated with lower risk for both morbidity and premature mortality. Finally, health care providers may be more attentive to persons with more pleasant affect.

As an alternative to the arguments above, which assume that PA directly affects health, PA may influence health primarily through its ability to ameliorate the potentially pathogenic influences of stressful life events. For example, Fredrickson (1998) suggests that positive emotions encourage exploration and creativity and result in the building of social, intellectual, and physical resources. Similarly, Salovey, Rothman, Detweiler, and Steward (2000) suggest that positive emotions generate psychological resources by promoting resilience, endurance, and optimism.

WHERE DO WE GO FROM HERE?

Some key strategies to move this literature forward include (a) using more sophisticated measures of PA to differentiate between dimensions of affect (e.g., activated vs. unactivated; discrete positive emotions); (b) including both PA and NA in studies in order to assess whether they have independent associations with health outcomes; (c) including social and cognitive factors that correlate with

PA, such as extraversion, personal control, purpose, self-esteem, and optimism, in order to assess whether these factors are responsible for associations attributed to PA; (d) including measures of self-reported health to exclude it as an alternative explanation; and (e) assessing alternative pathways through which PA could influence health.

Overall, we consider the literature associating trait PA with health provocative but not definitive. Nonetheless, the current findings should encourage those interested in affect and health to include PA as a potential predictor and to test the potential pathways that may link PA to health.

Recommended Reading

Lyubomirsky, S., King, L., & Diener, E. (2005). The benefits of frequent positive affect: Does happiness lead to success? *Psychological Bulletin, 131*, 803–855.
Pressman, S.D., & Cohen, S. (2005). (See References)
Salovey, P., Rothman, A.J., Detweiler, J.B., & Steward, W.T. (2000). (See References)

Acknowledgments—Preparation of this article was facilitated by support from Pittsburgh NIH Mind-Body Center (Grants HL65111 & HL65112), the John D. and Catherine T. MacArthur Foundation Network on Socioeconomic Status and Health, and a Postgraduate Scholarship from the Natural Science & Engineering Research Council of Canada.

Note

1. Address correspondence to Sheldon Cohen, Department of Psychology, Carnegie Mellon University, Pittsburgh, PA 15213; e-mail: scohen@cmu.edu.

References

Clark, L.A., Watson, D., & Leeka, J. (1989). Diurnal variation in the positive affects. *Motivation and Emotion, 13*, 205–234.
Cohen, S., Doyle, W.J., Turner, R.B., Alper, C.M., & Skoner, D.P. (2003). Emotional style and susceptibility to the common cold. *Psychosomatic Medicine, 65*, 652–657.
Danner, D.D., Snowdon, D.A., & Friesen, W.V. (2001). Positive emotions in early life and longevity: Findings from the nun study. *Journal of Personality & Social Psychology, 80*, 804–813.
Diener, E., & Emmons, R.A. (1985). The independence of positive and negative affect. *Journal of Personality and Social Psychology, 47*, 1105–1117.
Fredrickson, B.L. (1998). What good are positive emotions? *Review of General Psychology, 2*, 300–319.
Friedman, H.S., Tucker, J.S., Tomlinson-Keasey, C., Schwartz, J.E., Wingard, D.L., & Criqui, M.H. (1993). Does childhood personality predict longevity? *Journal of Personality & Social Psychology, 65*, 176–185.
Janoff-Bulman, R., & Marshall, G. (1982). Mortality, well-being, and control: A study of a population of institutionalized aged. *Personality & Social Psychology Bulletin, 8*, 691–698.
Klonoff-Cohen, H., Chu, E., Natarajan, L., & Sieber, W. (2001). A prospective study of stress among women undergoing in vitro fertilization or gamete intrafallopian transfer. *Fertility & Sterility, 76*, 675–687.
Koivumaa-Honkanen, H., Honkanen, R., Viinamaki, H., Heikkila, K., Kaprio, J., & Koskenvuo, M. (2000). Self-reported life satisfaction and 20-year mortality in healthy Finnish adults. *American Journal of Epidemiology, 152*, 983–991.
Middleton, R.A., & Byrd, E.K. (1996). Psychosocial factors and hospital readmission status of older persons with cardiovascular disease. *Journal of Applied Rehabilitation Counseling, 27*, 3–10.

Ostir, G.V., Markides, K.S., Peek, M.K., & Goodwin, J.S. (2001). The association between emotional well-being and the incidence of stroke in older adults. *Psychosomatic Medicine, 63*, 210–215.

Pennebaker, J.W. (1983). *The psychology of physical symptoms*. New York: Springer-Verlag.

Pressman, S.D., & Cohen, S. (2005). Does positive affect influence health? *Psychological Bulletin, 131*, 925–971.

Salovey, P., & Birnbaum, D. (1989). Influence of mood on health-relevant cognitions. *Journal of Personality & Social Psychology, 57*, 539–551.

Salovey, P., Rothman, A.J., Detweiler, J.B., & Steward, W.T. (2000). Emotional states and physical health. *American Psychologist, 55*, 110–121.

Stones, M.J., Dornan, B., & Kozma, A. (1989). The prediction of mortality in elderly institution residents. *Journals of Gerontology, 44*, P72–P79.

This article has been reprinted as it originally appeared in *Current Directions in Psychological Science*. Citation information for this article as originally published appears above.

Depression and Coronary Heart Disease: Complex Synergism of Mind, Body, and Environment

Nancy Frasure-Smith[1] and François Lespérance

McGill University, University of Montreal, Montreal Heart Institute, and Centre Hospitalier de l'Université de Montréal, Montreal, Quebec, Canada

Abstract

Beyond depression's impact on life quality, it is associated with both the incidence of coronary heart disease (CHD) and its prognosis. Depression is three times more common in CHD patients than in the general community. It is independently associated with at least a doubling in risk of subsequent cardiac events. Studies also show that it may precede the development of clinically evident CHD by many years. The mechanisms linking depression and CHD are currently unknown and likely to be complex. In addition to behavioral factors, changes in autonomic regulation, vascular disease of the brain, sub-chronic inflammation, reduced omega-3 free fatty acid levels, and enhanced platelet responsiveness may all be involved. Only one large clinical trial has attempted to alter CHD prognosis by treating depression. It succeeded in producing a small, but significant reduction in depression symptoms, but had no impact on subsequent CHD events. While debate continues about the causal relationship between CHD and depression, the best treatment strategy to improve prognosis in depressed CHD patients remains intensive modification of standard CHD risk factors in combination with treatment of depression to improve life quality.

Keywords

depression; coronary heart disease; risk factor; inflammation; omega-3

Major depression is the most prevalent psychiatric disorder. It is second only to coronary heart disease (CHD) as a cause of disability and early death in industrialized countries (Murray & Lopez, 1997). Because of expected changes in worldwide demographics, it is predicted that by 2020, CHD and depression will account for the greatest proportion of the global burden of disease. These statistics about depression are even more impressive because they do not include its very real impact on other illnesses, including CHD. Through changes in the hypothalamo-pituitary-adrenal axis,[2] the immune system, autonomic nervous system regulation, pain regulation, circadian rhythms, diet, and levels of physical activity, depression can affect the function of all body systems, and predispose to the development of other diseases. When depression occurs in someone with another medical illness, the pathophysiological consequences can be even more profound. Nowhere is the complex synergism between medical illness and depression better illustrated than in the study of patients with CHD.

Table 1. *Glossary of Terms Related to Coronary Heart Disease, Depression, and Their Physiological Mechanisms*

Arrhythmic death: Irregular beating of the heart is called an arrhythmia. In some cases, the heart rhythm becomes so erratic that the heart is no longer able to pump blood to the brain and the rest of the body, resulting in death.

Atherosclerosis: Atherosclerosis is sometimes called "hardening of the arteries." This process takes place over many years and can affect arteries all over the body, including those in the brain and the heart. In the atherosclerotic process, plaque, made up of cholesterol and other substances, forms on the inside walls of the arteries. This plaque has a membrane-like surface and a liquid cholesterol-rich center, and can rupture, leading to the formation of blood clots. In some cases, this process results in complete blockage of an artery, and the tissues receiving blood and oxygen from that artery are damaged or die.

Autonomic nervous system: The brain and the nerves that control the internal organs without one's awareness are called the autonomic nervous system. There are two parts to this system: the sympathetic and parasympathetic (or vagal) nervous systems.

Cardiac catheterization: Cardiac catheterization is a test in which a special dye is injected into the coronary arteries so that x-ray images can be taken to assess the degree and location of blockages.

Coronary angioplasty: Coronary angioplasty is an alternative to coronary bypass surgery in which a balloon is threaded into the heart arteries near coronary blockages and inflated to reduce the blockages without surgically opening the chest. Coronary bypass surgery involves using sections of vein from the leg or from noncardiac arteries in the chest to construct new pathways for blood flow to the heart that bypass blocked arteries.

Hypothalamo-pituitary-adrenal (HPA) axis: The system that coordinates the response to stress in the brain, the adrenal gland, and their chemical messengers is called the HPA axis.

Myocardial infarction (MI): When an artery providing blood and oxygen to the heart muscle becomes blocked for a few minutes or more, by rupture of atherosclerotic plaque and clot formation or because of spasm, some of the heart muscle dies. The result is a heart attack, or MI.

Parasympathetic (vagal) nervous system: The parasympathetic nervous system acts to conserve energy and allow relaxation and digestion of food. Its activation is associated with a decrease in heart rate.

Sympathetic nervous system: The sympathetic nervous system controls the body's "flight or fight" response. Activation of this system leads to an increase in heart rate.

Unstable angina: When the blockage of an artery is partial or intermittent and the heart muscle does not receive enough oxygen, the usual result is cardiac pain, referred to as angina. When this pain occurs at rest or cannot be treated with the patient's current medications, it is referred to as unstable angina.

Vascular disease of the brain: Atherosclerosis of brain arteries can cause neuronal death in the brain structures involved in mood regulation and cognition, leading to signs and symptoms of depression in some patients.

COMPLEX RELATIONSHIP BETWEEN DEPRESSION AND CHD

Major depression occurs in 15 to 20% of hospitalized CHD patients, with some 30 to 50% demonstrating at least some depression symptoms (Lespérance & Frasure-Smith, 2000). Estimates of the prevalence of depression are similar among post-myocardial infarction (post-MI) patients, as well as patients who have unstable angina or congestive heart failure, who are recovering from coronary bypass surgery, or who are hospitalized for cardiac catheterization or coronary angioplasty. These rates are about three times as high as in the general community. Despite its high prevalence, depression is often unrecognized in CHD patients. The symptoms of depression can reflect physical as well as psychological complaints, and it is difficult to determine whether fatigue, sleep problems, or difficulty concentrating are cardiac or depression related. In addition, some degree of depressed mood can be a normal reaction to the stresses associated with CHD. However, depression does not always lift with time. It frequently becomes a chronic condition that can interfere with treatment of CHD itself. Although the stigma associated with depression has decreased, patients, their families, and their doctors remain reluctant to seek advice from mental health professionals. Many patients resist the idea of additional medications or taking the time to participate in psychotherapy. Depression, like CHD, requires a long-term commitment from both physician and patient, and even with that commitment has only moderate rates of treatment success.

Beyond the ways in which depression and CHD can interact with and complicate reporting and recognition of symptoms, efforts to obtain treatment, provision of treatment, and compliance with treatment, there are even more sinister links between the two conditions. There is increasingly compelling evidence that depression is associated with worse prognosis in CHD patients.

IS DEPRESSION A CHD RISK FACTOR?

Because studies cannot randomly assign people to have or not have a particular potential risk factor, deciding whether variables are risk factors for CHD (i.e., increase the chances that healthy people will develop CHD or that CHD patients will worsen or die) involves making causal inferences from observational data indicating a statistical association between the putative risk factor and the disease. When evaluating causal relationships, it is important to consider the timing of the factors. That is, causes must precede effects. Causal inferences are strengthened if results are consistent across studies, if the statistical association between the risk factor and the outcome is strong, if there is evidence of a dose-response relationship (i.e., increasing level of risk is associated with increasing severity or rapidity of outcome), and if potentially confounding variables linked to both the risk and the outcome do not appear to explain the association (Grimes & Schultz, 2002). In addition, biologically plausible mechanisms for the link between the risk factor and the disease must exist. The final part of the puzzle is evidence from clinical trials that changing the risk factor results in a change in prognosis.

Over the past 20 years, an impressive body of research has shown that depression is associated with at least a doubling in risk of mortality and recurrent cardiac events in patients with CHD. The prognostic impact of depression is about as great as, and largely independent of, the impact of other major prognostic factors (e.g., the heart's pumping ability, severity of coronary atherosclerosis) used to estimate risk of mortality in these patients. Although not all recent prognostic studies have demonstrated independent links between depression and CHD outcomes (i.e., links that cannot be explained by third variables), none of the negative studies have had sample sizes large enough to detect a statistically significant doubling in risk, the level that is usually considered to constitute an important increase in CHD risk.

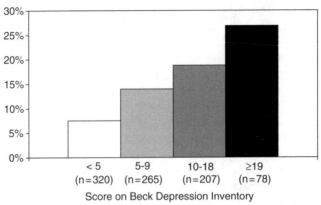

Fig. 1. Relation between cardiac deaths and depression among patients hospitalized for myocardial infarction. The graph shows the percentage of cardiac deaths over the 5 years following hospitalization as a function of level of depression symptoms (score on the Beck Depression Inventory) during hospitalization.

Our work, and that of other researchers, also indicates that there is a dose-response relationship between depression symptoms and long-term cardiac prognosis in post-MI patients. We administered the Beck Depression Inventory (BDI; Beck & Steer, 1987) to 896 patients during hospitalization for an acute MI and followed 870 of these patients for 5 years after hospital discharge (Lespérance, Frasure-Smith, Talajic, & Bourassa, 2002). Results showed a highly significant dose-response relationship between increasing BDI scores and long-term cardiac mortality (see Fig. 1). The increasing risk began to be apparent even below the usual level of symptoms considered to indicate depression (BDI score of 10 or higher), and was independent of the severity of cardiac disease (measured by various indices), as well as independent of age, sex, education, and marital status.

Beyond the consistent and strong evidence that depression increases risk in patients with CHD, a recent meta-analysis (statistical analysis combining the results of multiple independent studies) indicated that depression can also precede the development of CHD by many years (Rugulies, 2002). When the 13 studies included in this analysis were pooled, depression was found to increase the risk of developing CHD by a factor of about 1.6. Of all the psychosocial variables that have been studied as risk factors in CHD patients, including hostility, anxiety, and low social support, depression is the most prevalent; it is also the psychosocial risk factor that is best supported by epidemiological evidence (Rozanski, Blumenthal, & Kaplan, 1999).

HYPOTHESIZED MECHANISMS

Although many biological and behavioral mechanisms have been proposed to explain the link between CHD and depression (Joynt, Whellan, & O'Connor, 2003), their relative importance remains unknown. Some of the existing research supports the hypothesis that depression causes cardiac events, whereas other evidence suggests that CHD leads to depression. In addition, other risk factors may lead to both depression and CHD. Reciprocal causality may also be involved.

That is, depression might increase the risk of CHD, but once the cardiac disease is apparent, its multiple impacts on lifestyle and functioning could contribute to worsening depression. Finally, the development of CHD is a long process. Different sets of mechanisms may link depression and CHD at different points in the disease process.

Decreased heart rate variability is one of the mechanisms by which depression may lead to cardiac events. There is evidence that the beat-to-beat variation in heart rate is reduced in depression (Carney et al., 2001). Decreased heart rate variability is thought to reflect increased sympathetic tone, decreased vagal (parasympathetic nervous system) activity, or both. Post-MI patients, people with congestive heart failure, and diabetics all have reduced heart rate variability, and the greater the reduction in variability, the worse their prognosis. Depressed patients with CHD tend to have even more pronounced decreases in heart rate variability than nondepressed CHD patients. Thus, changes in heart rate variability may at least partially account for depression's negative association with cardiac prognosis.

Although it is also possible that depression and its physiological sequelae are not the cause of cardiac disease, but rather its consequence, the evidence for this mechanism is not very strong. Cardiologists frequently suggest that if patients are consciously or unconsciously aware of their cardiac prognosis, this can lead to depression. However, although indices of cardiac severity, such as poor pumping function and the number of blocked coronary arteries, are moderately associated with the level of depressive symptoms, depression's association with cardiac prognosis is statistically independent of these factors. The bulk of the evidence suggests that depression is associated with worse prognosis in patients with all levels of cardiac disease severity, and that cardiac disease severity does not explain the link between depression and cardiac prognosis.

There are at least four other models of the relation between depression and CHD: the vascular depression hypothesis, the cytokine model, the free fatty acid model, and the serotonin-transporter model. In each case, a common cause for depression and CHD is hypothesized to account for their apparent link. The vascular hypothesis of depression suggests that in advanced atherosclerosis, blockages in brain arteries may compromise blood supply. Reduced blood supply may produce loss or dysfunction of nerve cells in brain regions involved in mood and cognition, leading to depression (Alexopoulos et al., 1997). Similarly, atherosclerotic blockages in coronary arteries produce CHD. Thus, the link between depression and CHD, at least in the elderly, may be the result of generalized atherosclerosis.

The cytokine model of depression focuses on the inflammatory nature of the atherosclerotic process (Dantzer, Wollman, & Yirmiya, 2002). Atherosclerotic plaque, the buildup of cholesterol and other substances in the linings of the arteries, contains immune cells that produce cytokines, chemicals that orchestrate the inflammatory response and have widespread systemic effects. Cytokines can produce what is called sickness behavior, which includes loss of appetite and interest, fatigue, and social withdrawal. Note that these behaviors are closely related to depression. They are also associated with infection and fever. Although atherosclerosis is not an acute infection, but rather chronic, low-grade immune activation with a peak of activity at the time of a cardiac event, it is well established that increased levels of inflammatory markers predict worse cardiac prognosis. Intriguingly, patients with depression show patterns of immune activation similar to those seen in patients with CHD. It is possible that the heightened inflammatory activity in CHD patients also results in sickness behavior, depression, or both in some individuals.

A relative deficiency in the polyunsaturated omega-3 free fatty acids, found primarily in fatty fish, is associated with an increased risk of CHD, as well as with depression (Frasure-Smith, Lespérance, & Julien, 2004). International comparisons of CHD rates show the more fish in the average diet, the lower the incidence of CHD. In fact, trials of omega-3 supplementation and increased dietary intake of fish have been shown to reduce the risk of arrhythmic deaths in post-MI patients. Recent epidemiological studies have also shown that individuals with mood disorders have lower levels of omega-3 than individuals without psychiatric disorders. A few small clinical trials even suggest that omega-3 supplementation may have antidepressant properties. Thus, a relative deficiency of polyunsaturated omega-3 free fatty acids could be a risk factor for both CHD and depression, and a diet rich in omega-3 could be beneficial for both conditions.

Changes in blood clotting may also be a mechanism linking depression and CHD. Both MIs and episodes of unstable angina involve the formation of a blood clot within the arteries of the heart. This process is often triggered by the rupture of atherosclerotic plaque, which releases material that favors the activation and aggregation of blood platelets. Factors that facilitate platelet activation may help explain links between depression and CHD. Like nerve cells, platelets contain stores of serotonin and have the capacity to secrete, respond to, and reabsorb (reuptake) serotonin. One type of antidepressants, the selective serotonin reuptake inhibitors (SSRIs), is thought to affect depression by decreasing the reabsorption of serotonin into the platelets, thereby increasing its availability. In fact, there are studies suggesting heightened platelet activation and propensity to form blood clots are associated with depression, and some evidence that SSRIs may decrease platelet activation. Finally, it is plausible that there is a genetic predisposition to serotonin dysfunction in the brain that leads to depression, and that the same genetic predisposition independently leads to increased platelet activation and coronary events.

TREATMENT OF DEPRESSION IN CHD PATIENTS

Although there are multiple mechanisms that might link depression and CHD, and there is consistent, strong data that depression is associated with increased risk of cardiac events in CHD patients, as well as with the development of CHD in initially healthy individuals, there has been only one large randomized, controlled trial of whether treatment for depression can alter cardiac prognosis. In the Enhancing Recovery in Coronary Heart Disease (ENRICHD) study, more than 2,400 depressed or socially isolated post-MI patients were randomly assigned either to usual care from their physicians or to 6 months of cognitive-behavioral therapy[3] (CBT; ENRICHD Investigators, 2003). After 5 weeks, patients who did not respond to CBT were also prescribed sertraline (an SSRI). Results showed a statistically significant, but small difference in improvement in depression ratings between the CBT and usual-care groups. There was no group difference in cardiac outcome (death or nonfatal MI over an average follow-up of 29 months).

Although the ENRICHD results did not show an effect on cardiac outcome, they do not invalidate the extensive observational evidence of links between depression and CHD. There are many alternate explanations. Physicians of patients in the usual-care group were informed that their patients were depressed, and 36 months into the study, 21% of the usual-care patients had been treated with antidepressants, in comparison with 28% in the CBT group. Another recent study, SADHART (the Sertraline Anti-Depressant Heart Attack Randomized Trial), which involved 369 post-MI and unstable angina patients (Glassman et al., 2002), demonstrated that sertraline treatment for 24 weeks resulted in a statistically significant, but small improvement in depression symptoms in those patients with recurrent depression, especially if they initially had high levels of depression symptoms. Thus, in ENRICHD, the high proportion of antidepressant treatment in the usual-care group may have masked group differences in changes in depression symptoms and possibly cardiac events, particularly among patients with recurrent and severe depression. It is also possible that CBT does not have a strong enough impact on the pathophysiology of depression to influence cardiac events. Finally, if depression and CHD share a common cause, it is unlikely that treating one will affect the other. What may be required is treatment of the common causal factor.

Further research is needed to clarify the complex interplay of depression and cardiac disease, and to determine the most effective treatment strategies for improving both quality of life and prognosis in CHD patients. Adaptation and evaluation of existing interventions with a demonstrated impact on depression in noncardiac patients should be a high priority in research with CHD patients. For example, stepped care with individually tailored case management, in which different treatments are provided depending on patients' specific characteristics and responses, has a proven impact on depression in patients who are treated by general-practice physicians and would be a logical first step.

CONCLUSIONS

In summary, depression and CHD are complex, multifactorial diseases that involve multiple mechanisms in many systems, and these systems also interact with each other in complicated ways. Our knowledge of both conditions has grown enormously in the past decade, and recent advances in genetic research are likely to provide additional insights into new treatment options. Regardless of whether it is ever demonstrated that treating depression can influence prognosis, treatment of depression can reduce psychological burden and improve functioning for many CHD patients. However, until future trials suggest a different approach, the best strategy to reduce the impact of depression on cardiac prognosis is to ensure that depressed CHD patients also receive aggressive and comprehensive intervention to reduce their other cardiac risks.

Recommended Reading

Joynt, K.E., Whellan, D.J., & O'Connor, C.M. (2003). (See References)
Lespérance, F., & Frasure-Smith, N. (2000). (See References)
Rozanski, A., Blumenthal, J.A., & Kaplan, J. (1999). (See References)

Notes

1. Address correspondence to Nancy Frasure-Smith, Montreal Heart Institute, 5000 Bélanger, Montreal, Quebec, Canada; e-mail: nancy. frasure-smith@mcgill.ca.
2. For a glossary of terms related to CHD, depression, and their physiological mechanisms, see Table 1.
3. CBT is a structured form of psychotherapy that attempts to alter dysfunctional thinking patterns that can lead to negative emotions by making patients aware of these patterns and helping them to establish alternative interpretations to daily events and stressors.

References

Alexopoulos, G.S., Meyers, B.S., Young, R.C., Campbell, S., Silbersweig, D., & Charlson, M. (1997). 'Vascular depression' hypothesis. *Archives of General Psychiatry, 54*, 915–922.

Beck, A.T., & Steer, R.A. (1987). *Beck Depression Inventory manual.* Toronto, Ontario, Canada: Psychological Corp., Harcourt, Brace, Jovanovich.

Carney, R.M., Blumenthal, J.A., Stein, P.K., Watkins, L., Catellier, D., Berkman, L.F., Czajkowski, S.M., O'Connor, C., Stone, P.H., & Freedland, K.E. (2001). Depression, heart rate variability, and acute myocardial infarction. *Circulation, 104*, 2024–2028.

Dantzer, R., Wollman, E.E., & Yirmiya, R. (2002). Cytokines and depression: An update. *Brain, Behavior and Immunity, 16*, 501–502.

ENRICHD Investigators. (2003). Effects of treating depression and low perceived social support on clinical events after myocardial infarction. *Journal of the American Medical Association, 289*, 3106.

Frasure-Smith, N., Lespérance, F., & Julien, P. (2004). Major depression is associated with lower omega-3 fatty acid levels in patients with recent acute coronary syndromes. *Biological Psychiatry, 55*, 891–896.

Glassman, A.H., O'Connor, C.M., Califf, R., Swedberg, K., Schwartz, P., Bigger, T., Jr., Krishnan, K.R.R., van Zyl, L.T., Swenson, J.R., Finkel, M.S., Landau, C., Shapiro, P.A., Pepine, C.J., & Harrison, M., for the Sertraline Antidepressant Heart Attack Randomized Trial (SADHART) Group. (2002). Sertraline treatment of major depression in patients with acute MI or unstable angina. *Journal of the American Medical Association, 288*, 701–709.

Grimes, D.A., & Schultz, K.F. (2002). Bias and causal associations in observational research. *The Lancet, 359*, 248–252.

Joynt, K.E., Whellan, D.J., & O'Connor, C.M. (2003). Depression and cardiovascular disease: Mechanisms of interaction. *Biological Psychiatry, 54*, 248–261.

Lespérance, F., & Frasure-Smith, N. (2000). Depression in patients with cardiac disease: A practical review. *Journal of Psychosomatic Research, 48*, 379–391.

Lespérance, F., Frasure-Smith, N., Talajic, M., & Bourassa, M.G. (2002). Five-year risk of cardiac mortality in relation to initial severity and one-year changes in depression symptoms after myocardial infarction. *Circulation, 105*, 1049–1053.

Murray, C.J.L., & Lopez, A.D. (1997). Global mortality, disability, and the contribution of risk factors: Global Burden of Disease study. *The Lancet, 349*, 1436–1442.

Rozanski, A., Blumenthal, J.A., & Kaplan, J. (1999). Impact of psychological factors on the pathogenesis of cardiovascular disease and implications for therapy. *Circulation, 99*, 2192–2217.

Rugulies, R. (2002). Depression as a predictor for coronary heart disease: A review and meta-analysis. *American Journal of Preventive Medicine, 23*, 51–61.

This article has been reprinted as it originally appeared in *Current Directions in Psychological Science*. Citation information for this article as originally published appears above.

Buddhist and Psychological Perspectives on Emotions and Well-Being

Paul Ekman[1] and B. Alan Wallace
University of California, San Francisco

Richard J. Davidson
University of Wisconsin, Madison

Matthieu Ricard
Shechen Monastery, Katmandu, Nepal; and Santa Barbara Institute for Consciousness Studies, Santa Barbara, California

Abstract

Stimulated by a recent meeting between Western psychologists and the Dalai Lama on the topic of destructive emotions, we report on two issues: the achievement of enduring happiness, what Tibetan Buddhists call sukha, and the nature of afflictive and nonafflictive emotional states and traits. A Buddhist perspective on these issues is presented, along with discussion of the challenges the Buddhist view raises for empirical research and theory.

Keywords

Buddhism; consciousness

Buddhist thought, which arose more than 2,000 years ago in Asian cultures, holds assumptions that differ in important ways from modern psychology. The particular branch of Buddhist thinking we consider here is Indo-Tibetan, a tradition having roots in Indian thought and further developed by Tibetan theorists. It is a line of thinking that is more than 1,000 years old. Although different aspects of Buddhist thought have already influenced a number of psychologists, its challenges for research on emotion are not widely known. Some suggestive convergences between Buddhist thinking and, for example, findings in neurobiology, suggest the fruitfulness of integrating a Buddhist view into emotion research.

The traditional languages of Buddhism, such as Pali, Sanskrit, and Tibetan, have no word for "emotion" as such. Although discrepant from the modern psychological research tradition that has isolated emotion as a distinct mental process that can be studied apart from other processes, the fact that there is no term in Buddhism for emotion is quite consistent with what scientists have come to learn about the anatomy of the brain. Every region in the brain that has been identified with some aspect of emotion has also been identified with aspects of cognition (e.g., Davidson & Irwin, 1999). The circuitry that supports affect and the circuitry that supports cognition are completely intertwined—an anatomical arrangement consistent with the Buddhist view that these processes cannot be separated.

We have chosen two issues, the achievement of enduring happiness and the nature of afflictive emotions, to illustrate the usefulness of considering the

Buddhist perspective in work on emotion. Given the space allowed, we present illustrative examples of possible areas for research, rather than a more complete discussion.

This report is a collaborative effort of Buddhists (Matthieu Ricard and B. Alan Wallace) and psychologists (Paul Ekman and Richard J. Davidson). Our report grew out of an extraordinary meeting with His Holiness the Dalai Lama, in Dharamsala, India, in March 2000, that focused on destructive emotions.[2] The Buddhist authors wrote the sections titled "The Buddhist View," and the psychologist authors wrote the sections on research directions and theory.

ACHIEVING ENDURING HAPPINESS

The Buddhist View

Buddhists and psychologists alike believe that emotions strongly influence people's thoughts, words, and actions and that, at times, they help people in their pursuit of transient pleasures and satisfaction. From a Buddhist perspective, however, some emotions are conducive to genuine and enduring happiness and others are not. A Buddhist term for such happiness is *sukha*, which may be defined in this context as a state of flourishing that arises from mental balance and insight into the nature of reality. Rather than a fleeting emotion or mood aroused by sensory and conceptual stimuli, *sukha* is an enduring trait that arises from a mind in a state of equilibrium and entails a conceptually unstructured and unfiltered awareness of the true nature of reality. Many Buddhist contemplatives claim to have experienced *sukha*, which increases as a result of sustained training.

Similarly, the Buddhist concept of *duhkha*, often translated as "suffering," is not simply an unpleasant feeling. Rather, it refers most deeply to a basic vulnerability to suffering and pain due to misapprehending the nature of reality. (The terms *sukha* and *duhkha* are from Sanskrit, one of the primary languages of Buddhist literature.)

How is *sukha* to be realized? Buddhists believe that the radical transformation of consciousness necessary to realize *sukha* can occur by sustained training in attention, emotional balance, and mindfulness, so that one can learn to distinguish between the way things are as they appear to the senses and the conceptual superimpositions one projects upon them. As a result of such training, one perceives what is presented to the senses, including one's own mental states, in a way that is closer to their true nature, undistorted by the projections people habitually mistake for reality.

Such training results not only in shifts in fleeting emotions but also leads to changes in one's moods and eventually even changes in one's temperament. For more than two millennia, Buddhist practitioners have developed and tested ways of gradually cultivating those emotions that are conductive to the pursuit of *sukha* and of freeing themselves from emotions that are detrimental to this pursuit. The ideal here is not simply to achieve one's own individual happiness in isolation from others, but to incorporate the recognition of one's deep kinship with all beings, who share the same yearning to be free of suffering and to find a lasting state of well-being.

Two Research Directions

We have begun to examine highly experienced Buddhist practitioners, who presumably have achieved *sukha*, to determine whether that trait manifests itself in their biological activity during emotional episodes (Lutz, Greischar, Rawlings, Ricard, & Davidson, in press) or increases their sensitivity to the emotions of other people, and to see how their interactive style may transform the nature of conflictual interactions. Such study of Buddhism's most expert practitioners may change psychology's conception of what at least some human beings are capable of achieving.

Another possible area of research concerns the reliability of self-report about mental states. Although much of the research on emotion has presumed that research subjects and our patients during psychotherapy can readily report on their subjective experience through questionnaires and interviews, findings to date show that most people report only the most recent or most intense of their emotional experiences (e.g., Kahneman, Fredrickson, Schreiber, & Redelmeier, 1993; Rosenberg & Ekman, 1994) and are subject to bias. Research could determine whether those schooled in Buddhist practices could offer a more refined and complete account of their immediately past emotional experience, exhibiting fewer judgmental biases. In a related vein, other research has demonstrated that most people are poor predictors of what will make them happy (e.g., Wilson & Gilbert, in press). It would be interesting to determine whether those who have engaged in Buddhist contemplative practices sufficiently to achieve *sukha* are more accurate in affective forecasting.

AFFLICTIVE MENTAL STATES

The Buddhist View

Buddhism does not distinguish between emotions and other mental processes. Instead, it is concerned with understanding which types of mental activity are truly conducive to one's own and others' well-being, and which ones are harmful, especially in the long run.

In Buddhism, a clear distinction is made between affective states that are directly aroused by the experience of pleasurable stimuli (sensory, as well as aesthetic and intellectual) and *sukha*, which arises from the attentional, emotional, and cognitive balance of the mind. (For a similar distinction, see Sheldon, Ryan, Deci, & Kasser, 2004.) The experience of pleasure is contingent upon specific times, places, and circumstances, and can easily change into a neutral or unpleasant feeling. When one disengages from the pleasant stimulus, the resultant pleasure vanishes, whether or not it is connected to any afflictive state.

The initial challenge of Buddhist meditative practice is not merely to suppress, let alone repress, destructive mental states, but instead to identify how they arise, how they are experienced, and how they influence oneself and others over the long run. In addition, one learns to transform and finally free oneself from all afflictive states. This requires cultivating and refining one's ability to introspectively monitor one's own mental activities, enabling one to distinguish disruptive from nondisruptive thoughts and emotions. In Buddhism, rigorous, sustained training in mindfulness and introspection is conjoined with the cultivation of attentional stability and vividness.

In contrast to Aristotelian ethics, Buddhism rejects the notion that all emotions are healthy as long as they are not excessive or inappropriate to the time and place. Rather, Buddhism maintains that some mental states are afflictive regardless of their degree or the context in which they arise. Here we focus on three mental processes that are considered to be fundamental toxins of the mind.

The first of these is craving. This mental process is based on an unrealistic, reified distinction between self and others—or between subject and object more generally—as being absolutely separate and unrelated. Craving is concerned with acquiring or maintaining some desirable object or situation for "me" and "mine," which may be threatened by "the other." One assumes that desirable qualities are inherent in the object desired and then exaggerates these qualities, while ignoring or deemphasizing that object's undesirable aspects. Craving is therefore an unrealistic way of engaging with the world, and it is harmful whenever one identifies with this afflictive mental process, regardless of how strong it is or the circumstances under which it arises. Craving is said to be afflictive, for it disrupts the balance of the mind, easily giving rise to anxiety, misery, fear, and anger; and it is unrealistic in the sense that it falsely displaces the source of one's well being from one's own mind to objects.

Hatred is the second of the fundamental afflictions of the mind and is a reverse reflection of craving. That is, hatred, or malevolence, is driven by the wish to harm or destroy anything that obstructs the selfish pursuit of desirable objects and situations for me and mine. Hatred exaggerates the undesirable qualities of objects and deemphasizes their positive qualities. When the mind is obsessed with resentment, it is trapped in the deluded impression that the source of its dissatisfaction belongs entirely to the external object (just as, in the case of craving, the mind locates the source of satisfaction in desirable objects). But even though the trigger of one's resentment may be the external object, the actual source of this and all other kinds of mental distress is in the mind alone.

The third, most fundamental affliction of the mind is the delusion of grasping onto one's own and others' reified personal identities as real and concrete. According to Buddhism, the self is constantly in a state of dynamic flux, arises in different ways, and is profoundly interdependent with other people and the environment. However, people habitually obscure the actual nature of the self by superimposing on reality the concepts of permanence, singularity, and autonomy. As a result of misapprehending the self as independent, there arises a strong sense of the absolute separation of self and other. Then, craving naturally arises for the "I" and for what is mine, and repulsion arises toward the other. The erroneous belief in the absolute distinction of self and other thus acts as the basis for the derivative mental afflictions of craving, hatred, jealousy, and arrogance. Such toxins of the mind are regarded, in Buddhism, as the sources of all mental suffering.

Theoretical Issues and Research Directions

Psychologists do not distinguish between beneficial and harmful emotions. Those who take an evolutionary view of emotion (e.g., Cosmides & Tooby, 2000;

Ekman, 1992) have proposed that emotions were adaptive over the history of the species and remain adaptive today. Even those who categorize emotions as simply positive or negative (e.g., Watson, Clark, & Tellegen, 1988) do not propose that all of the negative emotions are harmful to oneself or to others. The goal in any psychologically informed attempt to improve one's emotional life is not to rid oneself of or transcend an emotion—not even hatred—but to regulate experience and action once an emotion is felt (Davidson, Jackson, & Kalin, 2000). (Note, however, that not all theorists consider hatred an emotion.)

One point of convergence between the Buddhist and psychological perspectives is that hostility, which is viewed in the West as a character or personality trait, is considered to be destructive to one's health. Impulsive chronic violence is also considered to be dysfunctional and is classified as pathological (Davidson, Putnam, & Larson, 2000). But neither of these is considered in psychology to be an emotion per se.

Rather than focusing on increasing consciousness of one's inner state, the emphasis in much of psychology is on learning how to reappraise situations (Lazarus, 1991) or how to control (regulate) emotional behavior and expressions (Gross, 1999; but see Ekman, 2003, for a psychological approach to enhancing awareness of emotions as they occur).

The growing literature based on self-report measures of well-being indicates that punctate events, even significant ones such as winning the lottery, phasically alter an individual's state of pleasure but do not change an individual's trait level of happiness. Buddhists agree that events such as winning the lottery would not alter an individual's dispositional level of happiness, but they do assert that happiness as a dispositional trait (*sukha*) can be cultivated through specific practices. Although the term trait positive affect as it has been used in the mood and temperament literature has some elements in common with *sukha*, it does not capture the essence of the Buddhist construct, which also includes a deep sense of well-being, a propensity toward compassion, reduced vulnerability to outer circumstances, and recognition of the interconnectedness with people and other living beings in one's environment. Moreover, *sukha* is a trait and not a state. It is a dispositional quality that permeates and pervades all experience and behavior.

Another important difference between Buddhism and psychological approaches is that the Buddhists provide a method for modifying affective traits and for cultivating *sukha* (Wallace, 2005), whereas in psychology the only methods for changing enduring affective traits are those that have been developed specifically to treat psychopathology. With a few notable exceptions (e.g., Seligman, 1998), no effort has been invested in cultivating positive attributes of mind in individuals who do not have mental disorders. Western approaches to changing enduring emotional states or traits do not involve the long-term persistent effort that is involved in all complex skill learning—for example, in becoming a chess master or learning to play a musical instrument. Typically, not even psychoanalysis or the most intensive forms of cognitive-behavior therapy involve the decades of training Buddhists consider necessary for the cultivation of *sukha*.

Buddhists, as we said, consider craving to be one of the primary toxins of the mind. Unlike psychologists, who restrict the idea of craving to states produced by substances of abuse or by strongly appetitive opportunities that offer the potential for abuse (e.g., gambling, sex), Buddhists use the term more generically to encompass the desire to acquire objects and situations for oneself. A growing body of neuroscientific literature has shown that activity of the neurotransmitter dopamine in a part of the brain called the nucleus accumbens is common to states of craving, including both pharmacologically induced addictions and activities such as gambling. Although activation of this system is highly reinforcing (i.e., it leads to the recurrence of behaviors associated with the system's activation), it is not associated with pleasure in the long run. Of course, what is not included in this neuroscientific framework is anything akin to the notion of *sukha*.

Buddhist contemplative practices are explicitly designed to counteract craving. It would thus be of great interest empirically to evaluate how effective these methods may be as interventions for addictive disorders, which are disorders of craving, and to determine if the brain systems associated with craving are altered by such training.

The Buddhist, but not Western, view considers hatred to be intrinsically harmful to people who experience it. This perspective suggests that it would be valuable to examine the different ways in which those who have been exposed to a major trauma react emotionally to the cause of their trauma—for example, how people whose children have been murdered react to the perpetrators once they are apprehended. In a study of such individuals, various biological, health, and social measures would provide information about the consequences of maintaining hatred or forgiveness toward the perpetrator.

JOINT CONCLUSION

Buddhist conceptions and practices that deal with emotional life make three very distinct contributions to psychology. Conceptually, they raise issues that have been ignored by many psychologists, calling on the field to make more finely nuanced distinctions in thinking about emotional experience. Methodologically, they offer practices that could help individuals report on their own internal experiences, and such practices might thereby provide crucial data that is much more detailed and comprehensive than that gathered by the techniques psychologists now use to study subjective emotional experience. Finally, Buddhist practices themselves offer a therapy, not just for the disturbed, but for all who seek to improve the quality of their lives. We hope what we have reported will serve to spark the interest of psychologists to learn more about this tradition.

Recommended Reading

Goleman, D. (2003). *Beyond destructive emotions: A scientific collaboration with the Dalai Lama.* New York: Bantam Books.

Teasdale, D., Segal, Z., & Williams, J.M. (1995). How does cognitive therapy prevent depressive relapse and why should attentional control (mindfulness) training help? *Behavior Research and Therapy, 33,* 25–39.

Wallace, B.A. (2005). (See References)

Acknowledgments—Paul Ekman's research was supported in part by a National Institute of Mental Health (NIMH) Senior Research Scientist Award, KO5-MH06092. Richard Davidson's work described in this article has been supported by NIMH Grants MN43454, MH40747, P50-MH522354, and P50-MH61083; by NIMH Research Scientist Award KO5-MH00875; by grants from the Research Network on Mind-Body Interaction of the John D. and Catherine T. MacArthur Foundation; and by support from the University of Wisconsin. The authors are grateful to the many colleagues who read and gave helpful suggestions on earlier drafts of this article, but especially to Daniel Goleman.

Notes

1. Address correspondence to Paul Ekman, P.O. Box 5211, Berkeley CA 94705; e-mail: paul@paulekman.com.

2. The participants at this meeting, besides the Dalai Lama, were Richard Davidson, Paul Ekman, Owen Flannagen, Daniel Goleman, Mark Greenberg, Thupten Jinpa, Matthieu Ricard, Jeanne Tsai, Francisco Varela, and Alan Wallace. We thank the Mind and Life Institute of Boulder, Colorado for organizing the meeting in India and a subsequent meeting during which we wrote this article.

References

Cosmides, L., & Tooby, J. (2000). Evolutionary psychology and the emotions. In M.L. Lewis & J. Haviland-Jones (Eds.), *Handbook of emotions* (2nd ed., pp. 3–134). New York: Guilford Press.

Davidson, R.J., & Irwin, W. The functional neuroanatomy of emotion and affective style. *Trends in Cognitive Science, 3*, 11–21.

Davidson, R.J., Jackson, D.C., & Kalin, N.H. (2000). Emotion, plasticity, context and regulation: Perspectives from affective neuroscience. *Psychological Bulletin, 126*, 890–906.

Davidson, R.J., Putnam, K.M., & Larson, C.L. (2000). Dysfunction in the neural circuitry of emotion regulation—a possible prelude to violence. *Science, 289*, 591–594.

Ekman, P. (1992). An argument for basic emotions. *Cognition and Emotion, 6*, 169–200.

Ekman, P. (2003). *Emotions revealed: Recognizing faces and feelings to improve communication and emotional life*. New York: Times Books.

Gross, J.J. (1999). The emerging field of emotion regulation: An integrative review. *Review of General Psychology, 2*, 271–299.

Kahneman, D., Fredrickson, B.L., Schreiber, C.A., & Redelmeier, D.A. (1993). When more pain is preferred to less: Adding a better end. *Psychological Science, 4*, 401–405.

Lazarus, R. (1991). *Emotion and adaptation*. New York: Oxford University Press.

Lutz, A., Greischar, L.L., Rawlings, N.B., Ricard, M., & Davidson, R.J. (in press). Long-term meditators self-induce high-amplitude gamma synchrony during mental practice. *Proceedings of the National Academy of Sciences, USA*.

Rosenberg, E.L., & Ekman, P. (1994). Coherence between expressive and experiential systems in emotion. *Cognition and Emotion, 8*, 201–229.

Seligman, M.E.P. (1998). *Learned optimism*. New York: Pocket Books.

Sheldon, M., Ryan, R.M., Deci, E.L., & Kasser, T. (2004). The independent effects of goal contents and motives on well-being: It's both what you pursue and why you pursue it. *Personality and Social Psychology Bulletin, 30*, 475–486.

Wallace, B.A. (2005). *Genuine happiness: Meditation as the path to fulfillment*. Hoboken, NJ: John Wiley and Sons.

Watson, D., Clark, L.A., & Tellegen, A. (1988). Development and validation of brief measures of positive and negative affect: The PANAS scales. *Journal of Personality and Social Psychology, 54*, 1063–1070.

Wilson, T., & Gilbert, D. (in press). Affective forecasting: Knowing what to want. *Current Directions in Psychological Science*.

Section 3: Critical Thinking Questions

1. Briefly describe the "critical period" hypothesis described by Barbara Sherwin. How might you imagine this hypothesis helps one to understand development in general? How about the etiology of mental illness?

2. Hormone replacement therapy (HRT) has been linked to an increased risk of breast cancer. How does one balance the knowledge that HRT may potentially prevent cognitive decline while simultaneously increasing one's risk for cancer? What does the author, Barbara Sherwin, have to say about this topic? What are some ethical questions raised by this research?

3. Frasure-Smith and Lespérance note that coronary heart disease and depression are major problems in industrialized countries. Can you think of some reasons why industrialization might contribute to the development of either or both of these health concerns? According to the Gottfredson and Dreary paper, what role might intelligence play in the co-occurrence of these diseases?

4. As our knowledge about the body and brain increases, physicians are able to focus on individual problems seemingly confined to one system (e.g. diseases like diabetes, cancer or major depression). The readings in this section suggest that each part of the body may affect others "downstream". What are the implications of a holistic approach to mental and physical health for treatment? What are the practical implications of such an approach?

5. What can we learn from a dialogue between western psychology and Buddhism? How might a Buddhist approach inform prevention, perception, and treatment of illness? Is it possible to incorporate a Buddhist approach into psychological science? Design a study that might yield some insights about human emotion from a Buddhist perspective.

This article has been reprinted as it originally appeared in *Current Directions in Psychological Science*. Citation information for this article as originally published appears above.

Section 4: Clinical Psychology: Investigation and Interpretation

Clinical psychology, the study of abnormal behavior, is the most prominent area of psychological inquiry. Importantly, clinical psychology is an ever expanding and changing field, where new diagnostic categories emerge and old diagnoses are discarded. How we think about abnormal behavior is shaped by individual (biological and temperamental) and social (environmental) variables.

Clinical psychology has benefited greatly from the development and application of non-invasive neurological investigation. Being able to "see" inside the brain has added a new dimension to our understanding of mental illness. As our society becomes more complex, we change the way we view mental disorder as well as how we treat it. Further, as our society becomes more "psychologically savvy" mental illness emerges as an integral part of the cultural dialogue. As you will learn, this increased awareness can have both positive and negative effects. In this section, you will read papers in which authors address issues in clinical psychology from biological, psychological and social perspectives.

In the first paper, Barry Jacobs (2005) presents a theory of clinical depression that emphasizes the role of neurogenesis, the growth of new neurons, in maintaining emotional health. Until recently, scholars believed that the adult brain was fully developed, a place where neurons might die but no new ones could emerge. To the contrary, although the majority of neural growth takes place before adulthood, new brain cells continue to appear well into adulthood. Jacobs investigates the role of neurogenesis in the precipitation and maintenance of major depressive episodes. Specifically, he argues that an event, such as stress, inhibits neurogenesis and thus makes a major depressive episode more likely. The role of neurogenesis in major depression might partially explain the perplexing success of anti-depressant medications.

Clinically-oriented psychological science might focus on the direction of a relationship between two variables. For example, the relationship between socio-economic status and mental health can be explained by two opposing theories, a) the social drift hypothesis (people with mental illness naturally drift downward on the socioeconomic ladder) and b) the sociogenic hypothesis (because living in poverty is more stressful, one is more likely to develop a mental illness). Which is "more" true? How do researchers determine the direction of this relationship? In the next paper, M. Lynne Cooper (2006) asks a similarly perplexing question, specifically, does drinking alcohol increase the likelihood of engaging in risky sexual behavior? Sexual risk taking poses a real public health hazard, resulting in undesirable outcomes such as sexually-transmitted diseases as well as unwanted pregnancies. Cooper reviews three explanations for the apparent relationship between alcohol and sexual risk taking. Individual variables such as a tendency for sensation-seeking might increase the likelihood that one will both drink alcohol and engage in risky sex, independently. Second, Cooper offers a "reverse causal explanation" and argues that perhaps individuals who wish to engage in sexual risk taking drink alcohol, intending to facilitate desired sexual behavior. Finally, Cooper explores a causal relationship and discusses how alcohol expectancies (both biological and psychological) might increase the likelihood of sexual risk taking. This paper offers an excellent example of the interaction of multiple factors (biological, psychological, and social) in promoting a specific behavior.

There is only one mental disorder in the Diagnostic and Statistical Manual for which there is one identifiable cause. To receive a diagnosis of post traumatic stress disorder (PTSD) one must be exposed to a seriously traumatic event, and suffer significant psychological consequences as a result. Fortunately, not everyone who experiences a severe trauma develops PTSD. Although enormous resources have been dedicated to investigating pathological responses to traumatic events, less attention has been paid to "resilience", or the ability to persevere in the event of trauma. George Bonanno (2005) reveals that resilience, not debilitation, is the most common response to trauma. Resilience, like PTSD, can take many different forms. As in the Cooper paper, individual differences in temperament or self-concept might make one more likely to be resilient in the aftermath of trauma.

A prominent part of our social dialogue includes psychological topics. People are interested in mental illness; they wonder about what makes one "abnormal" and worry about how to prevent and treat psychopathology. Mental illness in children is particularly troubling, and parents and educators typically absorb information about pertinent clinical psychology. The interest in psychological science has unfortunately not been accompanied by an understanding of how best to interpret scientific data. Autistic Disorder, or disorders in the Autism Spectrum are receiving a great deal of attention in the lay media. Morton Ann Gernsbacher, Michelle Dawson, and H. Hill Goldsmith (2005) offer a scientist's interpretation of the misleading assumption in the popular media that there is an "epidemic" of autism. They review several common misconceptions. One striking observation reveals that the diagnosis of autism has changed as scientists learn more about the syndrome. As a result, the category broadens, the diagnosis is less sensitive, and increasing numbers of children are likely to be labeled autistic. Thus, when one compares the prevalence of autism now, compared with the prevalence of autism 20 years ago, one must account for the broadening criteria when drawing conclusions. Gernsbacher, Dawson and Goldsmith point out the danger in labeling a psychological phenomenon an "epidemic". This alarmist language can be particularly harmful when parents and educators are making policy decisions based upon misinterpreted data.

While reading these papers, keep in mind the interaction of variables at multiple levels. Consider the role of the brain, both structure and function in mental illness. Remember that everyone is unique, thus individual differences contribute greatly to the manifestation of psychopathology. Finally, recall that the world in which we live is constantly changing and exerts a powerful influence on human behavior and its interpretation.

Depression: The Brain Finally Gets Into the Act

Barry L. Jacobs[1]
Princeton University

Abstract

The theory of clinical depression presented here integrates etiological factors, changes in specific structural and cellular substrates, ensuing symptomatology, and treatment and prevention. According to this theory, important etiological factors, such as stress, can suppress the production of new neurons in the adult human brain, thereby precipitating or maintaining a depressive episode. Most current treatments for depression are known to elevate brain serotonin neurotransmission, and such increases in serotonin have been shown to significantly augment the ongoing rate of neurogenesis, providing the neural substrate for new cognitions to be formed, and thereby facilitating recovery from the depressive episode. This theory also points to treatments that augment neurogenesis as new therapeutic opportunities.

Keywords

serotonin; adult brain neurogenesis; stress; clinical depression

When the history of mental illness is written, the 20th century will be remembered primarily not for its biomedical advances, but as the period when depression (along with the other major psychopathologies) was finally considered to be a disease and not a failure of character or a weakness of will. In part, this change is attributable to putting to rest, at least in the scientific community, the dogma of Cartesian duality of mind and body. Given that the mind is the manifestation of the brain, depression could be considered to be a somatic disorder, along with pathologies of the heart, kidney, and other organs.

HISTORICAL CONTEXT

This new perspective laid open the problem of depression to assault by investigators utilizing the modern biomedical armamentarium. Because of recent scientific advances at both the basic research and the clinical levels, it is the 21st century that will be remembered as the time when the major mental illnesses were finally understood at a deep, basic biological level, and when their treatments, and even prevention, were finally at hand.[2]

In the early years of modern biological psychiatry and psychology (1950s–1970s), neurobiological theories of depression focused on changes in patients such as elevated plasma levels of cortisol and corticosterone (hormones released from the upper portion of the adrenal gland), alterations in neurotransmitter-breakdown products found in the urine or cerebrospinal fluid, or lowered levels of neurotransmitters measured in plasma. In most of these cases, there was a heavy reliance on measures outside the central nervous system because of the general inaccessibility of brain measures. Thus, the search for the neural basis or pathophysiology of depression, in terms of either neurochemical or neuroanatomical-structural changes, came up largely empty.

More recently proposed neurobiological theories of depression attempt to directly relate precipitating events to changes in the brain, to classic symptomatology, and to coherent treatment strategies and even prevention. Such theories are especially attractive because they attempt to deal with the totality of the disease in a consistent and integrated manner. These theories go beyond simply pointing to "dysfunction in the left hemisphere" or "hypoactivity in the frontal lobes" and attempt to elucidate the neural and molecular mechanism underlying depression (Duman, Heninger, & Nestler, 1997; Jacobs, van Praag, & Gage, 2000; Manji, Drevets, & Charney, 2001). My colleagues and I have proposed one such theory, which focuses on the importance of neural changes in the brain for both the onset of and the recovery from depression (Jacobs et al., 2000).

NEUROPLASTICITY

One of the great conceptual leaps of modern neuroscience has been the notion of neuroplasticity. This is the idea that the adult brain can physically or morphologically change, not only in response to powerful toxins or trauma, but also in response to even subtle treatments or conditions. No less an intellect than the great Spanish neuroanatomist and Nobelist Ramon y Cajal believed that the morphology of the adult brain was essentially fixed. Scientists now know that even modest changes in the internal or external world can lead to structural changes in the brain. In fact, it is fair to say that the watchword for neuroscience in the past 20 to 30 years has become "plasticity."

Research in neuroplasticity has now shown that not only can neuronal morphology be altered, but also the actual number of neurons in the brain is not fixed. In the field of neurogenesis (the birth of new neurons), the work of Altman stands out as seminal. Altman was truly a scientist before his time (Altman & Das, 1965). In the early 1960s, he reported that two regions of the mammalian brain (most of his work was in rats), the olfactory bulb and the granule cell layer of dentate gyrus (DG; part of the hippocampal formation, which is a critical structure in the laying down of new cognitions), continue to generate new neurons in adulthood. In the context of the prevailing dogma of the immutability of the adult brain, this claim was heretical. And thus, not surprisingly, Altman's work was largely ignored and forgotten. It required more than 20 years for this topic to be reopened and reinvigorated. In the 1980s, Nottebohm reported that the overall size of certain regions of the bird brain, and the number of neurons in those areas, changed seasonally. Moreover, the increase in the number of brain cells appeared to coincide with the learning of new songs (Nottebohm, 1985). More than 10 years later, research groups led by Gould and Gage extended the concept of DG neurogenesis from birds and small mammals to monkeys, and eventually to humans (Erikssen et al., 1998; Gould, Cameron, Daniels, Wooley, & McEwen, 1994).

ADULT BRAIN NEUROGENESIS

Most neurons in the mammalian brain and spinal cord are generated during the pre- and perinatal periods of development. However, at least in the olfactory bulb, DG, and possibly some portions of the cerebral cortex areas, neurons continue to be born throughout life. These new neurons are derived primarily from progenitor cells that reside in the brain's subventricular zone, which lines the ventricles (fluid reservoirs of the brain), or in a layer of the hippocampal formation called the subgranular zone (lying immediately below the granule cell layer of the DG). Through a process that is as yet not well understood, a signal induces progenitor cells to enter the cell cycle and undergo mitosis (cell division). The entire process involves not only proliferation, but also migration and differentiation of brain cells. For the sake of economy, I use the terms proliferation and neurogenesis interchangeably because most new cells generated in the DG differentiate into neurons.

Our work in this field has focused on neurogenesis in the DG for several reasons: Neurogenesis occurs primarily in this structure, most studies of brain neurogenesis have been conducted on this region, this structure is known to play a critical role in brain information processing, and clinical evidence points to significant changes in the hippocampus in depression (as I discuss later). It is also well known that the hippocampus is linked to other brain structures, such as the amygdala, that play a more direct or central role in mood (affect).

STRESS

One of the cardinal features of depression is its recurrent nature. Some patients experience regular or periodic recurrence, whereas in other patients recurrence is aperiodic. It is tempting to speculate that such variation in mood might be attributable to the waning and waxing of some neural process in the brain.

In laboratory studies, the level of neurogenesis is quantified by treating animals with radioactive thymidine or bromodeoxyuridine (BrdU). These compounds are incorporated into the DNA of cells going through mitosis. Once these cells complete this process, their thymidine- or BrdU-labeled daughter cells in the brain can be identified and counted post mortem. A number of factors are known to positively and negatively influence neurogenesis in the DG. Stressors are the best known and most widely studied group of variables that strongly suppress DG neurogenesis. And almost always, this effect is attributable, in large part, to the release of hormones from the adrenal gland as part of the organism's general stress response. This fact was critical for our thinking, because stress and its related release of adrenal hormones are generally considered to be major etiological factors in clinical depression (Kendler, Karkowski, & Prescott, 1999).

SEROTONIN

The brain chemical most strongly associated with depression is serotonin (5-hydroxytryptamine). With the exception of psychotherapy, all effective treatments for depression are known to be directly or indirectly dependent on increasing brain serotonin. The best known of these are the eponymous SSRIs (serotonin-specific reuptake inhibitors), such as Paxil and Prozac. (These drugs act by preventing the serotonin that is released in the brain from being inactivated by being taken up by the brain cells that originally released it.) Thus, several years ago, we began to examine the effects of serotonin on cell proliferation in the DG of adult rats.

In our initial study, we found that the systemic administration of fenfluramine (which releases serotonin throughout the central nervous system) produced a powerful proliferative effect in the DG. We also found that this effect was completely prevented by prior administration of a drug that blocked serotonin's action at a specific site (5-HT$_{1A}$ receptor; Radley & Jacobs, 2002). Such drugs also significantly reduced spontaneous, or basal, levels of brain-cell production, suggesting that serotonin plays a role in DG cell proliferation under normal, or naturalistic, conditions. This line of work has been confirmed and extended by Daszuta and her colleagues (Brezun & Daszuta, 1999).

Next, we conducted an experiment that has the most direct relevance to the present theme. Systemic administration of the antidepressant drug fluoxetine (which is also known by the brand name Prozac) for 3 weeks produced a 70% increase in DG cell proliferation above that of control animals (Jacobs & Fornal, 1999). Two recent studies have confirmed and extended our results (Malberg, Eisch, Nestler, & Duman, 2000; Manev, Uz, Smalheiser, & Manev, 2001). They demonstrated that short-term administration of antidepressant drugs did not augment proliferation, an important finding because these drugs show clinical efficacy only after 4 to 6 weeks of daily administration. Electroconvulsive shocks (a powerful antidepressant treatment) given to rats also result in increased proliferation (Madsen et al., 2000).

The theory that follows from these experimental results is simple. Chronic, unremitting stress (a major etiological factor in depression) suppresses brain neurogenesis either by acting on adrenal hormones or by suppressing serotonin neurotransmission. This suppression of neurogenesis occurs most prominently in the hippocampus, but other brain areas may also be involved, either directly or indirectly. Recovery occurs, at least in part, when serotonin neurotransmission is increased, especially if the 5-HT$_{1A}$ receptor is activated, by any of a variety of methods (possibly including psychotherapy). Increased serotonin neurotransmission stimulates cell proliferation, and these recently born neurons provide the substrate for new cognitions to be formed.

This theory provides a ready explanation for the perplexing fact that antidepressant treatments typically require weeks to become effective. It is known that it takes several weeks for newly generated cells in the DG to fully mature and become integrated into the existing brain circuitry.

THE HIPPOCAMPUS

If this theory is valid, the hippocampus should show a special relationship to depression. A number of different pieces of evidence link clinical depression to changes in the hippocampus (Jacobs et al., 2000). However, this is not to suggest that change in the hippocampus is the only change in the brain associated with depression, nor do we suggest that alterations in the hippocampus underlie all of the observable aspects of depression.

Further clinical evidence supports an important role for the hippocampus in depression.

- The brains of depressed patients have smaller hippocampi than the brains of control subjects.
- Patients with Cushing's Syndrome (elevated levels of adrenal hormones in plasma) have a high incidence of depression. Additionally, patients administered such hormones for other medical reasons frequently become depressed.
- Temporal lobe epilepsy, which involves massive cell loss in and around the hippocampus, is often accompanied by depression.

DISCUSSION AND FUTURE DIRECTIONS

This work is firmly based on research in the burgeoning field of neurogenesis, which is a facet of stem-cell research, a topic that recently has become highly publicized and politicized. This area holds promise for treating human disease because it suggests that dead or damaged brain cells can be replaced with new, healthy neurons. Probably the most obvious candidate for this type of intervention is Parkinson's disease, in which the primary deficit is the loss of a particular type of brain cell (dopamine neurons) in a specific brain area (substantia nigra).

What would be a true test of the present theory? The first issue would be to determine whether DG neurogenesis wanes when patients go into depressive episodes and waxes as they emerge from these episodes (either spontaneously or following some type of therapy). Investigating this issue would require the development of new brain-imaging techniques, with greater resolution and specificity for particular cell types than is currently possible. Even if a relation between DG neurogenesis and waxing and waning of depression is confirmed in clinical studies, and I believe it will be, these data would be only correlative. In order to determine if there is a causal relationship between alterations of DG neurogenesis and depression, there would be a need to experimentally manipulate cell proliferation. Would the efficacy of antidepressant therapies be blunted by drugs that suppress neurogenesis? There would be obvious ethical concerns associated with such studies.

Perhaps researchers will find new drugs that more directly target augmentation of neurogenesis, and their potency as antidepressants could be evaluated. Also, nonpharmacological therapies that are known to affect neurogenesis, such as exercise, could be more fully evaluated for their antidepressant efficacy. Does the birth and death of brain cells lie at the heart of all types of clinical depression, regardless of etiology? If cell loss is critical, is it always mediated by increased release of adrenal hormones? If not, what other neurochemicals could mediate these deleterious effects and thus also become candidates for novel pharmacotherapies?

How important to depression are changes in neurogenesis in brain regions other than the hippocampus? The hippocampus is thought to be more involved in cognition than in affect or mood. However, a major difficulty that may be at the heart of depression is the patients' inability to form new cognitions about their condition and the future, and their resulting tendency to remain mired in a depressed state. Also, as mentioned earlier, the hippocampus has important connections to brain structures directly involved in mood (affect). Finally, there is no reason to restrict the present theory exclusively to the hippocampus, because neurogenesis may be a more general phenomenon in the brain.

In sum, this theory is representative of a new generation of approaches to understanding psychopathology from a specific neural perspective. Etiological factors lead to identifiable neural changes in particular brain structures, which in turn produce distinct symptomatology. This perspective suggests that therapies targeted at reversing these neural dysfunctions will be effective in treating mental illness.

Recommended Reading

Gross, C.G. (2000). Neurogenesis in the adult brain: Death of a dogma. *Nature Review Neuroscience, 1,* 67–73.
Jacobs, B.L., van Praag, H., & Gage, F.H. (2000). (See References)
Kendler, K.S., Gardner, C.O., & Prescott, C.A. (2002). Toward a comprehensive developmental model for major depression in women. *American Journal of Psychiatry, 15,* 1133–1145.

Acknowledgments—I thank Diane Ruble for helpful comments on an earlier draft of this manuscript. Preparation of this manuscript was supported by Grant MH 23433 from the National Institute of Mental Health.

Notes

1. Address correspondence to Barry L. Jacobs, Program in Neuroscience, Department of Psychology, Princeton University, Green Hall, Princeton, NJ 08544; e-mail: barryj@princeton.edu.

2. The importance of other aspects of psychiatric research in the past 50 years cannot be denied. This is the period in which psychopharmacology came into its own. In what many people consider a revolution, drugs were developed for the effective treatment of depression, bipolar illness, and schizophrenia.

References

Altman, J., & Das, G.D. (1965). Autoradiographic and histological evidence of postnatal hippocampal neurogenesis in rats. *Journal of Comparative Neurology, 124,* 319–335.
Brezun, J.M., & Daszuta, A. (1999). Depletion in serotonin decreases neurogenesis in the dentate gyrus and the subventricular zone of adult rats. *Neuroscience, 89,* 999–1002.
Duman, R.S., Heninger, G.R., & Nestler, E.J. (1997). A molecular and cellular theory of depression. *Archives of General Psychiatry, 54,* 597–606.
Eriksson, P.S., Perfilieva, E., Björk-Eriksson, T., Alborn, A.-M., Norberg, C., Peterson, D.A., & Gage, F.H. (1998). Neurogenesis in the adult human hippocampus. *Nature Medicine, 4,* 1313–1317.
Gould, E., Cameron, H.A., Daniels, D.C., Wooley, C.S., & McEwen, B.S. (1994). Adrenal hormones suppress cell division in the adult rat dentate gyrus. *Journal of Comparative Neurology, 340,* 551–565.
Jacobs, B.L., & Fornal, C.A. (1999). Chronic fluoxetine treatment increases hippocampal neurogenesis in rats: A novel theory of depression. *Society for Neuroscience Abstracts, 25,* 714.
Jacobs, B.L., van Praag, H., & Gage, F.H. (2000). Adult brain neurogenesis and psychiatry: A novel theory of depression. *Molecular Psychiatry, 5,* 262–269.

Kendler, K.S., Karkowski, L.M., & Prescott, C.A. (1999). Causal relationship between stressful life events and the onset of major depression. *American Journal of Psychiatry, 156*, 837–841.

Madsen, T.M., Treschow, A., Bengzon, J., Bolwig, T.G., Lindvall, O., & Tingström, A. (2000). Increased neurogenesis in a model of electroconvulsive therapy. *Biological Psychiatry, 47*, 1043–1049.

Malberg, J.E., Eisch, A.M., Nestler, E.J., & Duman, R.S. (2000). Chronic antidepressant treatment increases neurogenesis in adult rat hippocampus. *Journal of Neuroscience, 20*, 9104–9110.

Manev, H., Uz, T., Smalheiser, N.R., & Manev, R. (2001). Antidepressants alter cell proliferation in the adult brain in vivo and in neural cultures in vitro. *European Journal of Pharmacology, 411*, 67–70.

Manji, H.K., Drevets, W.C., & Charney, D.S. (2001). The cellular neurobiology of depression. *Nature Medicine, 7*, 541–547.

Nottebohm, F. (1985). Neuronal replacement in adulthood. *Annals of the New York Academy of Sciences, 457*, 143–161.

Radley, J.J., & Jacobs, B.L. (2002). 5-HT1A receptor antagonist administration decreases cell proliferation in the dentate gyrus. *Brain Research, 955*, 264–267.

This article has been reprinted as it originally appeared in *Current Directions in Psychological Science*. Citation information for this article as originally published appears above.

Three Reasons Not to Believe in an Autism Epidemic

Morton Ann Gernsbacher and H. Hill Goldsmith[1]
University of Wisconsin-Madison
Michelle Dawson
University of Montreal, Montreal, Quebec, Canada

Abstract

According to some lay groups, the nation is experiencing an autism epidemic—a rapid escalation in the prevalence of autism for unknown reasons. However, no sound scientific evidence indicates that the increasing number of diagnosed cases of autism arises from anything other than purposely broadened diagnostic criteria, coupled with deliberately greater public awareness and intentionally improved case finding. Why is the public perception so disconnected from the scientific evidence? In this article we review three primary sources of misunderstanding: lack of awareness about the changing diagnostic criteria, uncritical acceptance of a conclusion illogically drawn in a California-based study, and inattention to a crucial feature of the "child count" data reported annually by the U.S. Department of Education.

Keywords

autism; epidemiology; epidemic

If you have learned anything about autism lately from the popular media, you most likely have learned—erroneously—that there is "a mysterious upsurge" in the prevalence of autism (*New York Times,* October 20, 2002, Section 4, p. 10), creating a "baffling . . . outbreak" (CBSnews.com, October 18, 2002), in which new cases are "exploding in number" (*Time,* May 6, 2002, p. 48), and "no one knows why" (*USA Today,* May 17, 2004, p. 8D). At least a handful of U.S. Congress members decree on their .gov Web sites that the nation is facing an autism epidemic. Several national media have erroneously concluded that a set of data from California "confirms the autism epidemic," and the largest autism-advocacy organization in the world has expressed alarm over astronomical percentage increases in the number of autistic children served in the public schools since 1992. However, no sound scientific evidence indicates that the increase in the number of diagnosed cases of autism arises from anything other than intentionally broadened diagnostic criteria, coupled with deliberately greater public awareness and conscientiously improved case finding. How did public perception become so misaligned from scientific evidence? In this article, we review three major sources of misunderstanding.

THE CHANGING DIAGNOSIS OF AUTISM

The phenomenon of autism has existed most likely since the origins of human society. In retrospect, numerous historical figures—for instance, the 18th-century "wild boy of Aveyron"—fit autism diagnostic criteria but were not so diagnosed in their day (Frith, 1989). Only in the 1940s did a constellation of differences in social interaction, communication, and focused interests come to be categorized by Leo Kanner as "autism." However, another 40 years would elapse before American psychiatric practice incorporated criteria for autism into what was by then the third edition of its *Diagnostic and Statistical Manual of Mental Disorders* (*DSM-III*; American Psychiatric Association, APA, 1980). Thus, estimates of the prevalence of autism prior to 1980 were based on individual clinicians' (e.g., Kanner & Eisenberg, 1956) or specific researchers' (e.g., Rutter, 1978) conceptions—and fluctuated because of factors that continue to introduce variation into current-day estimates (e.g., variation in the size of the population sampled and the manner of identification).

Autism has remained in the *DSM* (under the title, Pervasive Developmental Disorders), but not without modification through subsequent editions. Whereas the 1980 *DSM-III* entry required satisfying six mandatory criteria, the more recent 1994 *DSM-IV* (APA, 1994) offers 16 optional criteria—only half of which need to be met. Moreover, the severe phrasing of the 1980 mandatory criteria contrasts with the more inclusive phrasing of the 1994 optional criteria. For instance, to qualify for a diagnosis according to the 1980 criteria an individual needed to exhibit "*a pervasive lack of responsiveness* to other people" (emphasis added; APA, 1980, p. 89); in contrast, according to 1994 criteria an individual must demonstrate only "a lack of spontaneous seeking to share . . . achievements with other people" (APA, 1994, p. 70) and peer relationships less sophisticated than would be predicted by the individual's developmental level. The 1980 mandatory criteria of "*gross deficits* in language development" (emphasis added; APA, 1980, p. 89) and "if speech is present, peculiar speech patterns such as immediate and delayed echolalia, metaphorical language, pronominal reversal" (APA, 1980, p. 89) were replaced by the 1994 options of difficulty "sustain[ing] a conversation" (APA, 1994, p. 70) or "lack of varied . . . social imitative play" (p. 70). "*Bizarre responses* to various aspects of the environment" (emphasis added; APA, 1980, p. 90) became "persistent preoccupation with parts of objects" (APA, 1994, p. 71).

Furthermore, whereas the earlier 1980 (*DSM-III*) entry comprised only two diagnostic categories (infantile autism and childhood onset pervasive developmental disorder), the more recent 1994 (*DSM-IV*) entry comprises five. Three of those five categories connote what is commonly called autism: Autistic Disorder, Pervasive Developmental Disorder Not Otherwise Specified (PDDNOS), and Asperger's Disorder. Autistic Disorder requires meeting half of the 16 criteria, but Asperger's Disorder, which did not enter the *DSM* until 1994, involves only two thirds of that half, and PDDNOS, which entered the *DSM* in 1987, is defined by subthreshold symptoms. Therefore, Asperger's Disorder and PDDNOS are often considered "milder variants." These milder variants can account for nearly three fourths of current autism diagnoses (Chakrabarti & Fombonne, 2001). Consider also the recent practice of codiagnosing autism alongside known medical and genetic conditions (e.g., Down syndrome, Tourette's syndrome, and cerebral palsy; Gillberg & Coleman, 2000); the contemporary recognition that autism can exist among people at every level of measured intelligence (Baird et al., 2000), the deliberate efforts to identify autism in younger and younger children (Filipek et al., 2000), and the speculation that many individuals who would meet present-day criteria were previously mis- or undiagnosed (Wing & Potter, 2002), including some of the most accomplished, albeit idiosyncratic, historical figures such as Isaac Newton, Lewis Carroll, W.B. Yeats, Thomas Jefferson, and Bill Gates (Fitzgerald, 2004).

THE CALIFORNIA DATA

In California, persons diagnosed with autism (and other developmental disabilities) qualify for services administered by the statewide Department of Developmental Services (DDS). In 1999, the California DDS reported that from 1987 to 1998 the number of individuals served under the category of "autism" had increased by 273% (California DDS, 1999). Alarmed by this 273% increase, the California legislature commissioned the University of California Medical Investigation of Neurodevelopmental Disorders (M.I.N.D.) Institute to determine whether the increase could be explained by changes in diagnostic criteria. The M.I.N.D. Institute (2002) concluded, on the basis of data we describe next, that there was "no evidence that a loosening in the diagnostic criteria has contributed to the increased number of autism clients served by the [California DDS] Regional Centers" (p. 5). Although this unrefereed conclusion made national headlines and continues to be articulated on innumerable Web sites, it is unwarranted.

The study involved two samples of children who had been served under the California DDS category of "autism": One sample was born between 1983 and 1985 (the earlier cohort); the other sample was born between 1993 and 1995 (the more recent cohort). Both cohorts were assessed with the same autism diagnostic instrument (an interview conducted with care providers). However, the autism diagnostic instrument was based on *DSM-IV* criteria—criteria that were not even published until 1994. When the same percentage of children in the earlier and the more recent cohort met the more recent *DSM-IV* criteria, the researchers imprudently concluded that the "observed increase in autism cases cannot be explained by a loosening in the criteria used to make the diagnosis" (M.I.N.D. Institute, 2002, p. 7).

To understand the fallacy of the conclusion, consider the following analogy, based on male height and graphically illustrated in Figure 1. Suppose the criterion for "tall" was 74.5 in. and taller in the mid-1980s, but the criterion was loosened to 72 in. and taller in the mid-1990s. A diagnostic instrument based on the looser, more recent criterion of 72 in. would identify males who met the 74.5-in. criterion as well as those who met the 72-in. criterion.[2] Although a perfectly reliable diagnostic instrument based on a looser criterion would identify 100% of the individuals who meet the looser criterion along with 100% of the individuals who meet the more restricted criterion, a highly reliable instrument might identify about 90% of each group; this is the percentage of each cohort in the California study who met the more recent autism criteria.

Most crucially, broadening the criterion will result in a dramatic increase in diagnosed cases. For instance, census data allow us to estimate that 2,778 males in McClennan County, Texas would be called tall by the more restricted 74.5-in. criterion, and 10,360 males would be called tall by the broader 72-in. criterion;

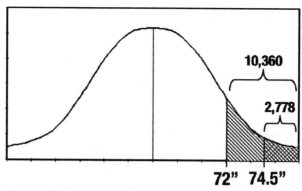

Fig. 1. Distribution of male height in McClennan County, Texas. Shaded areas represent segments of the population defined as "tall" according to two standards: men over 74.5 in. (2,778) versus men over 72 in. (10,360).

if those two criteria had been applied a decade apart, a 273% increase in the number of males called tall would have emerged—without any real increase in Texans' height. In the same way, the 273% increase from 2,778 versus 10,360 California children who received services for "autism" in 1987 versus 1998 could well be a function of broadened criteria.

As we have already detailed, the commonly applied diagnostic criteria for autism broadened nationally from the 1980s to the 1990s; thus, it would be unusual if the criteria used for eligibility in California had not also broadened during this time. Two further aspects of the California data suggest that the criteria must have broadened. First, children in the more recent cohort were dramatically less likely to have intellectual impairment: Whereas 61% of the children in the earlier cohort were identified as having intellectual impairments, only 27% of the children in the more recent cohort were so identified. The lower rate of intellectual impairment in the more recent cohort matches recent epidemiological data, and the difference between the two rates suggests a major difference between the two cohorts (e.g., that the more recent cohort was drawn from a less cognitively impaired population).

Second, on two of the three dimensions measured by the autism diagnostic instrument, the children in the more recent cohort were, on average, less symptomatic than the children from the earlier cohort. The researchers stated that although these differences were statistically significant (i.e., they exceeded the criterion of a statistical test), they were likely not clinically significant (i.e., they were likely not of significance to the clinical presentation); therefore, the researchers suggested that these differences should not be taken as evidence that the diagnostic criteria had broadened. However, refer again to the tallness analogy: Comparing two cohorts of males in McClennan County diagnosed according to our more restricted (74.5-in.) versus our broader (72-in.) criterion would probably result in a statistically significant difference between the two cohorts' average height—but the difference would be just about an inch (i.e., most likely not a clinically significant difference).

THE "CHILD COUNT" DATA

The purpose of the federal Individuals With Disabilities Education Act (IDEA), passed in 1991, is to ensure that all children with disabilities are provided a free, appropriate, public education including an individually designed program. Schools comply with the IDEA by reporting to the federal Department of Education an annual "child count" of the number of children with disabilities served. It is the data from these annual child counts that have been the most egregiously misused in arguments for an autism epidemic.

For example, in October 2003, the Autism Society of America sent its 20,000 members the following electronic message: "Figures from the most recent U. S. Department of Education's 2002 Report to Congress on IDEA reveal that the number of students with autism [ages 6 to 21] in America's schools *jumped an alarming 1,354% in the eight-year period from the school year 1991-92 to 2000-01*" (emphasis added). What the Autism Society failed to note is the following fact (available in the *Report to Congress,* immediately under the autism data entries): Prior to the 1991–1992 school year, there was no child count of students with autism; autism did not even exist as an IDEA reporting category. Moreover, in 1991–1992, use of the autism reporting category was optional (it was required only in subsequent years).

Whenever a new category is introduced, if it is viable, increases in its usage will ensue. Consider another IDEA reporting category introduced along with autism in 1991–1992: "traumatic brain injury." From 1991–1992 to 2000–2001, this category soared an astronomical 5,059%. Likewise, the reporting category "developmental delay," which was introduced only in 1997–1998, grew 663% in only 3 years.

After the initial year, the number of children reported under the IDEA category of autism has increased by approximately 23% annually. Why the continuing annual increase? As is the case with new options in the marketplace, like cellular phones and high-speed Internet, new reporting categories in the annual child count are not capitalized upon instantaneously; they require incrementally magnified awareness and augmentation or reallocation of resources. Currently no state reports the number of children with autism that would be expected based on the results of three recent, large-scale epidemiological studies, which identified 5.8 to 6.7 children per 1,000 for the broader autism spectrum (Baird et al., 2000; Bertrand et al., 2001; Chakrabarti & Fombonne, 2001). In 2002–2003, front-runners Oregon and Minnesota reported 4.3 and 3.5 children with autism per 1,000, respectively, while Colorado, Mississippi, and New Mexico reported only 0.8, 0.7, and 0.7 children with autism per 1,000. Thus, most likely IDEA child counts will continue to increase until the number reported by each state approaches the number of children identified in the epidemiological studies.

Why do states vary so widely in the number of children reported (or served)? Each state's department of education specifies its own diagnostic criteria, and states differ (as do school districts within states, and individual schools within school districts) in the value given to a diagnosis in terms of services received. States also vary from year to year in the number of children served and reported. For instance, Massachusetts historically reported the lowest percentage of children with autism: only 0.4 or 0.5 per 1,000 from 1992 through 2001. Then, in 2002, Massachusetts reported a 400% increase in one year, when it began using student-level data (i.e., actually counting the students) rather than applying a ratio, which was calculated in 1992, based on the proportion of students in each disability classification as reported in 1992. In their 2002 IDEA report to Congress, Massachusetts state officials warned that the increase will continue for several years as "districts better understand how to submit their data at the student level" (IDEA, 2002, p. 4) and "all districts comply completely with the new reporting methods" (IDEA, 2002, p. 4).

OTHER REASONS NOT TO BELIEVE IN AN AUTISM EPIDEMIC

In this article we have detailed three reasons why some lay-persons mistakenly believe that there is an autism epidemic. They are unaware of the purposeful broadening of diagnostic criteria, coupled with deliberately greater public awareness; they accept the unwarranted conclusions of the M.I.N.D. Institute study; and they fail to realize that autism was not even an IDEA reporting category until the early 1990s and incremental increases will most likely continue until the schools are identifying and serving the number of children identified in epidemiological studies. Apart from a desire to be aligned with scientific reasoning, there are other reasons not to believe in an autism epidemic.

Epidemics solicit causes; false epidemics solicit false causes. Google *autism* and *epidemic* to witness the range of suspected causes of the mythical autism epidemic. Epidemics also connote danger. What message do we send autistic children and adults when we call their increasing number an epidemic? A pandemic? A scourge? Realizing that the increasing prevalence rates are most likely due to non-catastrophic mechanisms, such as purposely broader diagnostic criteria and greater public awareness, should not, however, diminish societal responsibility to support the increasing numbers of individuals being diagnosed with autism. Neither should enthusiasm for scientific inquiry into the variety and extent of human behavioral, neuroanatomical, and genotypic diversity in our population be dampened.

Recommended Reading

Fombonne, E. (2003). Epidemiological surveys of autism and other pervasive developmental disorders: An update. *Journal of Autism and Developmental Disorders, 33*, 365–382.

Institute of Medicine. (2004). *Immunization safety review: Vaccines and autism*. Washington, DC: National Academies Press.

Wing, L., & Potter, D. (2002). (See References)

Notes

1. Address correspondence to Morton Ann Gernsbacher, Department of Psychology, University of Wisconsin-Madison, 1202 W. Johnson St., Madison, WI 53706; e-mail: MAGernsb@wisc.edu.

2. Wing and Potter (2002) provide a similar illustration. The same percentage of children who met Kanner's earlier, more restricted criteria met *DSM-IV*'s more recent,

broadened criteria; if the child was autistic according to Kanner's restricted criteria, the child was autistic according to *DSM-IV*'s broadened criteria. Of course, the reverse was not true. Only 33 to 45% of the children who met more recent *DSM-IV* criteria met earlier Kanner criteria.

References

American Psychiatric Association. (1980). *Diagnostic and statistical manual of mental disorders* (3rd ed.). Washington, DC: Author.

American Psychiatric Association. (1994). *Diagnostic and statistical manual of mental disorders* (4th ed.). Washington, DC: Author.

Baird, G., Charman, T., Baron-Cohen, S., Cox, A., Swettenham, J., Wheelwright, S., & Drew, A. (2000). A screening instrument for autism at 18 months of age: A 6 year follow-up study. *Journal of the American Academy of Child and Adolescent Psychiatry, 39,* 694–702.

Bertrand, J., Mars, A., Boyle, C., Bove, F., Yeargin-Allsopp, M., & Decoufle, P. (2001). Prevalence of autism in a United States population: The Brick Township, New Jersey, investigation. *Pediatrics, 108,* 1155–1161.

California Department of Developmental Services. (1999). *Changes in the population with autism and pervasive developmental disorders in California's developmental services system: 1987–1998. A report to the legislature.* Sacramento, CA: California Health and Human Services Agency.

Chakrabarti, S., & Fombonne, E. (2001). Pervasive developmental disorders in preschool children. *Journal of the American Medical Association, 285,* 3093–3099.

Filipek, P.A., Accardo, P.J., Ashwal, S., Baranek, G.T., Cook, E.H. Jr., Dawson, G., Gordon, B., Gravel, J.S., Johnson, C.P., Kallen, R.J., Levy, S.E., Minshew, N.J., Ozonoff, S., Prizant, B.M., Rapin, I., Rogers, S.J., Stone, W.L., Teplin, S.W., Tuchman, R.F., & Volkmar, F.R. (2000). Practice parameter: Screening and diagnosis of autism: Report of the Quality Standards Subcommittee of the American Academy of Neurology and the Child Neurology Society. *Neurology, 55,* 468–479.

Fitzgerald, M. (2004). *Autism and creativity: Is there a link between autism in men and exceptional ability?* London: Brunner-Routledge.

Frith, U. (1989). *Autism: Explaining the enigma.* Oxford, England: Blackwell.

Gillberg, C., & Coleman, M. (2000). *The biology of the autistic syndromes* (3rd ed.). London: MacKeith Press.

IDEA. (2002). *Data Notes for IDEA, Part B.* Retrieved April 22, 2005, from IDEAdata Web side: http://www.ideadata.org/docs/bdatanotes2002.doc

Kanner, L., & Eisenberg, J. (1956). Early infantile autism 1943–1955. *American Journal of Orthopsychiatry, 26,* 55–65.

M.I.N.D. Institute. (2002). *Report to the Legislature on the principal findings from The Epidemiology of Autism in California: A Comprehensive Pilot Study.* Davis: University of California-Davis.

Rutter, M. (1978). Diagnosis and definition. In M. Rutter & E. Schopler (Eds.), *Autism: A reappraisal of concepts and treatments* (pp. 1–25). New York: Plenum Press.

U.S. Department of Education. (2002). *Twenty-fourth annual report to Congress on the implementation of the Individuals With Disabilities Education Act.* Washington, DC: Author.

Wing, L., & Potter, D. (2002). The epidemiology of autistic spectrum disorders: Is the prevalence rising? *Mental Retardation and Developmental Disabilities Research Reviews, 8,* 151–162.

This article has been reprinted as it originally appeared in *Current Directions in Psychological Science.* Citation information for this article as originally published appears above.

Resilience in the Face of Potential Trauma

George A. Bonanno[1]

Teachers College, Columbia University

Abstract

Until recently, resilience among adults exposed to potentially traumatic events was thought to occur rarely and in either pathological or exceptionally healthy individuals. Recent research indicates, however, that the most common reaction among adults exposed to such events is a relatively stable pattern of healthy functioning coupled with the enduring capacity for positive emotion and generative experiences. A surprising finding is that there is no single resilient type. Rather, there appear to be multiple and sometimes unexpected ways to be resilient, and sometimes resilience is achieved by means that are not fully adaptive under normal circumstances. For example, people who characteristically use self-enhancing biases often incur social liabilities but show resilient outcomes when confronted with extreme adversity. Directions for further research are considered.

Keywords

loss; grief; trauma; resilience; coping

Life is filled with peril. During the normal course of their lives, most adults face one or more potentially traumatic events (e.g., violent or life-threatening occurrences or the death of close friends or relatives). Following such events, many people find it difficult to concentrate; they may feel anxious, confused, and depressed; and they may not eat or sleep properly. Some people have such strong and enduring reactions that they are unable to function normally for years afterward. It should come as no surprise that these dramatic reactions have dominated the literatures on loss and trauma. Until recently, the opposite reaction—the maintenance of a relative stable trajectory of healthy functioning following exposure to a potential trauma—has received scant attention. When theorists have considered such a pattern, they have typically viewed it either as an aberration resulting from extreme denial or as a sign of exceptional emotional strength (e.g., McFarlane & Yehuda, 1996).

RESILIENCE (NOT RECOVERY) IS THE MOST COMMON RESPONSE TO POTENTIAL TRAUMA

Over a decade ago, my colleagues and I began an ongoing investigation of this supposedly rare response, and the means by which people might achieve such presumably superficial (or exemplary) functioning in the aftermath of a potentially traumatic event. The results of our research have consistently challenged the prevailing view on the subject. We took as our starting point the burgeoning developmental literature on resilience. Developmental researchers and theorists had for several decades highlighted various protective factors (e.g., ego-resiliency, the presence of supportive relationships) that promote healthy trajectories among

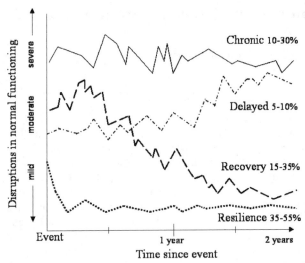

Fig. 1. Prototypical trajectories of disruption in normal functioning during the 2-year period following a loss or potential trauma.

children exposed to unfavorable life circumstances such as poverty (e.g., Garmezy, 1991; Rutter, 1987). We sought to adapt this body of research to the study of resilient outcomes among adults in otherwise normal circumstances who are exposed to isolated and potentially highly disruptive events.

Our research led to three primary conclusions, each mirroring but also extending the insights gained from developmental research. First, resilience following potentially traumatic events represents a distinct outcome trajectory from that typically associated with recovery from trauma. Historically, there have been few attempts to distinguish subgroups within the broad category of individuals exposed to potential trauma who do not develop post-traumatic stress disorder (PTSD). When resilience had been considered, it was often in terms of factors that "favor a path to recovery" (McFarlane & Yehuda, 1996, p. 158). However, studies have now demonstrated that resilience and recovery are discrete and empirically separable outcome trajectories following a dramatic event such as the death of a spouse (e.g., Bonanno, Wortman et al., 2002) or direct exposure to terrorist attack (e.g., Bonanno, Rennicke, & Dekel, in press). Figure 1 depicts the prototypical resilience and recovery trajectories, as well as trajectories representing chronic and delayed symptom elevations (discussed later).

In this framework, recovery is defined by moderate to severe initial elevations in psychological symptoms that significantly disrupt normal functioning and that decline only gradually over the course of many months before returning to pre-trauma levels. In contrast, resilience is characterized by relatively mild and short-lived disruptions and a stable trajectory of healthy functioning across time. A key point is that even though resilient individuals may experience an initial, brief spike in distress (Bonanno, Moskowitz, Papa, & Folkman, 2005) or may struggle for a short period to maintain psychological equilibrium (e.g., several weeks of sporadic difficulty concentrating, intermittent sleeplessness, or daily variability in levels of well-being; Bisconti et al., in press), they nonetheless manage to keep functioning effectively at or near their normal levels. For example, resilience has been linked to the continued fulfillment of personal and social responsibilities and the capacity for positive emotions and generative experiences (e.g., engaging in new creative activities or new relationships), both immediately and in the months following exposure to a potentially traumatic event (Bonanno & Keltner, 1997; Bonanno, Wortman et al., 2002; Bonanno, Rennicke, & Dekel, in press; Fredrickson et al., 2003).

A second conclusion that emerges from our research is that resilience is typically the most common outcome following exposure to a potentially traumatic event. It has been widely assumed in the literature that the most common response to such an occurrence is an initial but sizeable elevation in trauma symptoms followed by gradual resolution and recovery (McFarlane & Yehuda, 1996). However, although symptom levels tend to vary for different potentially traumatic events, resilience has consistently emerged as the most common outcome trajectory. In one study, for example, over half of the people in a sample of middle-aged individuals who had lost their spouses showed a stable, low level of symptoms; and stable low symptoms were observed in more than a third of a group of gay men who were bereaved after providing care for a partner dying of AIDS, a considerably more stressful context (Bonanno, Moskowitz et al., 2005). Resilience was also readily observed in a random phone-dialing survey of Manhattan residents following the September 11 terrorist attack (Bonanno, Galea, Bucciarelli, & Vlahov, 2005). Following conventions established in the study of subthreshold depression, we defined a mild to moderate trauma reaction as two or more PTSD symptoms and resilience as one or no PTSD symptoms in the first 6 months following the attack. Over 65% in the New York metropolitan area were resilient. Among people with more concentrated exposure (e.g., those who had either witnessed the attack in person or who were in the World Trade Center during the attack), the proportion showing resilience was still over 50%. Finally, even among people who were physically injured in the attack, a group for whom the estimated proportion of PTSD was extremely high (26.1%), one third (32.8%) of the individuals were resilient.

In establishing the validity of the resilient trajectory it is imperative to distinguish stable, healthy functioning from denial or other forms of superficial adjustment. To this end, several studies have now documented links between resilience and generally high functioning prior to a potentially traumatic event (Bonanno, Wortman, et al., 2002; Bonanno, Moskowitz et al., 2005). Several studies have also documented resilient outcomes using relatively objective measures that go beyond participant self-report, including structured clinical interviews and anonymous ratings of functioning from participants' friends or relatives (e.g., Bonanno, Rennicke, & Dekel, in press; Bonanno, Moskowitz et al., 2005). For example, we (Bonanno, Rennicke, & Dekel, in press) recruited the friends and relatives of high-exposure survivors of the World Trade Center terrorist attack and asked them to assign the survivors to either the resilience trajectory or one of the other outcome trajectories depicted in Figure 1. The assignments of friends and relatives closely matched the survivors' actual symptom levels over time, and thus provided important validation for the resilience trajectory.

THE HETEROGENEITY OF RESILIENCE: FLEXIBLE AND PRAGMATIC COPING

A third conclusion to emerge from our research, again extending the conclusions of developmental researchers, is that there are multiple and sometimes unexpected factors that might promote a resilient outcome. At the most general level, many of the same characteristics that promote healthy development should also foster adult resilience. These would include both situational factors, such as supportive relationships, and individual factors, such as the capacity to adapt flexibly to challenges (Block & Block, 1980). The capacity for adaptive flexibility was mirrored in a recent study associating resilience among New York City college students in the aftermath of September 11 with flexibility in emotion regulation, defined as the ability to effectively enhance or suppress emotional expression when instructed to do so (Bonanno, Papa, LaLande, Westphal, & Coifman, 2004).

In addition to these general health-promoting factors, however, our research also underscores a crucial point of departure from the developmental literature. Childhood resilience is typically understood in response to corrosive environments, such as poverty or enduring abuse. By contrast, adult resilience is more often a matter of coping with an isolated and usually (but not always) brief potentially traumatic event. The key point is that whereas corrosive environments require longer-term adaptive solutions, isolated events often oblige a more pragmatic form of coping, a "whatever it takes" approach, which may involve behaviors and strategies that are less effective or even maladaptive in other contexts. For instance, considerable research attests to the health benefits of expressing negative emotions. Although most resilient bereaved individuals express at least some negative emotion while talking about their loss, they nonetheless express relatively less negative emotion and greater positive emotion than other bereaved individuals (e.g., Bonanno & Keltner, 1997), thereby minimizing the impact of the loss while "increasing continued contact with and support from important people in the social environment" (p. 134).

Another example of pragmatic coping is illustrated by trait self-enhancement, the tendency toward self-serving biases in perception and attribution (e.g., overestimating one's own positive qualities). People given to self-serving biases tend to be narcissistic and to evoke negative reactions in other people. However, they also have high self-esteem and cope well with isolated potential traumas. Our research team examined self-enhancement among people dealing with two powerful stressor events, the premature death of a spouse and exposure to urban combat during the recent civil war in Bosnia (Bonanno, Field, Kovacevic, & Kaltman, 2002). In both samples, trait self-enhancement was positively associated with ratings of functioning made by mental health experts. In the bereavement study, however, untrained observers rated self-enhancers relatively unfavorably (lower on positive traits, e.g., honest; and higher on negative traits, e.g., self-centered). Yet, these negative impressions did not appear to interfere with self-enhancers' ability to maintain a high level of functioning after the loss.

This same pattern of findings was observed among high-exposure survivors of the September 11 attack (Bonanno et al., in press). Trait self-enhancement was more prevalent among individuals exhibiting the resilient trajectory, whether established by self-reported symptoms or ratings from friends or relatives. Self-enhancers also had greater positive affect and were rated by their friends and relatives as having consistently higher levels of mental and physical health, goal accomplishment, and coping ability. However, self-enhancers' friends and relatives also rated them as decreasing in social adjustment over the 18 months after September 11 and, among those with the highest levels of exposure, as less honest. This mixed pattern of findings suggests again that self-enhancers are able to maintain generally high levels of functioning in most areas except their social relations. Interestingly, however, self-enhancers themselves perceived their social relationships in relatively more positive terms than other participants, and this factor fully mediated their low levels of PTSD symptoms. In other words, self-enhancers appear to be blissfully unaware of the critical reactions they can evoke in others, and this type of self-serving bias evidently plays a crucial role in their ability to maintain stable levels of healthy functioning in other areas following a potentially traumatic event.

DIRECTIONS FOR FUTURE RESEARCH

The study of adult resilience is nascent and there are myriad questions for future research. An obvious imperative is to learn how the various costs and benefits of resilience vary across different types and durations of potentially traumatic events. Is there a point, for example, when the long-term costs of a particular type of coping might outweigh whatever crucial short-term advantages it provides? Might such trade-offs vary by gender or culture? Western, independence-oriented societies, for example, tend to focus more heavily than collectivist societies on the personal experience of trauma. However, little is known about the extent that loss and trauma reactions vary across cultures. A recent comparative study showed that bereaved people in China recovered more quickly from loss than did bereaved Americans (Bonanno, Papa et al., 2005). However, as is typical of Chinese culture, Chinese bereaved also reported more physical symptoms than Americans. These data raise the intriguing questions of whether resilience has different meanings in different cultural contexts and, perhaps even more important, whether different cultures may learn from each other about effective and not-so-effective ways of coping with extreme adversity.

These questions in turn raise multiple practical and philosophical uncertainties about whether resilience can or should be learned. On the one hand, the observed link between resilient outcomes and personality variables suggests that resilient traits may be relatively fixed and not easily inculcated in others. And, given the social costs associated with some of the traits found in resilient people (e.g., self-enhancement), the advantage of simply imitating resilient individuals is questionable. On the other hand, a more promising avenue for training people to cope resiliently with trauma is suggested by the evidence linking resilience to flexible adaptation (Block & Block, 1980; Bonanno et al., 2004). Because adaptive flexibility can be manipulated experimentally (e.g., people's ability to engage in various cognitive or emotional processes can be measured under different stress or conditions; Bonanno et al., 2004), it should be possible to systematically examine the stability of such a trait over time and the conditions under which it might be learned or enhanced.

A related question pertains to how resilient individuals might view their own effectiveness at coping with potential trauma. Although at least some resilient individuals are surprised at how well they cope (Bonanno, Wortman et al., 2002), it seems likely that others (e.g., self-enhancers) might overestimate their own resilience. This issue is particularly intriguing in relation to the distinction between stable resilience and delayed reactions. Although delayed reactions are not typically observed during bereavement (e.g., Bonanno, Wortman et al., 2002), a small subset of individuals exposed to potentially traumatic events (5–10%) typically exhibit delayed PTSD. Preliminary evidence indicates that delayed-PTSD responders have higher initial symptom levels than do resilient individuals (e.g., Bonanno et al., in press). Further evidence of this distinction would hold potentially important diagnostic implications for early intervention.

Finally, another question pertains to how resilient individuals experience the crucial early weeks after an extreme stressor event. A recent study by Bisconti, Bergeman, and Boker (in press) shed some welcome light on this issue by examining daily well-being ratings in the early months after the death of a spouse. Although resilient bereaved typically show only mild and relatively short-lived overall decreases in well-being, examination of their daily ratings indicated marked variability across the first 3 weeks and then a more stable but still variable period that endured through the second month of bereavement. Perhaps similar research using larger samples and Internet methods might illuminate how resilient individuals manage to continue functioning and meeting the ongoing demands of their lives while nonetheless struggling, at least for a short period, to maintain self-regulatory equilibrium.

Recommended Readings

Bonanno, G.A. (2004). Loss, trauma, and human resilience: Have we underestimated the human capacity to thrive after extremely aversive events. *American Psychologist, 59,* 20–28.

Bonanno, G.A., & Kaltman, S. (2001). The varieties of grief experience. *Clinical Psychology Review, 21,* 705–734.

Gilbert, D.T., Pinel, E.C., Wilson, T.D., Blumberg, S.J., & Wheatley, T. (1998). Immune neglect: A source of durability bias in affective forecasting. *Journal of Personality and Social Psychology, 75,* 617–638.

Luthar, S.S. (in press). Resilient adaptation. In D. Cicchetti & D.J. Cohen (Eds.), *Developmental psychopathology: Risk, disorder, and adaptation.* New York: Wiley.

Acknowledgments—This research was supported by grants from the National Institutes of Health (R29-MH57274) and the National Science Foundation (BCS-0202772 and BCS-0337643).

Note

1. Address correspondence to George A. Bonanno, Clinical Psychology Program, 525 West 120th St., Box 218, Teachers College, Columbia University, New York, NY 10027; e-mail: gab38@columbia.edu.

References

Bisconti, T.L., Bergeman, C.S., & Boker, S.M. (in press). Social support as a predictor of variability: An examination of recent widows' adjustment trajectories. *Psychology and Aging.*

Block, J.H., & Block, J. (1980). The role of ego-control and ego-resiliency in the organization of behavior. In W.A. Collins (Ed.), *The Minnesota Symposia on Child Psychology* (Vol. 13, pp. 39–101). Hillsdale, NJ: Erlbaum.

Bonanno, G.A., Field, N.P., Kovacevic, A., & Kaltman, S. (2002). Self-enhancement as a buffer against extreme adversity: Civil war in Bosnia and traumatic loss in the United States. *Personality and Social Psychology Bulletin, 28*, 184–196.

Bonanno, G.A., Galea, S., Bucciarelli, A., & Vlahov, D. (2005). Psychological resilience after disaster: New York City in the aftermath of the September 11th terrorist attack. Manuscript submitted for publication.

Bonanno, G.A., & Keltner, D. (1997). Facial expressions of emotion and the course of conjugal bereavement. *Journal of Abnormal Psychology, 106*, 126–137.

Bonanno, G.A., Moskowitz, J.T., Papa, A., & Folkman, S. (2005). Resilience to loss in bereaved spouses, bereaved parents, and bereaved gay men. *Journal of Personality and Social Psychology, 88*, 827–843.

Bonanno, G.A., Papa, A., Lalande, K., Nanping, Z., & Noll, J.G. (2005). Grief processing and deliberate grief avoidance: A prospective comparison of bereaved spouses and parents in the United States and China. *Journal of Consulting and Clinical Psychology, 73*, 86–98.

Bonanno, G.A., Papa, A., LaLande, K., Westphal, M., & Coifman, K. (2004). The importance of being flexible: The ability to both enhance and suppress emotional expression predicts long-term adjustment. *Psychological Science, 15*, 482–487.

Bonanno, G.A., Rennicke, C., & Dekel, S. (in press). Self-enhancement among high-exposure survivors of the September 11th terrorist attack: Resilience or social maladjustment? *Journal of Personality and Social Psychology.*

Bonanno, G.A., Wortman, C.B., Lehman, D.R., Tweed, R.G., Haring, M., Sonnega, J., Carr, D., & Neese, R.M. (2002). Resilience to loss and chronic grief: A prospective study from pre-loss to 18 months post-loss. *Journal of Personality and Social Psychology, 83*, 1150–1164.

Fredrickson, B.L., Tugade, M.M., Waugh, C.E., & Larkin, G.R. (2003). What good are positive emotions in crisis? A prospective study of resilience and emotion following the terrorist attacks on the United States on September 11th, 2001. *Journal of Personality and Social Psychology, 84*, 365–376.

Garmezy, N. (1991). Resilience and vulnerability to adverse developmental outcomes associated with poverty. *American Behavioral Scientist, 34*, 416–430.

McFarlane, A.C., & Yehuda, R. (1996). Resilience, vulnerability, and the course of posttraumatic reactions. In B.A. van der Kolk, A.C. McFarlane, & L. Weisaeth (Eds.), *Traumatic stress* (pp. 155–181). New York: Guilford.

Rutter, M. (1987). Psychosocial resilience and protective mechanisms. *American Journal of Orthopsychiatry, 57*, 316–331.

This article has been reprinted as it originally appeared in *Current Directions in Psychological Science*. Citation information for this article as originally published appears above.

Does Drinking Promote Risky Sexual Behavior?: A Complex Answer to a Simple Question

M. Lynne Cooper[1]

University of Missouri–Columbia

Abstract

The present review argues that, popular lore notwithstanding, the well-documented association between usual patterns of alcohol use and risky sex reflects multiple underlying processes that are both causal and noncausal (spurious) in nature. It is further argued that even alcohol's acute causal effects on sexual behavior are more variable than they are commonly assumed to be. Drinking can promote, inhibit, or have no effect on behavior, depending on the interplay of factors governing behavior in a particular situation and the content of individually held beliefs about alcohol's effects.

Keywords

alcohol; risky sex; condom use

With the advent of AIDS, efforts to understand the causes of sexual risk-taking have assumed great urgency. In this context, alcohol and its potential disinhibiting effects have received much attention. In the past 20 years, more than 600 studies have been conducted on the link between drinking and risky sex, and drinking proximal to intercourse has become a standard target of intervention efforts aimed at reducing risky sexual behaviors. Targeting drinking as part of a strategy to reduce risky sex can only be effective if drinking causally promotes such behaviors, however. Does the evidence support this connection? Conventional wisdom aside, the answer to this question is surprisingly complex.

BACKGROUND

The belief that alcohol causally disinhibits sexual behavior is firmly ingrained in our culture. Most people believe that drinking increases the likelihood of sexual activity, enhances sexual experience, and promotes riskier sexual behavior. Many also attribute risky sexual experiences to the fact that they were drinking and report drinking (or plying their partner with alcohol) to exploit alcohol's alleged disinhibiting effects on sexual behavior.

Consistent with popular belief, the overwhelming majority of studies do find an association between the two behaviors (Cooper, 2002; Leigh & Stall, 1993). The typical study examines the cross-sectional association between usual patterns of drinking and risky sex. For example, in such studies, individuals who drink consistently report more partners than those who abstain do. Owing to design limitations, however, these studies tell us little about the underlying causal relationship. Such data cannot even establish a temporal link between drinking and risky sex, a minimum condition for attributing causality to acute alcohol effects.

Thus, although people are quick to infer a causal connection between the two behaviors, multiple interpretations are possible. Three will be considered here.

THIRD-VARIABLE EXPLANATIONS

Third variable explanations that involve stable (possibly genetically based) features of the individual or of his or her life situation offer one important explanation. For example, a person might both drink and have risky sex to satisfy sensation-seeking needs, because of poor impulse control or coping skills, or in an effort to cope with negative emotions. Consistent with this possibility, Cooper, Wood, Orcutt, and Albino (2003) showed that one third of the statistical overlap (modeled by a higher-order factor) among diverse risk behaviors, including alcohol use and risky sex, could be explained by low impulse control and an avoidant style of coping with negative emotions. Thrill seeking accounted for a much smaller proportion of the overlap, and significantly predicted the overlap only among white (not black) adolescents. In addition, avoidance coping predicted the onset of drinking among initially abstinent youth, and in interaction with impulsivity it predicted the onset of sexual behavior among those who were initially virgins. Thus, avoidance coping and impulsivity appear to be important common causes that partially account for the link between drinking and risky sex. Although thrill seeking was not a strong predictor in our randomly constituted, biracial adolescent sample, closely related measures (e.g., sensation seeking) have been shown to fully account for the association between drinking and risky sex in some high-risk samples (e.g., heavy drinkers, gay or bisexual men).

An individual might also drink and have risky sex as part of a lifestyle, such as being single or living in a fraternity house, where both behaviors are tacitly or explicitly encouraged. Consistent with this possibility, perceptions of peer norms related to drinking and sex are among the most robust predictors of involvement in both behaviors among youth. Similarly, characteristics of one's home environment—e.g., living in a single-parent or conflict-ridden household—have also been found to predict both behaviors. Thus, direct evidence showing that co-variation between the two behaviors can be explained by third variables, and indirect evidence showing that involvement in both behaviors is linked to the same putative causal factors, support the contention that the association between drinking and risky sex is at least partly due to the influence of underlying common causes.

REVERSE CAUSAL EXPLANATIONS

Reverse causal explanations posit that the intention or desire to engage in risky sex causes one to drink when sexual opportunity is perceived. Consistent with this possibility, surveys of college students reveal that up to one half of undergraduates report drinking more than usual to make it easier to have sex and giving their partners alcohol to increase the likelihood of sex (Cooper, 2002). Alternatively, an individual might plan a romantic evening and drink to enhance that experience or plan to pick someone up at a party and drink to provide an excuse (to oneself or others) for behavior that might later be seen as inappropriate. Although different motives (to disinhibit, enhance, or excuse) presumably underlie drinking in each scenario, all accounts nevertheless assume that people who drink strategically hold relevant beliefs about alcohol's capacity to facilitate the desired sexual outcome. Supporting this notion, Dermen and I (Dermen & Cooper, 1994) found that people who believe that alcohol enhances or disinhibits sex are more likely to drink, and to drink to intoxication, in sexual or potentially sexual situations (e.g., on a date). Thus, for at least some people, the intention or desire to have sex may precede and cause drinking, rather than the reverse.

CAUSAL EXPLANATIONS

Two prominent theories depict alcohol as a cause of disinhibited social behaviors: alcohol myopia and expectancy theories. Alcohol-myopia theory (Steele & Josephs, 1990) posits that disinhibited behavior results from an interaction of diminished cognitive capabilities and the specific cues that influence behavior in a given situation. Because alcohol narrows the range of cues perceived and limits the ability to process and extract meaning from these cues, intoxication renders a person susceptible to momentary pressures. Simple, highly salient cues (e.g., sexual arousal) continue to be processed, whereas more distal, complex ones (e.g., fear of pregnancy) are no longer adequately processed. Consequently, alcohol creates a "myopia" in which incompletely processed aspects of immediate experience exert undue influence on behavior and emotion. Accordingly, alcohol has its strongest effect when a behavior is controlled by instigating and inhibiting cues that are strong and nearly equal in force—a circumstance known as inhibition conflict.

In support of this model, Steele and Josephs conducted a meta-analysis (a method for statistically combining effects) of 34 experimental studies testing alcohol's effects on social behavior. Results revealed a small (.14) average standardized effect for alcohol under low-inhibition-conflict conditions versus a large effect (1.06) under high-conflict conditions. Thus, consistent with alcohol-myopia theory, intoxicated participants behaved more extremely than sober ones did primarily under high-conflict conditions.

Whereas alcohol-myopia theory emphasizes pharmacological mechanisms, expectancy theory emphasizes psychological ones. According to this view, an individual's behavior after drinking is driven by pre-existing beliefs (expectancies) about alcohol's effects on behavior, much like a self-fulfilling prophecy (Hull & Bond, 1986). The role of expectancies has been investigated experimentally in studies that independently manipulate alcohol content and expectancy set (the belief that alcohol has been consumed). In a meta-analysis of 36 such studies, Hull and Bond found that people who believed they had consumed alcohol (but had not) behaved similarly to those who had consumed alcohol (and didn't know it). Indeed, expectancy effects were significant and only slightly smaller than alcohol-content effects (.27 vs. .35). Expectancy theory thus highlights the role of individually held beliefs about alcohol's effects, and suggests by extension that alcohol effects on behavior may vary as a function of these beliefs.

The foregoing indicates that alcohol intoxication can cause more extreme social behavior through both pharmacological and psychological mechanisms.

Contrary to popular opinion, these effects are not immutable, but are contingent on the nature of instigating and inhibiting cues governing momentary behavior, on the content of one's beliefs about alcohol effects, or possibly on a combination of both. Theoretically, then, alcohol intoxication should lead to riskier sexual behavior only under certain conditions or among certain people, a contention that existing evidence largely supports.

A SELECTIVE REVIEW OF NATURALISTIC STUDIES OF DRINKING AND RISKY SEX

From a public health perspective, one of the most important issues concerns alcohol's potential to facilitate the occurrence of intercourse, especially with new or casual partners. To investigate this issue, Orcutt and I (Cooper & Orcutt, 1997) examined the link between drinking and intercourse on two first-date occasions in a large, representative sample of adolescents. Although these data are correlational, the within-subjects design allowed us to compare a person's behavior on two occasions that, for many, differed in the presence versus absence of alcohol, thus helping us rule out stable individual differences between drinkers and nondrinkers as an alternative explanation for observed differences in sexual behavior. As Figure 1 illustrates, our results showed that rates of intercourse were higher when the male partner drank and lower when he abstained. Interestingly, however, parallel analyses revealed no such relationship for drinking by the female partner.

Drawing on alcohol-myopia theory, we reasoned that the psychological conditions necessary for alcohol-related disinhibition existed only among men. Specifically, if males experienced a type of conflict in which dominant cues favored behavioral action while peripheral cues favored behavioral inhibition, we would expect (due to the greater difficulty of accessing and processing peripheral

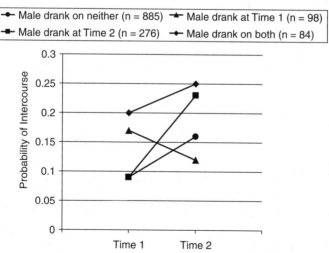

Fig. 1. Male couple-member alcohol use and probability of intercourse on two first-date occasions. From Cooper & Orcutt (1997).

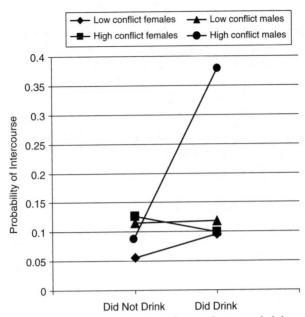

Fig. 2. Alcohol use, gender, and perceived conflict predicting probability of intercourse on the most recent first date. From Cooper & Orcutt (1997).

cues) alcohol-related disinhibition. In contrast, if females experienced a type of conflict in which dominant cues favored inhibition and peripheral ones activation, then decreased processing of peripheral cues should not disinhibit behavior. Consistent with this logic, we found that men perceived more benefits relative to costs of having sex on their most recent first date, whereas women perceived more costs relative to benefits. Moreover, only the perception of increasing costs predicted conflict among men (for whom benefits were more salient), whereas the reverse was true among women. Thus, men and women appeared to experience qualitatively different forms of conflict about having sex on their most recent first date. Moreover, consistent with the idea that the type of conflict conducive to alcohol-related disinhibition occurred only among men, rates of intercourse on the date were significantly elevated only among highly conflicted men who drank alcohol (Fig. 2).

Together these data indicate that how alcohol affects sexual behavior is determined by the content and relative strength of competing cues that inhibit or activate behavior, and they raise the possibility that alcohol might even promote safer behavior under the right circumstances! Recent experimental evidence lends strong support to this idea, showing that when the potential costs of having sex with an attractive new partner were made salient, intoxicated individuals reported more cautious intentions than did sober ones (MacDonald, Fong, Zanna, & Martineau, 2000).

A second key question from a public health perspective is whether drinking reduces condom use. Somewhat surprisingly, most naturalistic studies directly testing the link between drinking on a specific intercourse occasion and condom use on that occasion find no relationship. Indeed in a quantitative analysis of 29 such tests (Cooper, 2002), alcohol was associated with lower rates of condom (and birth-control) use only under circumscribed conditions: at first intercourse but not on subsequent intercourse occasions, in younger but not older samples, and in studies conducted earlier rather than more recently (Leigh, 2002, reports similar results).

One plausible interpretation of these findings is that few people experience the type of conflict conducive to alcohol-related disinhibition of condom use, though such conflict may have been common in the past and may still be common among sexually inexperienced, younger adolescents. Although no study has directly tested these ideas, a study conducted by Dermen and me (Dermen & Cooper, 2000) provides indirect support. We examined feelings of conflict about using a condom on four occasions of intercourse across two different samples (one of college students; one of community-residing young adults, aged 19–25), and found that fewer than 15% of participants were highly conflicted about using a condom on each occasion. Moreover, although drinking did not predict lower overall rates of condom use on any of these occasions, it predicted significantly lower rates (in three of four tests) among those who felt conflicted about using a condom on that occasion.

In short, these data suggest that drinking can undermine safe sex behaviors, but that it does not invariably do so. Rather, alcohol can promote, inhibit, or have no effect on risky sexual behaviors depending on the specific constellation of salient cues in the moment.

THE ROLE OF ALCOHOL EXPECTANCIES

Although the preponderance of evidence suggests that inhibition conflict plays the larger role in accounting for alcohol's acute causal effects on risky sexual behavior, expectancies also appear important. As previously discussed, those who believe that alcohol disinhibits or enhances sexual experience are more likely to drink in (potentially) sexual situations, suggesting that expectancies are instrumental in setting up situations that may lead to alcohol-related disinhibition of sex. Expectancies (in the absence of alcohol) have also been shown to influence other aspects of sexual experience that could indirectly promote risky behaviors. For example, a recently conducted experiment in which participants were paired with previously unknown, opposite-sex partners found that participants who thought they had consumed alcohol (though none had been consumed) reported greater sexual arousal, perceived their partners as more sexually disinhibited, and showed erotic slides (presumed to be a behavioral analog of sexual interest) to their partners significantly longer, but only if they also held strong beliefs about alcohol's capacity to disinhibit or enhance sexual experience (George, Stoner, Norris, Lopez, & Lehman, 2000). These data suggest that expectancies, once activated by alcohol consumption, may strengthen instigating cues for sex, thereby bringing an individual for whom costs might otherwise greatly outweigh benefits into a state of high inhibition conflict. Finally, expectancies have also been shown to interact with feelings of conflict to jointly predict alcohol-related disinhibition of risky sexual behavior (Dermen & Cooper, 2000). Thus, expectancies and actual alcohol content might work in tandem to disinhibit risky sexual behavior in real-world situations where the two processes always co-occur.

CONCLUSIONS AND FUTURE DIRECTIONS

The relationship between alcohol use and risky sex is complex. It cannot be explained by a single mechanism, but instead reflects multiple underlying causal and noncausal processes. Moreover, even the causal portion of this relationship is not manifest as a main effect but as an interaction.

These complexities have important implications for both research and intervention efforts. The multiplicity of plausible causal mechanisms highlights the need for diverse methodological approaches for exploring alternative models, and for greater sophistication in framing research questions. Rather than focusing on which model better accounts for the link between drinking and risky sex, future research should focus on delineating the conditions under which, and the individuals for whom, different causal (and noncausal) processes are most likely to operate.

At the same time, researchers trying to unravel alcohol's acute effects must adopt more sophisticated methods for studying the complex interplay between drinking, individually held expectancies, and situational cues. Diary methods in which people report on both behaviors across multiple days provide an important and ecologically valid approach for examining this relationship. Such methods not only enable more accurate assessment of the behaviors themselves but also provide a window onto the motivations, emotions, and cognitions that subtly shape these behaviors and set the stage for alcohol's variable effects across individuals and situations.

The existence of multiple causal models also points to the need for diverse intervention strategies, and raises the possibility that different strategies will be optimally effective among individuals for whom different causal processes dominate. For example, among people who chronically drink and engage in risky behaviors, the relationship between drinking and risky sex may primarily reflect the influence of underlying common causes. For such individuals, universal change strategies targeting these common causes should be maximally efficacious. Alternatively, carefully designed interventions aimed at reducing drinking (or manipulating risk cues) in settings where drinking and encountering potential partners co-occur (e.g., college bars) could lower sexual risks associated with alcohol use among those who are most vulnerable to acute intoxication effects, situational influences, or both. To be maximally effective, interventions must be carefully tailored for different populations and circumstances in which different underlying causal processes predominate.

Recommended Reading

Cooper, M.L. (2002). (See References)
George, W.H., & Stoner, S.A. (2000). Understanding acute alcohol effects on sexual behavior. *Annual Review of Sex Research, 11*, 92–122.
Leigh, B.C., & Stall, R. (1993). (See References)
Weinhardt, L.S., & Carey, M.P. (2000). Does alcohol lead to sexual risk behavior? Findings from event-level research. *Annual Review of Sex Research, 11*, 125–157.

Note

1. Address correspondence to M. Lynne Cooper, 105 McAlester Hall, University of Missouri, Columbia, MO, 65211; e-mail: cooperm@missouri.edu.

References

Cooper, M.L. (2002). Alcohol use and risky sexual behavior among college students and youth. *Journal of Studies on Alcohol, 14*(Suppl.), 101–117.

Cooper, M.L., & Orcutt, H.K. (1997). Drinking and sexual experiences on first dates among adolescents. *Journal of Abnormal Psychology, 106*, 191–202.

Cooper, M.L., Wood, P.K., Orcutt, H.K., & Albino, A.W. (2003). Personality and predisposition to engage in risky or problem behaviors during adolescence. *Journal of Personality and Social Psychology, 84*, 390–410.

Dermen, K.H., & Cooper, M.L. (1994). Sex-related alcohol expectancies among adolescents. *Psychology of Addictive Behaviors, 8*, 161–168.

Dermen, K.H., & Cooper, M.L. (2000). Inhibition conflict and alcohol expectancy as moderators of alcohol's relationship to condom use. *Experimental and Clinical Psychopharmacology, 8*, 198–206.

George, W.H., Stoner, S.A., Norris, J., Lopez, P.A., & Lehman, G.L. (2000). Alcohol expectancies and sexuality: A self-fulfilling prophecy analysis of dyadic perceptions and behavior. *Journal of Studies on Alcohol, 61*, 168–176.

Hull, J.G., & Bond, C.F. (1986). Social and behavioral consequences of alcohol consumption and expectancy: A meta-analysis. *Psychological Bulletin, 99*, 347–360.

Leigh, B.C. (2002). Alcohol and condom use: A meta-analysis of event-level studies. *Sexually Transmitted Disease, 29*, 476–482.

Leigh, B.C., & Stall, R. (1993). Substance use and risky sexual behavior for exposure to HIV: Issues in methodology. *American Psychologist, 48*, 1035–1045.

MacDonald, T.K., Fong, G.T., Zanna, M.P., & Martineau, A.M. (2000). Alcohol myopia and condom use: Can alcohol intoxication be associated with more prudent behavior? *Journal of Personality and Social Psychology, 78*, 605–619.

Steele, C.M., & Josephs, R.A. (1990). Alcohol myopia: Its prized and dangerous effects. *American Psychologist, 45*, 921–932.

Section 4: Critical Thinking Questions

1. The "Cartesian duality of mind and body" means that one's mind is something separate from one's body. What are the implications of this statement for mental illness? What are the implications for mental illness if the statement is not true? What do you think about Decartes view? Do you agree or disagree with him?

2. Stem-cell research is a hotly debated topic in political and scientific circles. According to the Jacobs paper, how might stem-cell research be used to help treat mental disorders? What are the ethical implications of such research?

3. The Diagnostic and Statistical Manual of Mental Disorders is a dynamic text, meaning that it changes as scientists obtain new information. How does this help our understanding of psychopathology? How might it unintentionally hinder our view of mental illness?

4. What are some of the problems associated with the broadening of the diagnostic criteria for mental illness in general? What are some of the benefits?

5. Briefly define "alcohol myopia" theory. How might this theory differentially predict the behavior of males and females? How might this inform alcohol education on college campuses?

6. In clinical psychology, there is a focus on "abnormal" behaviors. Meaning, clinicians typically study and treat those who have vastly different emotional experiences from otherwise emotionally healthy people. What can we learn from studying the mentally-well? How might this inform our understanding of psychopathology? How do you think George Bonano would answer this question?

7. The term "epidemic" connotes danger, fear, and contagion. What effect might this have on the identification, assessment and treatment of children with social and developmental delays? What is an alternative way of conveying the importance of early identification of mental illness without unreasonable alarm?

This article has been reprinted as it originally appeared in *Current Directions in Psychological Science*. Citation information for this article as originally published appears above.

Section 5: Individual Differences

People differ from each other—that is clear. How and why they differ is less clear and is the subject of the study of personality and individual differences. The study of individual differences is fascinating because it entails examining persons from multiple perspectives. As reflected in this section, researchers who study individual differences are immensely interested in understanding "the whole person" from both a between-person perspective (what differentiates males from females?; extraverts from introverts?) and a within-person perspective (how variable is one's self-esteem over time?). Recent studies suggest that there are aspects of the person that are durable, while other aspects are more malleable. This section includes articles that illustrate multiple ways to understand dimensions of individual differences.

Rothbart (2007) asks, "What are the origins of human personality" and argues that the study of temperament is necessary to fully understand personality development. In her research, she investigates the interplay of social (e.g., parenting effects) and cognitive factors (e.g., effortful control) in shaping one's temperament. She argues that temperament is ultimately linked to individual differences in personality. Under what conditions does one deviate from their characteristic disposition? This question is asked by Sweeny, Carroll, & Schepperd (2006) who draw from previous literature to examine when and why people shift from their typical optimistic outlook. She also reports on the costs and benefits of this personality shift. Demonstrating the variability of personality over time, Robins and Trzesniewski (2005) track the development of self-esteem over the lifespan. Their research shows that self-esteem rises and dips at different points in one's life and that there are gender differences in this patterning. Even still, they find that there is "rank order stability" in self-esteem over time, which speaks to the impervious nature of self-esteem. Also investigating gender differences, Susan Nolen-Hoeksema (2001) reviews the literature to find some explanation for why females experience more depression than males from adolescence to adulthood. Her paper shows that differences in stress experiences (a social explanation) and reactivity to stress (a biological and cognitive explanation) can explain female vulnerability to depression. Finally, studies of personality and individual differences have important applications to everyday life. Timothy Smith (2006) investigates how personality affects physical health, with a specific focus on chronic anger/hostility and neuroticism/negative affectivity. In his paper, he underscores the importance of using precise measurement tools to assess traits related to health outcomes. He also recommends that newer research should investigate mechanisms that underlie the associations between personality and health.

Personality as Risk and Resilience in Physical Health

Timothy W. Smith[1]
University of Utah

Abstract

Research on the association between personality characteristics and subsequent physical health has produced several consistent findings and identified other tentative relationships. Chronic anger/hostility and neuroticism/negative affectivity are the best established personality risk factors for poor health. Optimism, social dominance, and other traits also appear to influence risk. Several mechanisms have been identified as possibly underlying these effects, but few have been evaluated definitively. Future research may be well served by incorporation of concepts and methods from current personality research.

Keywords

personality and health; psychosomatics; stress

The fascinating notion that personality influences physical health lies at the heart of several fields. Thirty years ago this hypothesis was central in the emergence of health psychology and behavioral medicine, as it was previously for psychosomatic medicine. Studies in which personality traits predicted health outcomes such as longevity and the onset of serious illness also contributed to the resurgence of personality research in recent decades, as those studies addressed the criticism that personality variables have limited predictive utility.

Suggestions that personality influences disease appear over centuries of medical writing (Smith & Gallo, 2001). Yet, the view that connections between "mind and body" are more fiction than fact is prominent in the recent history of medicine, as when an editor of the *New England Journal of Medicine* described the hypothesis that personality and related psychological factors influence the development of medical disease as "folklore" (Angell, 1985). A growing body of research has challenged such skepticism. Yet, methodological and conceptual issues often limit the kinds of conclusions that can be drawn, thus creating an agenda for future research.

TRAITS LINKED TO HEALTH

Dozens of purportedly distinct personality characteristics have been studied as influences on health. The following review summarizes the most compelling evidence.

Beyond Type A: Hostility and Dominance

The groundbreaking work of M. Friedman and Rosenman (1959) on Type A behavior and coronary heart disease (CHD) is perhaps the most well-known example of the personality–health hypothesis. Two decades of research following their description of the Type A behavior pattern (i.e., competitiveness, achievement striving, impatience, hostility, excessive job involvement, and emphatic speech) generally supported its role as a risk factor. Several failures to replicate later challenged this conclusion, even though the literature as a whole demonstrated an association. The failures to replicate led researchers to examine individual elements within the multifaceted Type A construct, as inconsistent associations between the pattern and CHD might indicate that only some components influenced health. Hostility soon emerged as the most unhealthy Type A characteristic. Although negative findings have also appeared in this literature, many subsequent studies have supported an association of individual differences in the tendency to experience anger, cynical or suspicious beliefs, and antagonistic interpersonal behavior with asymptomatic atherosclerosis, the incidence of CHD, and mortality from cardiovascular and other causes (Smith, Glazer, Ruiz, & Gallo, 2004).

Other studies indicate another unhealthy aspect of the Type A pattern. A socially dominant style including loud, rapid, and emphatic speech and a tendency to "cut off" and "talk over" others during social interaction is associated with CHD risk (Houston, Chesney, Black, Cates, & Hecker, 1992). Other prospective studies have supported an association between dominance and subsequent health (cf. Smith, Gallo, & Ruiz, 2003), as do the results of nonhuman primate models of atherosclerosis (Kaplan & Manuck, 1998).

Negative Affectivity, Neuroticism, and Risk

Individual differences in the experience of negative emotions (e.g., anxiety, sadness) have long been suspected as contributing to poor health. This trait is represented in major personality taxonomies, commonly labeled neuroticism or negative affectivity. An early and influential review concluded that this broad dimension conferred vulnerability to disease (H.S. Friedman & Booth-Kewley, 1987). However, critical responses to the review's conclusions suggested that this effect may have been overestimated through the inclusion of studies relying on health-outcome measures that combined illness behavior (e.g., somatic complaints) and actual illness (e.g., diagnosed diseases or mortality). As a result, the apparent association between neuroticism and subsequent disease might have reflected—at least in part—an association between this trait and somatic complaints rather than objectively defined disease. However, subsequent well-designed prospective studies have consistently supported the prior conclusion (Suls & Bunde, 2005); neuroticism and negative affectivity are associated with reduced longevity and increased incidence of objectively diagnosed serious illness.

Personality as Resilience: Optimism and Conscientiousness

The tendency to hold optimistic—as opposed to pessimistic or even hopeless—beliefs about the future has been found to be associated with better health in several prospective studies. These effects include lower incidence of CHD (Kubzanky, Sparrow, Vokonas, & Kawachi, 2001), better prognosis following heart surgery (Scheier et al., 1999), and greater longevity (Giltay, Kamphuis, Kalmijin, Zitman, & Kromhout, 2006). Previous research has suggested that some of the apparent association between optimism and health could actually involve shared variance with neuroticism and the related tendency toward excessive somatic complaints. However, recent studies support a prospective association with objective health outcomes. In some studies these effects have been independent of measures of negative affectivity or neuroticism, although in others it is unclear if the possible overlap between these traits and optimism could contribute to observed associations with objective health outcomes. Conscientiousness has been found to predict longevity, even when this trait is measured during childhood (H.S. Friedman et al., 1995). Among patients with chronic medical illness, conscientiousness is associated with longer survival (Christensen et al., 2002).

CURRENT ISSUES

Several issues have complicated efforts to translate the hypothesis that personality influences health into testable forms. These considerations are important in the critical evaluation of existing research.

Assessing Health, Measuring Personality, and Testing Associations

Burgeoning interest in personality and health research led to the use of a variety of methodological approaches. The most informative studies use unambiguous outcomes (e.g., mortality, objectively diagnosed disease) and prospective designs. Prospective designs reduce the likelihood that associations reflect the consequences of disease rather than potential causes. A concurrent association between serious illness and negative affect could reflect psychological reactions to disease rather than contributions to its emergence in the first place. Developments in medical imaging have created opportunities for more informative cross-sectional designs by quantifying disease states that are not yet apparent. Through ultrasound and computed tomography procedures, serious but asymptomatic disease (e.g., carotid artery plaque, coronary artery calcification) can be measured in otherwise healthy individuals. In such studies, associations between psychological variables and disease are less likely to reflect consequences of disease than they are in designs comparing individuals with and without clinically apparent conditions. Nonetheless, prospective designs provide the clearest information.

In quantifying physical health, outcomes such as mortality and objectively diagnosed disease avoid ambiguities associated with symptom reports, self-ratings of health, or utilization of health care. These latter indicators involve illness behavior— things people do when sick—rather than actual disease. Importantly, illness behavior is sometimes excessive, as when somatic complaints are extreme for a given level of disease severity, and sometimes less extreme than expected, as in stoicism or denial. Somatic complaints, self-ratings of health and disability, and utilization of health care are important outcomes in their own right. However, they are ambiguous because associations between personality and actual disease are difficult to distinguish from those involving only illness behavior.

Personality measures used in this area have also been problematic. Scales are often developed for individual studies, with minimal attention to psychometric concerns (e.g., scale structure, reliability, validity). Evidence of construct validity is often lacking. For example, different scales with similar labels might not actually assess the same trait, and scales with distinct names may actually assess a single characteristic. This has unfortunate implications for a cumulative science of personality and health; sometimes there is little evidence that intended constructs—rather than other traits inadvertently assessed—are involved in an observed association.

Associations Are Not Explanations: Evaluating Mechanisms

Associations between personality and subsequent health raise the question of mechanisms underlying these effects (see Fig. 1). *Health behavior models* suggest that personality traits are associated with health habits, such as smoking or imprudent diet. These habits, in turn, could mediate associations between personality and health. This effect of personality could be consistent over time and across situations, or personality could moderate the extent to which health behaviors (e.g., exercise, eating) change in response to stress. Hostility is associated with a variety of negative health behaviors. Yet, its association with subsequent morbidity and mortality generally remains significant when measures of health behavior are controlled (Smith et al., 2004). Conscientiousness is associated with prudent health behavior (Bogg & Roberts, 2004), but there is evidence that it affects subsequent health independently of this mechanism (H.S. Friedman et al., 1995)

Interactional stress moderation models suggest that personality influences both appraisals of potentially stressful circumstances and coping responses. Appraisals and coping, in turn, alter physiological processes involved in disease etiology. That is, personality moderates physiological responses to stressors in such a way as to influence the likelihood of subsequent disease. Hostile persons generally respond to social stressors with larger physiological reactions (i.e., increases in heart rate and blood pressure; release of catecholamines and cortisol) than those of their more agreeable counterparts, and they display heightened inflammatory activity (Smith et al., 2004). Assertion of dominance during social interaction consistently evokes heightened blood pressure and heart rate (Smith et al., 2003). Chronic negative emotions have been associated with suppressed immune functioning, heightened inflammation, and alterations in autonomic functioning, and optimism is associated with better immune functioning and lower ambulatory blood pressure (Smith & Gallo, 2001).

The *transactional stress moderation model* posits similar pathways but suggests that personality also influences exposure to stressful circumstances. Through decisions to enter or avoid situations, unintentional evocation of responses from other persons, and intentional impacts on others, personality characteristics can alter the frequency, severity, and duration of stressful circumstances (e.g., interpersonal conflict), as well as the availability of stress-reducing resources (e.g., social support). The physiological effects of varying levels of stress exposure could contribute to the effects of personality on health. Hostility and neuroticism have both been linked extensively to increased exposure to interpersonal stressors and reduced levels of social support.

Constitutional predisposition models suggest that underlying genetic or constitutional factors (e.g., temperament, psycho-biological responsiveness, etc.) influence social behavior, emotional traits, and other indicators of personality, as well as pathophysiological processes in disease development. In this view, personality

Health Behavior Model

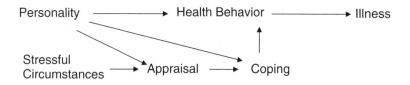

Interactional Stress Moderation Model

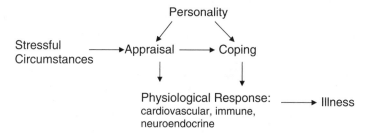

Transactional Stress Moderation Model

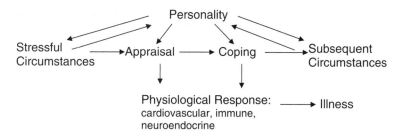

Constitutional Predisposition Model

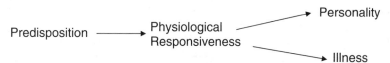

Fig. 1. Models of mechanisms linking personality and health. In the *health behavior model*, personality traits influence health behavior (e.g., smoking, exercise, sleep) or changes in health behavior in response to stressful life circumstances or events. In the *interactional stress moderation model*, personality factors influence appraisal and coping in response to stressful circumstances, which in turn influence physiological responses contributing to illness. The *transactional stress moderation model* extends the interactional model by including the bidirectional effect of personality on exposure to stressful life circumstances and the availability of stress-reducing resources. In the *constitutional predisposition model*, underlying genetic or other psychobiologic factors influence both personality characteristics and the development of illness.

and disease are causally unrelated co-effects of an underlying third variable. For example, trait anger, cynicism, and aggressiveness show significant heritability, and molecular-genetic studies have identified possible candidate genes, suggesting that an underlying constitutional factor could influence the expression of hostility and contribute to disease risk (Smith et al., 2004).

To date, tests of these mechanisms are largely preliminary. Associations between personality and mechanisms or between mechanisms and health have been the main focus. Few studies include more complete mediational tests. Given the common assessment of health behavior in epidemiological research, there have been more mediational tests of this mechanism than of the stress-moderational or constitutional models. Generally, results indicate that health behavior does not provide a complete explanation of associations between personality and health, although some studies support this model.

CONCLUSIONS AND FUTURE DIRECTIONS

Consistent evidence from well-controlled prospective studies indicates that neuroticism/negative affectivity and anger/hostility are associated with important health outcomes. Smaller literatures suggest similar effects for dominance and optimism, and several other traits (e.g., conscientiousness) have received at least some support. It is difficult to reconcile these robust effects with the view that the personality–health hypothesis represents "folklore." Indeed, studies of personality and health may be an essential component of a comprehensive understanding of health and disease.

Plausible mechanisms that potentially underlie these associations have been described, but the literature includes very few compelling tests of these mediational hypotheses. The identification of such mechanisms is essential for the wider acceptance in the biomedical community of personality as an influence on health. That is, the elucidation of mechanisms will be important not only for the advance of basic science and its translation into risk-reducing intervention; the issue of mechanisms is also important for the credibility of the general perspective that personality can influence health. Yet, isolation of one or even a small number of critical mechanisms may be an unrealistic goal. Many of the diseases studied in this research area have complex etiologies that change across stages within their potentially decades-long development and course. The importance of personality traits in such evolving health outcomes may reflect the fact that they are related to multiple, potentially complex and changing mechanisms over long periods of time. Hence, the traditional medical approach in which individual risk factors are related to a specific aspect of disease etiology through a precisely defined mechanism may be a poor model for the ways in which long-standing and far-reaching personality traits influence the development and course of disease over a span of many years. Instead, personality may be related to "bundled" mechanisms involving multiple health behaviors, exposure to several sources of environmental stress, and a variety of interrelated psychophysiological influences on health.

Three major viewpoints in personality psychology have made important contributions to research in this area and are essential in its future (Smith & Gallo, 2001). The predominant trait approach, the Five Factor Model (FFM), may be particularly useful. FFM traits have been used as predictors of health outcomes, but perhaps more importantly this well-established taxonomy can serve as a set of clearly defined personality constructs with well-validated measures (i.e., nomological net) in evaluating, comparing, and contrasting measures and constructs used in health research. In this way, the FFM could bring order to an unwieldy proliferation of constructs and scales and perhaps identify a smaller number of traits that influence health individually or in interactive combinations. The broad traits of the FFM might be seen as posing a threat to the identification of more specific personality influences on health, as when anxiety, anger, and depressive symptoms are subsumed within neuroticism or negative affectivity (Suls & Bunde, 2005). However, versions of the FFM that examine facets within the broader traits can provide such specificity while still maintaining the integrative value of this taxonomy.

The FFM is best suited for describing *which* personality characteristics are associated with health. The social-cognitive perspective provides valuable concepts and methods for describing *how* individuals come to encounter and respond to situations in ways that ultimately affect their health. Rather than broad and static traits, as in the FFM, social-cognitive approaches include smaller, more dynamic units of cognition, affect, and social behavior that describe personality processes. Optimism is the social-cognitive construct most clearly linked to subsequent health, but this perspective provides a generally applicable set of concepts for explicating psychological mechanisms linking personality with health-relevant processes and outcomes.

Current personality-and-health research is typically conducted separately from research on social-environmental risk factors, such as social support or interpersonal conflict. Parsing risk factors as characteristics either of persons or the social contexts they inhabit poses an impediment to an integrative science of psychosocial risk. A third perspective—the interpersonal approach—is useful in this regard. It assumes that personality and recurring features of the social environment are typically two aspects of a single phenomenon. It includes a structural model of social behavior—the interpersonal circumplex—that conceptualizes social situations and personality through common dimensions (i.e., friendliness versus hostility, dominance versus submissiveness). It also includes an account of reciprocal influences between individuals and social situations. Through these concepts and related measures, the interpersonal approach may facilitate a comprehensive perspective on psychosocial risk factors for physical illness (Smith et al., 2004). Each of these perspectives in current personality psychology can contribute to the ultimate goal of research on personality and health—a scientifically informed approach to identifying, explicating, and reducing psychosocial risk for physical illness.

Recommended Reading

Schneiderman, N., Ironson, G., & Siegel, S.D. (2005). Stress and health: Psychological, behavioral, and biological determinants. *Annual Review of Clinical Psychology, 1,* 607–628.

Smith, T.W., & MacKenzie, J. (2006). Personality and risk of physical illness. *Annual Review of Clinical Psychology, 2,* 435–467.

Suls, J., & Bunde, J. (2005). (See References)

Note

1. Address correspondence to Timothy W. Smith, Department of Psychology, University of Utah, 390 South 1530 East (room 502), Salt Lake City, UT 84112; e-mail: tim.smith@psych.utah.edu.

References

Angell, M. (1985). Disease as a reflection of the psyche. *New England Journal of Medicine, 312,* 1570–1572.

Bogg, T., & Roberts, B.W. (2004). Conscientiousness and health-related behaviors: A meta-analysis of the leading behavioral contributors to mortality. *Psychological Bulletin, 130,* 887–919.

Christensen, A.J., Ehlers, S.L., Wiebe, J.S., Moran, P.J., Raichle, K., Femeyhough, K., & Lawton, W.J. (2002). Patient personality and mortality: A 4-year prospective examination of chronic renal insufficiency. *Health Psychology, 21,* 315–320.

Friedman, H.S., & Booth Kewley, S. (1987). The "disease-prone personality": A meta-analytic review of the construct. *American Psychologist, 42,* 539–555.

Friedman, H.S., Tucker, J.S., Schwartz, J.E., Martin, L.R., Tomlinson-Keasey, C., Wingard, D.L., & Criqui, M.H. (1995). Childhood conscientiousness and longevity: Health behaviors and cause of death. *Journal of Personality and Social Psychology, 68,* 696–703.

Friedman, M., & Rosenman, R.H. (1959). Association of a specific overt behavior pattern with increases in blood cholesterol, blood clotting time, incidence of arcus senilis and clinical coronary artery disease. *Journal of the American Medical Association, 169,* 1286–1296.

Giltay, E.J., Kamphuis, M.H., Kalmijin, S., Zitman, F.G., & Kromhout, D. (2006). Dispositional optimism and the risk of cardiovascular death: The Zutphen Elderly Study. *Archives of Internal Medicine, 166,* 431–436.

Houston, B.K., Chesney, M.A., Black, G.W., Cates, D.S., & Hecker, M.L. (1992). Behavioral clusters and coronary heart disease risk. *Psychosomatic Medicine, 54,* 447–461.

Kaplan, J.R., & Manuck, S.B. (1998). Monkeys, aggression, and the pathobiology of atherosclerosis. *Aggressive Behavior, 24,* 323–334.

Kubzansky, L.D., Sparrow, D., Vokonas, P., & Kawachi, I. (2001). Is the glass half empty or half full? A prospective study of optimism and coronary heart disease in the Normative Aging Study. *Psychosomatic Medicine, 63,* 910–916.

Scheier, M.F., Matthews, K.A., Owens, J.F., Schulz, R., Bridges, M.W., Magovern, G.J., & Carver, C.S. (1999). Optimism and rehospitalization after coronary artery bypass graft surgery. *Archives of Internal Medicine, 159,* 829–835.

Smith, T.W., & Gallo, L.C. (2001). Personality traits as risk factors for physical illness. In A. Baum, T. Revenson, & J. Singer (Eds.), *Handbook of health psychology* (pp. 139–172). Hillsdale, NJ: Erlbaum.

Smith, T.W., Gallo, L.C., & Ruiz, J.M. (2003). Toward a social psycho-physiology of cardiovascular reactivity: Interpersonal concepts and methods in the study of stress and coronary disease. In J. Suls & K. Wallston (Eds.), *Social psychological foundations of health and illness* (pp. 335–366). Oxford, England: Blackwell.

Smith, T.W., Glazer, K., Ruiz, J.M., & Gallo, L.C. (2004). Hostility, anger, aggressiveness and coronary heart disease: An interpersonal perspective on personality, emotion and health. *Journal of Personality, 72,* 1217–1270.

Suls, J., & Bunde, J. (2005). Anger, anxiety, and depression as risk factors for cardiovascular disease: The problems and implications of overlapping affective dimensions. *Psychological Bulletin, 131,* 260–300.

This article has been reprinted as it originally appeared in *Current Directions in Psychological Science*. Citation information for this article as originally published appears above.

Is Optimism Always Best?: Future Outlooks and Preparedness

Kate Sweeny[1] and James A. Shepperd
University of Florida
Patrick J. Carroll
The Ohio State University

Abstract

Although people generally appear optimistic about the future, they shift from optimism under certain circumstances. Drawing from a recent review of the literature, we describe how both optimism and shifts from optimism serve the common goal of preparedness, which includes a readiness to deal with setbacks and a readiness to take advantage of opportunities. Shifts from optimism occur in response to available information and to the possibility that things may not turn out as hoped. People tend to shift from optimism when feedback is anticipated in the near future, when the outcome is important, when negative outcomes are easily imagined, and when the outcomes are uncontrollable. In addition, people with low self-esteem shift from optimism more readily than do people with high self-esteem. Finally, both optimism and shifts from optimism have unique benefits in terms of preparedness.

Keywords

optimism; pessimism; expectations; preparedness

In general, people are optimistic about the future, and for good reason. An optimistic outlook appears to provide numerous benefits (Scheier & Carver, 1993). It is linked to greater persistence toward goals and to better coping and adjustment. Optimism facilitates health benefits including reduced levels of postpartum depression, better recovery from alcoholism, and bolstered cardiovascular and immune-system functioning (see Shepperd, Carroll, & Sweeny, in press, for a review). Furthermore, optimism carries social benefits, at least in Western cultures. In general, optimistic people are better liked than pessimistic people (Helweg-Larsen, Sadeghian, & Webb, 2002). Finally, it feels good to believe that the future will be bright; believing otherwise can lead to anxiety.

Given the benefits of optimism, an optimistic outlook appears to be the status quo for most people in most instances. One might thus expect people to embrace optimism under all circumstances. However, mounting evidence suggests that people will shelve their optimism at the moment of truth in favor of a more realistic or even pessimistic outlook. For example, students in one study were pessimistic about their performance on an exam moments before receiving their grades (Shepperd, Ouellette, & Fernandez, 1996). Although past research generally overlooks the potential benefits of moving away from optimism at the moment of truth, we propose that optimism and shifts from optimism serve a similar goal: the need for preparedness (Carroll, Sweeny, & Shepperd, 2006). Importantly, our discussion of optimism is less concerned with whether predictions about the future are objectively optimistic relative to some external criterion, such as the population base rate, than in how predictions at one point in time compare with predictions at another point in time. For our purposes, optimism and pessimism refer to relative expectations about the future at a moment in time, not a dispositional tendency to view the future in a particular way.

FUTURE OUTLOOKS AND THE NEED TO PREPARE

We propose that a need for preparedness governs fluctuations in future outlooks (Carroll et al., 2006). Preparedness is a goal state of readiness to respond to uncertain outcomes. It includes being prepared for possible setbacks should they occur, but also being prepared to take advantage of opportunities when they arise. In most circumstances, optimism best serves the goal of preparedness by organizing thoughts and activity around goal pursuit and persistence and the acquisition of opportunities and resources. Optimism fosters a positive mindset to undertake challenges with the confidence that one can succeed. However, in other circumstances, a shift from optimism best serves the goal of preparedness by directing thoughts and actions toward assessing and responding to changes in the local environment. Of course, when danger has passed or worst-case scenarios become less dire, shifts toward optimism can also serve the need for preparedness by directing energy toward goal attainment. Finally, a pessimistic outlook can facilitate preparation for possible undesired outcomes. As the moment of truth draws near, pessimism directs cognitions and activity toward avoiding undesired outcomes or minimizing their consequences.

WHY DO PEOPLE SHIFT FROM OPTIMISM?

Given the evidence suggesting that optimism is the status quo, what prompts people to depart from optimism? We suggest two broad reasons for departures from optimism, both of which serve the larger need of preparedness (Fig. 1; Carroll et al., 2006). The first is a response to information and the second is a response to the possibility that things might not turn out as hoped. It is noteworthy that these explanations are not mutually exclusive; people may shift from optimism for multiple reasons.

Responding to Available Information

Sometimes people depart from optimism in response to information bearing on the accuracy of their predictions. The information can take three forms (Carroll et al., 2006). First, sometimes people gain new information that prompts them to adjust their predictions to prepare for what lies ahead. As the moment of truth draws near, people often gain greater understanding of the circumstances that might influence their outcomes and, perhaps, a better a sense of what outcomes are realistic and what outcomes are not. Second, people sometimes revise their outlooks as a result of more careful consideration or scrutiny of existing information. The greater scrutiny may arise from increased accountability concerns, whereby people feel pressure (either internally or externally generated) to justify or defend their outlook, or from the fact that as events draw near, people shift the

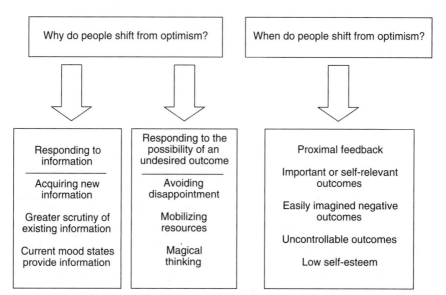

Fig. 1. Why and when people shift from optimism. People shift from optimism in response to information and in response to the possibility of undesired consequences. Situational and personal factors can make shifts from optimism more likely to occur.

way they construe events. Whereas people construe distant events abstractly and focus more on what they would like to happen, they construe near events concretely and focus more on what is likely to happen (Trope & Liberman, 2003). Third, current mood can be a source of information. As events and outcomes draw near, people often experience an increase in anxiety and may draw inferences about themselves and their likely outcomes based on their current anxiety (Schwartz & Clore, 1988).

To put these explanations in context, consider college students' predictions about their starting salaries. College seniors in one study shifted their salary predictions in their first post-graduation job from optimism 4 months prior to graduation to realism 2 weeks prior to graduation. Sophomores and juniors, by contrast, showed no such shift in predictions (Shepperd et al., 1996). Undoubtedly, the seniors recalibrated their predictions in part due to gaining greater information about starting salaries either from their own interview experience or from the experiences of friends. Furthermore, as their senior year drew to a close, the seniors may have felt growing pressure to explain their overly optimistic salary expectations to themselves and others, and they may have focused more on the difficulties of the application and interview process and less on the dream of making millions. Finally, the seniors may have interpreted increasing anxiety about the job market as evidence that their original expectations were too high.

Responding to the Possibility of an Undesired Outcome

Not all shifts in outlook reflect a response to information. In some instances, a shift from optimism reflects a response to the possibility that things may not turn out as hoped. That is, people sometimes position themselves for the possibility of an undesired outcome. This category of response also has three manifestations (Fig. 1; Carroll et al., 2006).

The first manifestation is an attempt to prepare for possible disappointment. People's expectations strongly influence their feelings about their outcomes. When outcomes exceed expectations, people feel elated; when outcomes fall short of expectations, people feel disappointed (Shepperd & McNulty, 2002). Thus, people may shift their expectations downward to avoid disappointment. Second, people may shift from optimism in an effort to mobilize energy toward avoiding undesired outcomes or toward minimizing their consequences. In some instances, this mobilization reflects the cognitive strategy of defensive pessimism, in which some people use pessimism and the resulting anxiety to prompt preventative behavior (Norem & Cantor, 1986). The third manifestation is a form of magical thinking in which people perhaps believe that making optimistic predictions diminishes the likelihood that the desired outcome will occur. People may thus voice less optimistic or even pessimistic predictions to avoid "jinxing" a forthcoming outcome.

To put the second category of explanations in context, imagine a woman who finds a lump in her breast. She may adopt negative expectations (i.e., believing that the lump indicates cancer) to avoid being caught off guard and to minimize negative feelings if her suspicions are correct. Adopting negative expectations may also prompt her to take action by making an appointment with her doctor or scheduling a mammogram. Finally, she may believe that she could "jinx" herself and make a negative outcome more likely by assuming the best.

WHEN DO PEOPLE SHIFT FROM OPTIMISM?

Figure 1 also identifies a number of factors that moderate when people shift from optimism (Carroll et al., 2006). These factors are conditions under which people are likely to shift, and they may occur alone or in tandem in a particular situation. First, people shift from optimism when they anticipate information or feedback bearing on the accuracy of their outlook. The more proximal the feedback (i.e., as the moment of truth draws near), the more inclined people are to shelve their optimism. For example, students applying to graduate school may be confident of attaining admission into the most prestigious programs when the application deadlines are months away. However, these students may adopt more moderate expectations as they prepare for the GRE and struggle through the application process. When the process is complete (i.e., applications are in the mail), these students may further lower their expectations as they realize that their fate is now out of their hands. Finally, all optimism may vanish the day the graduate school admission letter arrives in the mail. Research documents this shift from optimism in domains ranging from exam predictions to expectations about testing positive for a disease. Figure 2 illustrates the typical pattern seen in exam-score estimates.

Second, people are more likely to shift from optimism when the outcome is personally consequential or important. Thus, for example, people are more likely to shift from optimism when awaiting test results for a serious disease than for a

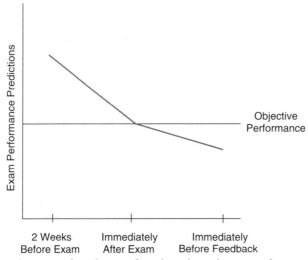

Fig. 2. Typical pattern of predictions for a hypothetical exam performance over time, relative to actual performance.

nonserious disease. Of course, outcome importance is somewhat subjective. Two people may regard the same potential outcome quite differently. A C on an exam may be disastrous for a student in danger of losing a scholarship but only a minor annoyance for another student not facing such dire consequences. As might be expected, the former student is more likely than the latter student to depart from optimism (Shepperd, Findley-Klein, Kwavnick, Walker, & Perez, 2000).

Third, people shift from optimism to the extent that they can easily imagine an alternative, worse outcome. The easier it is to imagine an undesired outcome, the more likely people are to shelve their optimism. Indeed, inducing people to imagine undesired outcomes can prompt a shift from optimism in future predictions (Sanna, 1999). Fourth, people shift from optimism when they perceive their future outcomes as beyond their control. For example, at the beginning of a semester, students may predict that they will receive As in their courses because they plan to attend all of their classes and spend each night studying. As the final exam looms and all opportunities for control are diminished, students may be less optimistic about their chances for success. Similarly, people are more likely to be optimistic when they can control the impact of an undesirable outcome, even if they cannot prevent the outcome from occurring. For example, people are less likely to believe that they will contract diseases that can be prevented or even treated effectively with medication; they are more pessimistic about contracting diseases that cannot be prevented or treated.

Finally, people low in self-esteem lower their estimates more over time than do people high in self-esteem. The effect of self-esteem on future outlooks may arise for several reasons. First, people with low self-esteem may be less certain of their abilities and thus more sensitive to situational cues (such as declining control) that suggest things may turn out badly. Second, they may think more about things that could lead to undesirable outcomes—that is, they may more readily

173

mentally simulate undesirable outcomes when anticipating feedback. Third, people with low self-esteem are more reactive to feedback, and this reactivity may incline them to proactively regulate affect by shifting from optimism in anticipation of feedback. That is, they may be particularly inclined to prepare themselves for possible bad news by expecting the worst (Shepperd et al., 1996).

COSTS AND BENEFITS OF DEPARTURES FROM OPTIMISM

Although the benefits of optimism are well-documented, shifting from optimism also has benefits (Shepperd, Sweeny, & Carroll, 2006). First, a less optimistic outlook can make people feel better about the outcomes they experience. As noted earlier, people feel elated when outcomes exceed expectations, and shifting from optimism (i.e., lowering expectations) can increase elation in response to outcomes. Conversely, people feel disappointed when outcomes fall short of expectations. A shift from optimism allows people to prepare for and ultimately avoid potential disappointment by anticipating bad news. Second, a pessimistic outlook can prompt preparatory actions that reduce the likelihood of an undesired outcome, diminish the negative consequences, and expedite recovery.

Of course, a downward shift in outlook can have costs. Adopting a negative outlook forfeits the physical, mental, and emotional benefits of optimism, and embracing a pessimistic outlook can trigger negative affect and anxiety. The anxiety can be debilitating to the extent that people become preoccupied with thoughts of possible bad news and unable to manage other aspects of their life. For example, people who are obsessed with the possibility that a loved one may be injured or killed or that every minor health concern will turn out to be fatal may be unable to meet the demands of everyday life. Furthermore, people making predictions about the future must wrestle with an array of competing goals, and these goals may make pessimism undesirable. For example, a gymnast awaiting one set of scores while preparing for his or her next routine may forego pessimism in order to remain confident for the upcoming performance.

SUMMARY AND FUTURE DIRECTIONS

Future outlooks are important because they influence how people feel about their outcomes and because they prompt activity directed at facilitating desired outcomes and avoiding or mitigating undesired outcomes. Although an optimistic outlook has numerous benefits and appears to be the ambient state for most people at most times, a downward shift from optimism also offers benefits. People who are overly optimistic about the future are ill-prepared to respond to setbacks that may occur. When available information indicates that expectations are inaccurate, shifting expectations prepares people to deal with the most likely outcomes. Likewise, when an undesired outcome seems possible, shifting expectations downward prepares people by providing protection from an emotional blow. Ultimately, we suggest that a balance between optimism and pessimism best serves the demands of preparedness. People should be optimistic enough to take advantage of the many benefits of a positive outlook, but they should also sufficiently temper that optimism so that they can motivate preventative action and avoid being caught off guard (Sweeny & Shepperd, in press).

Finally, we acknowledge many unanswered questions. First, the developmental processes that lead people to adjust their future outlooks downward from optimism are largely unknown. Do children learn about the consequences of holding different future outlooks from experience, or is this understanding a natural consequence of increased cognitive abilities? Second, all published research exploring shifts in future outlooks comes from investigators in Western cultures, and although the need for preparedness is likely universal, the specific strategies people use to achieve this end and the costs and benefits of these strategies may vary cross-culturally. Third, some of the presumed consequences of shifting from optimism are speculative and require empirical confirmation. These questions aside, recognizing that optimism is not always beneficial will likely yield new insights into how people can best prepare for future outcomes.

Recommended Readings

Carroll, P.J., Sweeny, K., & Shepperd, J.A. (2006). (See References)
Shepperd, J.A., Ouellette, J.A., & Fernandez, J.K. (1996). (See References)
Sanna, L.J., & Chang, E. (2006). *Judgments over time: The interplay of thoughts, feelings and behaviors.* New York: Oxford University Press.

Acknowledgments—We thank two anonymous reviewers for their helpful comments on an earlier version of this manuscript.

Note

1. Address correspondence to Kate Sweeny, Department of Psychology, PO Box 112250, University of Florida, Gainesville, FL 32611-2250; e-mail: kdockery@ufl.edu.

References

Carroll, P.J., Sweeny, K., & Shepperd, J.A. (2006). Forsaking optimism. *Review of General Psychology, 10,* 56–73.
Helweg-Larsen, M., Sadeghian, P., & Webb, M.A. (2002). The stigma of being pessimistically biased. *Journal of Social and Clinical Psychology, 21,* 92–107.
Norem, J.K., & Cantor, N. (1986). Defensive pessimism: Harnessing anxiety and motivation. *Journal of Personality and Social Psychology, 51,* 1208–1217.
Sanna, L.J. (1999). Mental simulations, affect, and subjective confidence: Timing is everything. *Psychological Science, 10,* 339–345.
Scheier, M., & Carver, C. (1993). On the power of positive thinking: The benefits of being optimistic. *Current Directions in Psychological Science, 2,* 26–30.
Schwartz, N., & Clore, G.L. (1988). How do I feel about it? Informative functions of affective states. In K. Fiedler & J. Forgas (Eds.), *Affect, cognition, and social behavior* (pp. 44–62). Toronto: Hogrefe.
Shepperd, J.A., Carroll, P.J., & Sweeny, K. (in press). A functional approach to explaining fluctuations in future outlooks: From self-enhancement to self-criticism. In E. Chang & L. Sanna (Eds.), *The complexities of self-criticism and self-enhancement: Theory, research and clinical implications.* Washington, DC: American Psychological Association.
Shepperd, J.A., Findley-Klein, C., Kwavnick, K.D., Walker, D., & Perez, S. (2000). Bracing for loss. *Journal of Personality and Social Psychology, 78,* 620–634.

Shepperd, J.,& McNulty, J. (2002). The affective consequences of expected and unexpected outcomes. *Psychological Science, 13*, 85–88.

Shepperd, J.A., Ouellette, J.A., & Fernandez, J.K. (1996). Abandoning unrealistic optimism: Performance estimates and the temporal proximity of self-relevant feedback. *Journal of Personality and Social Psychology, 70*, 844–855.

Shepperd, J.A., Sweeny, K., & Carroll, P.J. (2006). Abandoning optimism in predictions about the future. In L.J. Sanna & E. Chang (Eds.), *Judgments over time: The interplay of thoughts, feelings and behaviors* (pp. 13–33). New York: Oxford University Press.

Sweeny, K., & Shepperd, J.A. (in press). Do people brace sensibly? Risk judgments and risk prevalence. *Personality and Social Psychology Bulletin.*

Trope, Y., & Liberman, N. (2003). Temporal construal. *Psychological Review, 110*, 403–421.

This article has been reprinted as it originally appeared in *Current Directions in Psychological Science*. Citation information for this article as originally published appears above.

Temperament, Development, and Personality

Mary K. Rothbart[1]
University of Oregon

Abstract

Understanding temperament is central to our understanding of development, and temperament constructs are linked to individual differences in both personality and underlying neural function. In this article, I review findings on the structure of temperament, its relation to the Big Five traits of personality, and its links to development and psychopathology. In addition, I discuss the relation of temperament to conscience, empathy, aggression, and the development of behavior problems, and describe the relation between effortful control and neural networks of executive attention. Finally, I present research on training executive attention.

Keywords

temperament; development; personality; neural networks; attention training

What are the origins of human personality? Are they chiefly the result of the child's reinforcement history? The child's learned attributions about the social world? The child's genes? Or is there more to understand than would result from a simple choice between nature and nurture? Concepts of temperament are necessary to understand the origins of personality development. Temperament describes the initial state from which personality develops and links individual differences in behavior to underlying neural networks. Temperament and experience together "grow" a personality, which will include the child's developing cognitions about self, others, and the physical and social world, as well as his or her values, attitudes, and coping strategies.

From early infancy, children show considerable variability in their reactions to the environment. One child is fearful, has only a brief attention span, and cries even at moderately stimulating play; another child enjoys vigorous play, is not easily distracted, and seeks out exciting events. These reactions, together with the mechanisms that regulate them, constitute the child's temperament. Temperament is defined as individual differences in emotional, motor, and attentional reactivity measured by latency, intensity, and recovery of response, and self-regulation processes such as effortful control that modulate reactivity (Rothbart & Derryberry, 1981). These differences are biologically based and are linked to an individual's genetic endowment (Posner, Rothbart, & Sheese, 2007).

The study of temperament is as old as the Hindu Upanishads and as recent as yesterday's studies in molecular genetics. Considerable advances have been made in recent years in our understanding of the structure of temperament, its development, and its relation to aspects of personality and neural structure (see reviews by Posner & Rothbart, 2007a; Rothbart & Bates, 2006). In this article, I present a general description of temperament followed by a more detailed discussion of the broad temperament construct of effortful control (EC). EC describes children's ability to choose a course of action under conditions of conflict, to plan for the future, and to detect errors. This construct emerged initially from sophisticated psychometric studies of parent reports and has also been measured in the laboratory (Rothbart & Bates, 2006). EC has been linked to important developmental outcomes, including the development of conscience and of behavior problems. In addition, EC is related to the executive attention network as identified in imaging studies. It also involves specific genes (Posner et al., 2007).

Here, I review the research on the structure of temperament, its relation to the Big Five personality traits, and its links to outcomes in personality and psychopathology (Rothbart & Posner, 2006). I describe the links between EC, executive attention, and brain networks related to executive attention and discuss their modifiability by experience.

THE STRUCTURE OF TEMPERAMENT

Many psychologists are aware of the nine dimensions of temperament identified by the New York Longitudinal Study, taken from interviews with parents about their infants (Thomas & Chess, 1977). These included activity level, approach/withdrawal, intensity, threshold, adaptability, rhythmicity, mood, attention span persistence, and distractibility. More recently, psychometric studies have refined these categories (Rothbart & Bates, 2006). Temperament dimensions that have now emerged show strong similarities to the structure of temperament in other animals, including the defensive reactions of fear and anger, approach reactions of activity and pleasure to high intensity stimulation, and attentional scales of duration of orienting in infancy and of EC in toddlerhood. Recent research with the Children's Behavior Questionnaire (Rothbart, Ahadi, Hershey, & Fisher, 2001), a parent report measure for children 3 to 7 years of age, also identified three broad dimensions of temperament described in Table 1 and depicted in Figure 1.

These dimensions of temperament are related to the Big Five personality factors of Extraversion (extraversion/surgency), Neuroticism (negative affectivity), and Conscientiousness (EC). The Openness and Agreeableness factors have been found to relate to the adult temperamental dimensions of perceptual sensitivity and affiliation (Evans & Rothbart, 2007). It is important to remember, however, that temperament theory goes beyond a list of unrelated traits or broad dimensions. Of central importance are the interactions between children's reactive impulses and their efforts to control them. In particular, researchers are interested in the relations among EC, extraversion/surgency, and negative affectivity.

Very similar broad dimensions of temperament have been found across cultures, and different correlations among these dimensions in the United States and China are shown in Figure 1 (Ahadi, Rothbart, & Ye, 1993). In the United States, but not in China, children high in EC showed lower negative affectivity. In China, but not in the United States, children high in EC showed lower extraversion/surgency. These differences may be related to culturally valued behaviors (low distress in the United States; low outgoing behavior in China), guiding development. Basic biological processes of temperament appear to be shared across cultures, but outcomes vary depending on cultural values and the child's experiences.

Table 1. *Definitions of Temperament in the Children's Behavior Questionnaire and the Early Adolescent Temperament Questionnaire*

Broad dimensions/ Temperament scales	Scale definitions
Effortful control	
Attention Control	The capacity to focus attention as well as to shift attention when desired
Inhibitory Control	The capacity to plan future action and to suppress inappropriate responses
Perceptual Sensitivity	Detection or perceptual awareness of slight, low-intensity stimulation in the environment
Low-Intensity Pleasure	Pleasure derived from activities or stimuli involving low intensity, rate, complexity, novelty, and incongruity
Negative affectivity	
Frustration	Negative affect related to interruption of ongoing tasks or goal blocking
Fear	Negative affect related to anticipation of distress
Discomfort	Negative affect related to sensory qualities of stimulation, including intensity, rate, or complexity of light, movement, sound, or texture
Sadness	Negative affect and lowered mood and energy related to exposure to suffering, disappointment, and object loss
Soothability	Rate of recovery from peak distress, excitement, or general arousal
Extraversion/surgency	
Activity	Level of gross motor activity including rate and extent of locomotion
Low—Shyness	Behavioral inhibition to novelty and challenge, especially social
High-Intensity Pleasure	Pleasure derived from activities involving high intensity or novelty
Smiling & Laughter	Positive affect in response to changes in stimulus intensity, rate, complexity, and incongruity
Impulsivity	Speed of response initiation
Positive Anticipation	Positive excitement and anticipation for expected pleasurable activities
Affiliation[a]	Desire for warmth and closeness with others, independent of shyness or extraversion

Note. Subscales are grouped according to their broad dimensions.
[a]In Early Adolescent Temperament Questionnaire only.

DEVELOPMENT OF TEMPERAMENT

Temperament characteristics can be seen in the newborn and measured in the fetus. The newborn shows distress and avoidant movements, and by 2 to 3 months, approach reactions are evidenced in smiling, laughter, and body movement. Physical approach is seen when developing motor systems permit, usually by 4 to 6 months. Anger or frustration is seen at 2 to 3 months, and fear in the form of behavioral inhibition appears to be differentiated from general distress proneness by 7 to 10 months. Fear in infancy predicts children's later fearfulness and low aggression; anger predicts later higher frustration and aggression. Fear thus appears to act as a control on both approach and aggression (Rothbart & Bates, 2006).

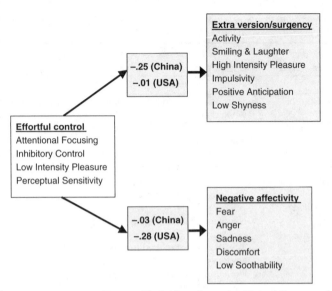

Fig. 1. Temperament in 6- to 7-year-old children from the United States and China as evaluated by the Children's Behavior Questionnaire. The similar overall temperament structure suggests that the basic building blocks of temperament are the same in both cultures; but their relationships differ, as shown by the correlations in the middle boxes.

Fear is a reactive dimension that also contains regulatory components (behavioral inhibition or withdrawal from threatening stimulation). As noted above, behavioral fear develops later than approach responses. Although fear serves to inhibit approach and aggression, it may also capture attention (Rothbart & Sheese, 2007). A second, attentional control system, EC, allows more flexible inhibition of action (not eating a rich dessert), facilitation of action (eating more vegetables instead), detection of errors, and planning. EC as measured in laboratory tasks develops strongly over the preschool and into the school years. By 30 months, children show consistency in performance across tasks and considerable stability of EC is found thereafter (Kochanska, Murray, & Harlan, 2000; Rothbart, Sheese, & Posner, in press).

TEMPERAMENT AND SOCIALIZATION-RELEVANT CHARACTERISTICS

Temperament is consistently related to important social behaviors such as empathy and conscience. In my research, infant fear predicted parent-reported guilt, empathy, and low aggression at age 6 to 7 years. In Kochanska, Aksan, and Joy's (2007) research, more fearful children developed greater conscience during the preschool years than less fearful children did. Fear provides internal cues of discomfort that can be attributed to conscience rather than to external reward or coercion. The relation between temperament and conscience was also affected by parenting. Fearful children who received gentle and nonpunitive socialization developed greater conscience than did fearful children whose parents were

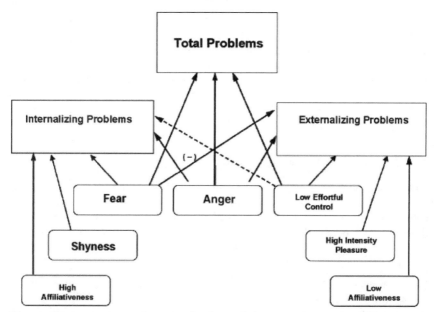

Fig. 2. Temperament in relation to developing behavior problems. Internalizing problems refers to anxious, inhibited, depressed, and withdrawn behavior; externalizing problems refers to disruptive, aggressive, and hyperactive behavior. The broken line denotes a weak relation.

punitive. For more fearless children, conscience depended on another aspect of parenting. More fearless children who had positive relations with their parents developed greater conscience than fearless children whose relations with their parents were less positive.

EC also positively predicts conscience (Kochanska et al., 2000), as well as empathy, guilt, and low aggressiveness. EC may provide the attentional flexibility needed to react to negative feelings in others without being overwhelmed by them (empathy) and to relate these feelings to responsibility for one's own actions (conscience). Thus, two control systems, one emotional (fear) and one attentional (EC), appear to influence the development of conscience: Fear provides the distress and reactive inhibition components, and EC provides the attentional flexibility needed to link distress cues, action, and moral principles. A review by Eisenberg, Smith, Sadovsky, and Spinrad (2004) provides important additional findings relating EC to social and personality development.

Temperament is also an important contributor to a lower incidence of behavior problems, and this is found even when there is no overlap in content between the temperament and psychopathology measures (Rothbart & Bates, 2006). Figure 2 depicts relations reported in the literature, including a recent study by Ormel et al. (2005), which used the Early Adolescent Temperament Questionnaire–Revised to relate temperament at 10 to 11 years to the development of behavior problems at 12 to 14 years. Extraversion/surgency is related to greater externalizing problems (acting out) and to fewer internalizing problems (fear, sadness, low self-esteem). Anger and frustration predict both internalizing and externalizing problems, but fear is more strongly related to internalizing and anger to externalizing difficulties. The new scale of Affiliativeness in the Early Adolescent Temperament Questionnaire predicted both high internalizing and low externalizing problems. Low EC is a consistent and strong predictor of externalizing problems and a less strong predictor of internalizing problems. EC also moderates the effects of negative affectivity on problems; highly negative children will be less likely to show problems when they have higher EC (Rothbart & Bates, 2006; Rothbart & Posner, 2006).

NEURAL CORRELATES OF TEMPERAMENT

One exciting aspect of temperament is that it can be studied at multiple levels. Reactive temperament, for example, has been related to neural structure, especially to the functioning of the amygdala and (for extraversion/surgency) to dopamine systems (Rothbart & Posner, 2006). In the laboratory, researchers have studied the brain's attentional networks, which develop over time and are related to individual differences in EC. Monitoring and resolving conflict between incompatible responses have been linked to specific executive attention networks in the brain (Posner & Rothbart, 2007b). A basic measure of conflict resolution is provided by the Stroop task, in which the name of a word conflicts with the name of the color it is printed in. Tasks such as the Attention Networks Test (ANT) present flanking stimuli that distract from the task of responding to a central stimulus. Stroop and flanker tasks used in adult imaging studies activate the anterior cingulate and lateral prefrontal areas of the brain, which are parts of the executive attention network (Posner & Rothbart, 2007a; Rothbart et al., in press).

When Stroop and flanker tasks are adapted for children as markers of executive attention development, researchers can trace brain function through children's performance. For toddlers, the spatial conflict task is used. Here the child must match an animal picture (dog or cat) cue with a picture of the same animal on one of two response keys. The location of the key can be directly below the cue or on the opposite side. There is a strong tendency to respond on the same side as the cue and the child must overcome this conflict to make the correct response. (see Posner & Rothbart, 2007a). At 30 months (the age when Kochanska et al., 2000, found EC tasks to be related), children moved from repeatedly performing the same incorrect response to showing more accurate performance. By 3 years, they showed high accuracy but were slower in the conflicting condition, as is found in adults. Preschool children who performed well on the tasks also scored higher in measures of EC and lower on impulsivity and were less prone to frustration (as evaluated by the Children's Behavior Questionnaire). By age 7, the rapid period of development of executive attention appears to be complete.

TRAINING AND GENETICS OF EXECUTIVE ATTENTION

Given the central importance of EC and executive attention to development, can these systems be influenced by experience? Previously, researchers in our laboratory created a set of training exercises to help preschool children develop executive attention skills (Rueda, Rothbart, McCandliss, Saccamanno, & Posner, 2005). Exercises were adapted from tasks used to train monkeys for space travel.

Fig. 3. Attention-training exercise (the cat seeking grass). As the extent of the mud (the dark gray area around the perimeter of the picture) increases, the extent of the grass (the white patch on the right) decreases. When the grass area becomes very small, the children are using the cat as a cursor to be moved from one spot to another.

Children ranging in age from 4 to 6 years were trained to use a joystick as they controlled the movement of a cat on the screen. They were instructed to guide the cat to the grass without getting in the mud (see Fig. 3). Over trials, the grass area shrinks and the mud area expands, so that the child is effectively moving the cat as a cursor. Children then learn how to have the cat move to intercept the travel of a duck, who either visibly swims across a pond or dives into it, and are trained on working-memory and Stroop-like conflict tasks.

These exercises were completed in five training sessions, with pre- and posttraining assessments including the ANT described previously and the Kaufman-Brief Intelligence Test. During ANT performance, 128 channels of electroencephalography were also recorded. We wished to measure the negative brain response arising around 200 milliseconds following the target (N2), which in adults arises in the anterior cingulate and is related to conflict performance.

Both 4- and 6-year-old children who had undergone training performed better on conflict trials than did children in the control group, but performance was highly variable and the difference did not reach statistical significance. Analysis of the N2 data, however, indicated that the trained children showed a more adultlike response. Intelligence scores of trained children were also higher after this brief training. Temperament measures were not affected, but both EC and children's distress proneness may be influenced if longer training programs were used, as in preschool settings (Posner & Rothbart, 2007a).

Executive attention efficiency has also been related to alleles (variants) of specific genes in both adults and children (Posner et al., 2007), and in children, genetic alleles have been related to parent reports of negative affectivity, EC, and extraversion/surgency. Researchers at the University of Oregon have also recently found an interaction between specific genes and parenting in the prediction of children's temperament. Research on genes and the development of temperament and personality will be of great interest in future studies.

FUTURE DIRECTIONS

This article provides a brief review of advances in our understanding of temperament and development. These advances have been considerable, but much remains to be learned. Future studies will explore temperament in relation to how children experience their social and physical world and their development of situation-specific behavior. Genetic analyses will allow for a much more differentiated study of temperament in relation to experience in children's development. By studying temperament at behavioral, mental, and brain-network levels and by investigating children's variability, development, and psychopathology, researchers will make increasing progress in this area (Posner & Rothbart, 2007b).

Recommended Reading

Eisenberg, N., Smith, C.L., Sadovsky, A., & Spinrad, T.L. (2004). (See References)
Kochanska, G., Murray, K.T., & Harlan, E.T. (2000). (See References)
Posner, M.I., & Rothbart, M.K. (2007a). (See References)
Rothbart, M.K., & Bates, J.E. (2006). (See References)
Rothbart, M.K., & Posner, M.I. (2006). (See References)

Acknowledgments—The research reported here was supported by National Institutes of Mental Health Grants MH43361 and MH01471 and by a McDonnell Foundation grant. The author wishes to thank Michael Posner and Myron Rothbart for their help in developing this review.

Note

1. Address correspondence to Mary K. Rothbart, Department of Psychology, University of Oregon, Eugene, OR 97403-1227; e-mail: maryroth@uoregon.edu.

References

Ahadi, S., Rothbart, M.K., & Ye, R. (1993). Children's temperament in the United States and China: Similarities and differences. *European Journal of Personality, 7*, 359–378.
Eisenberg, N., Smith, C.L., Sadovsky, A., & Spinrad, T.L. (2004). Effortful control: Relations with emotion regulation, adjustment, and socialization in childhood. In R.F. Baumeister & K.D. Vohs (Eds.), *Handbook of self-regulation: Research, theory, and applications* (pp. 259–282). New York: Guilford.
Evans, D., & Rothbart, M.K. (2007). Developing a model for adult temperament. *Journal of Research in Personality, 41*, 868–888.
Kochanska, G., Aksan, N., & Joy, M.E. (2007). Children's fearfulness as a moderator of parenting in early socialization: Two longitudinal studies. *Developmental Psychology, 43*, 222–237.

Kochanska, G., Murray, K.T., & Harlan, E.T. (2000). Effortful control in early childhood: Continuity and change, antecedents, and implications for social development. *Developmental Psychology, 36,* 220–232.

Ormel, A.J., Oldehinkel, A.J., Ferdinand, R.F., Hartman, C.A., de Winter, A.F., & Veenstra, R. (2005). Internalizing and externalizing problems in adolescence: General and dimension-specific effects of familial loadings and preadolescent temperament traits. *Psychological Medicine, 35,* 1825–1835.

Posner, M.I., & Rothbart, M.K. (2007a). *Educating the human brain.* Washington, DC: American Psychological Association.

Posner, M.I., & Rothbart, M.K. (2007b). Research on attentional networks as a model for the integration of psychological science. *Annual Review of Psychology, 58,* 1–23.

Posner, M.I., Rothbart, M.K., & Sheese, B.E. (2007). Attention genes. *Developmental Science, 10,* 24–29.

Rothbart, M.K., Ahadi, S.A., Hershey, K., & Fisher, P. (2001). Investigations of temperament at three to seven years: The Children's Behavior Questionnaire. *Child Development, 72,* 1394–1408.

Rothbart, M.K., & Bates, J.E. (2006). Temperament. In W. Damon, R. Lerner, & N. Eisenberg (Eds.), *Handbook of child psychology: Vol. 3. Social, emotional, and personality development* (6th ed., pp. 99–166). New York: Wiley.

Rothbart, M.K., & Derryberry, D. (1981). Development of individual differences in temperament. In M.E. Lamb & A. Brown (Eds.), *Advances in developmental psychology* (Vol. 1, pp. 37–86). Hillsdale, NJ: Erlbaum.

Rothbart, M.K., & Posner, M.I. (2006). Temperament, attention, and developmental psychopathology. In D. Cicchetti & D. Cohen (Eds.), *Developmental psychopathology: Vol. 2. Developmental Neuroscience* (2nd ed., pp. 465–501). New York: Wiley.

Rothbart, M.K., & Sheese, B.E. (2007). Temperament and emotion regulation. In J.J. Gross (Ed.), *Handbook of emotion regulation* (pp. 331–350). New York: Guilford.

Rothbart, M.K., Sheese, B.E., & Posner, M.I. (in press). Executive attention and effortful control: Linking temperament, brain networks, and genes. *Perspectives in Developmental Psychology.*

Rueda, M.R., Rothbart, M.K., McCandliss, B.D., Saccamanno, L., & Posner, M.I. (2005). Training, maturation, and genetic influences on the development of executive attention. *Proceedings of the National Academy of Sciences, USA, 102,* 14931–14936.

Thomas, A., & Chess, S. (1977). *Temperament and development.* New York: Bruner/Mazel.

This article has been reprinted as it originally appeared in *Current Directions in Psychological Science*. Citation information for this article as originally published appears above.

Self-Esteem Development Across the Lifespan

Richard W. Robins[1]
Department of Psychology, University of California, Davis
Kali H. Trzesniewski
Institute of Psychiatry, King's College, London, United Kingdom

Abstract

After decades of debate, a consensus is emerging about the way self-esteem develops across the lifespan. On average, self-esteem is relatively high in childhood, drops during adolescence (particularly for girls), rises gradually throughout adulthood, and then declines sharply in old age. Despite these general age differences, individuals tend to maintain their ordering relative to one another: Individuals who have relatively high self-esteem at one point in time tend to have relatively high self-esteem years later. This type of stability (i.e., rank-order stability) is somewhat lower during childhood and old age than during adulthood, but the overall level of stability is comparable to that found for other personality characteristics. Directions for further research include (a) replication of the basic trajectory using more sophisticated longitudinal designs, (b) identification of the mediating mechanisms underlying self-esteem change, (c) the development of an integrative theoretical model of the life-course trajectory of self-esteem.

Keywords

self-esteem; development; change; stability

As he was nearing the end of his life, Michelangelo began working on what many people believe to be his most important work, the Florentine Pietà. After working intensely for almost a decade, he entered his studio one day and took a sledgehammer to the sculpture. He broke away the hands and legs and nearly shattered the work before his assistants dragged him away. Why did Michelangelo attempt to destroy one of his greatest creations, a statue that has been described as among the finest works of the Renaissance? Disillusioned and isolated in the last decades of his life, Michelangelo had a heightened sense of perfectionism that was exacerbated by his failure to live up to the expectations of his father, who viewed being a sculptor as akin to being a manual laborer. Michelangelo, it seems, had self-esteem issues. Was Michelangelo's low self-esteem normative for someone his age? Was he likely to have been plagued by self-doubts throughout his life? An emerging body of evidence is beginning to offer answers to these kinds of questions.

In this article, we review the current state of scientific evidence regarding the development of self-esteem across the lifespan.[2] After decades of debate, a consensus is emerging about the way self-esteem changes from childhood to old age. We focus here on two forms of change: (a) normative changes in self-esteem, which reflect whether individuals, on average, increase or decrease over time (assessed by mean differences in self-esteem across age groups); and (b) the stability of individual differences in self-esteem, which reflect the degree to which the relative ordering of individuals is maintained over time (assessed by correlations between self-esteem scores across two time points, i.e., test–retest correlations).[3]

THE NORMATIVE TRAJECTORY OF SELF-ESTEEM ACROSS THE LIFESPAN

As we go through life, our self-esteem inevitably waxes and wanes. These fluctuations in self-esteem reflect changes in our social environment as well as maturational changes such as puberty and cognitive declines in old age. When these changes are experienced by most individuals at about the same age and influence individuals in a similar manner, they will produce normative shifts in self-esteem across developmental periods.

The findings from three recent studies—a meta-analysis of 86 published articles (Trzesniewski, Donnellan, & Robins, 2001; see also Twenge & Campbell, 2001); a large, cross-sectional study of individuals aged 9 to 90 (Robins, Trzesniewski, Tracy, Gosling, & Potter, 2002); and a cohort-sequential longitudinal study of individuals aged 25 to 96 (Trzesniewski & Robins, 2004)—paint a portrait of the normative trajectory of self-esteem across the lifespan (see Fig. 1). Below, we summarize the major changes that occur from childhood to old age.

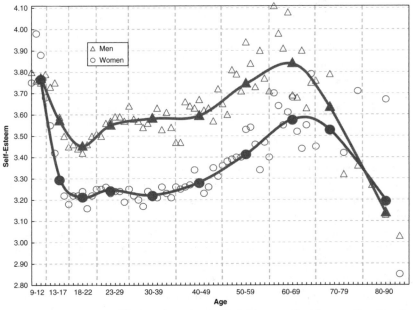

Fig. 1. Mean level of self-esteem for males and females across the lifespan. Also plotted are year-by-year means, separately for males (open triangles) and females (open circles). From "Global Self-Esteem Across the Lifespan," by R.W. Robins, K.H. Trzesniewski, J.L. Tracy, S.D. Gosling, and J. Potter, 2002, *Psychology and Aging, 17*, p. 428. Copyright 2002 by the American Psychological Association. Reprinted with permisson.

Childhood

Young children have relatively high self-esteem, which gradually declines over the course of childhood. Researchers have speculated that children have high self-esteem because their self-views are unrealistically positive. As children develop cognitively, they begin to base their self-evaluations on external feedback and social comparisons, and thus form a more balanced and accurate appraisal of their academic competence, social skills, attractiveness, and other personal characteristics. For example, as children move from preschool to elementary school they receive more negative feedback from teachers, parents, and peers, and their self-evaluations correspondingly become more negative.

Adolescence

Self-esteem continues to decline during adolescence. Researchers have attributed the adolescent decline to body image and other problems associated with puberty, the emerging capacity to think abstractly about one's self and one's future and therefore to acknowledge missed opportunities and failed expectations, and the transition from grade school to the more academically challenging and socially complex context of junior high school.

Adulthood

Self-esteem increases gradually throughout adulthood, peaking sometime around the late 60s. Over the course of adulthood, individuals increasingly occupy positions of power and status, which might promote feelings of self-worth. Many lifespan theorists have suggested that midlife is characterized by peaks in achievement, mastery, and control over self and environment (e.g., Erikson, 1985). Consistent with these theoretical speculations, the personality changes that occur during adulthood tend to reflect increasing levels of maturity and adjustment, as indicated by higher levels of conscientiousness and emotional stability (Trzesniewski, Robins, Roberts, & Caspi, 2004).

Old Age

Self-esteem declines in old age. The few studies of self-esteem in old age suggest that self-esteem begins to drop around age 70 (about the age when Michelangelo began working on the Florentine Pietà). This decline may be due to the dramatic confluence of changes that occur in old age, including changes in roles (e.g., retirement), relationships (e.g., the loss of a spouse), and physical functioning (e.g., health problems), as well as a drop in socioeconomic status. The old-age decline may also reflect a shift toward a more modest, humble, and balanced view of the self in old age (Erikson, 1985). That is, older individuals may maintain a deep-seated sense of their own worth, but their self-esteem scores drop because they are increasingly willing to acknowledge their faults and limitations and have a diminished need to present themselves in a positive light to others. Consistent with this interpretation, narcissism tends to decline with age (Foster, Campbell, & Twenge, 2003).

Gender Differences

Overall, males and females follow essentially the same trajectory: For both genders, self-esteem is relatively high in childhood, drops during adolescence, rises gradually throughout adulthood, and then declines in old age. Nonetheless, there are some interesting gender divergences. Although boys and girls report similar levels of self-esteem during childhood, a gender gap emerges by adolescence, such that adolescent boys have higher self-esteem than adolescent girls (Kling, Hyde, Showers, & Buswell, 1999; Robins et al., 2002). This gender gap persists throughout adulthood, and then narrows and perhaps even disappears in old age (Kling et al., 1999; Robins et al., 2002). Researchers have offered numerous explanations for the gender difference, ranging from maturational changes associated with puberty to social-contextual factors associated with the differential treatment of boys and girls in the classroom or gender differences in body image ideals. However, no generally accepted integrative theoretical model exists.

RANK-ORDER STABILITY OF SELF-ESTEEM

Over the past several decades, researchers have debated the degree to which self-esteem should be thought of as a trait-like construct that remains relatively stable over time or as a state-like process that continually fluctuates in response to environmental and situational stimuli. If self-esteem is more state-like over the long term than other personality characteristics, then it may not be a useful predictor of important real-world outcomes.

The findings of a recent meta-analysis support the claim that self-esteem is a stable, trait-like construct (Trzesniewski, Donnellan, & Robins, 2003). The stability of self-esteem across all age groups, as determined by test-retest correlations, is comparable to that of the major dimensions of personality, including Extraversion, Agreeableness, Conscientiousness, Neuroticism, and Openness to Experience (Roberts & DelVecchio, 2000). Thus, individuals who have relatively high self-esteem at one point in time tend to have high self-esteem years later; likewise those with low self-esteem earlier in life tend to have low self-esteem later.

However, self-esteem is more stable in some periods of life than in others. Stability is relatively low during early childhood, increases throughout adolescence and early adulthood, and then declines during midlife and old age. This curvilinear trend holds for men and women, for U.S. and non-U.S. participants, and for different self-esteem scales.

The lower levels of stability found during childhood and old age may reflect the dramatic life changes, shifting social circumstances, and relatively rapid maturational changes that characterize both the beginning and end of life. For example, during old age, important life events such as retirement and becoming a grandparent may transform one's sense of self, producing higher levels of self-esteem in some individuals and lower levels in others. These life events can lead to lower levels of self-esteem stability if they are experienced at different ages (e.g., some people retire earlier than others) or differentially affect individuals (e.g., only some retirees decline in self-esteem). Moreover, Erikson (1985) noted

that as individuals grow older they begin to review their lifelong accomplishments and experiences, leading in some cases to more critical self-appraisals
(ego despair) and in other cases to increased self-acceptance (ego integrity).
Thus, a developmental shift toward greater self-reflection in old age may produce
increases in self-esteem for some individuals but decreases for others.

IMPLICATIONS

Until recently, the self-esteem literature had been caught in a quagmire of conflicting findings and there was little agreement about the way self-esteem develops. The research reviewed in this article will hopefully move the field toward
consensus, and help address questions such as: When in the lifespan is self-
esteem relatively high or low? Is self-esteem more like a state (relatively transi-
tory) or more like a trait (relatively unchanging)?

Understanding the trajectory of self-esteem may provide insights into the
underlying processes that shape self-esteem development. For example, the fact
that self-esteem drops during both adolescence and old age suggests that there
might be something common to both periods (e.g., the confluence of multiple
social and physical changes) that negatively affects self-esteem.

Knowledge about self-esteem development also has implications for the timing of interventions. For example, the normative trajectory of self-esteem across the
lifespan suggests that interventions should be timed for pre- or early adolescence
because by late adolescence much of the drop in self-esteem has already occurred.
Moreover, developmental periods during which rank-order stability is relatively low
may be ideal targets of intervention programs because self-esteem may be particularly malleable during these times of relative upheaval in the self-concept.

CONCLUSIONS AND FUTURE DIRECTIONS

Research accumulating over the past several years paints an increasingly clear
picture of the trajectory of self-esteem across the lifespan. Self-esteem shows
remarkable continuity given the vast array of experiences that impinge upon a
lived life. At the same time, self-esteem also shows systematic changes that are
meaningfully connected to age-related life experiences and contexts. These normative changes illustrate the role of the self as an organizing psychological construct that influences how individuals orient their behavior to meet new
demands in their environment and new developmental challenges.

Several difficult but tractable issues remain. First, some of the findings
reported here require further replication and exploration. In particular, relatively
few studies have documented the decline in self-esteem during old age. Establishing the robustness of this effect is important given inconsistent findings in
the literature about whether emotional well-being and other aspects of adjustment drop during old age (Mroczek, 2001). In addition, a more fine-grained
analysis of age trends might reveal important fluctuations (e.g., changes from
early to late adulthood) that were obscured in the present studies.

Second, although the methodological quality of self-esteem research has
increased dramatically over the past decade, there is still room for improvement.

Greater attention should be paid to measurement issues, including analyses of whether self-esteem scales show different forms of measurement invariance (e.g., does the meaning of self-esteem items vary across age groups?). The use of more representative samples would increase the generalizability of the findings and allow for a deeper exploration into the potential moderating effects of gender, race, ethnicity, and social class. Sophisticated statistical models should be used to better understand dynamic, reciprocal causal influences (e.g., is self-esteem a cause or consequence of important life experiences; e.g., Ferrer & McArdle, 2003). Cohort-sequential longitudinal studies, in which individuals from different age groups are followed over time, are needed to tease apart aging and cohort effects (e.g., will all older individuals develop lower self-esteem or just the particular cohort of individuals who experienced the Great Depression and other life events unique to that cohort?). Finally, genetically informed designs are needed to explore the mutual influence of nature and nurture on self-esteem development; researchers have yet to appreciate the profound implications of the finding that global self-esteem, like most traits, has a genetic basis (e.g., McGuire et al., 1999).

Third, research is needed on the mediating mechanisms underlying self-esteem change. Chronological age has no causal force per se. We need to understand what else changes with age that might produce changes in self-esteem at different developmental periods. One approach is to document the social-contextual factors associated with chronological age, such as the key social roles and events that define and shape one's position in the life course. However, it is important to recognize that such factors can only influence self-esteem through intrapsychic mechanisms, such as perceptions of control and agency and feelings of pride and shame, which shape the way people react to and internalize the events that occur in their lives. In our view, the best way to understand self-esteem development is to understand the self-evaluative mechanisms that drive the self system—that is, the cognitive and affective processes presumed to play a role in how self-evaluations are formed, maintained, and changed. Although experimental studies have linked a number of self-evaluative processes to short-term changes in self-evaluation, we know little about the influence of such processes on self-esteem change over long periods of time. Lifespan research on the self should draw on this experimental work to develop hypotheses about long-term change in self-esteem and explore how self-evaluative processes documented in the lab play out in real-world contexts.

Finally, the literature on self-esteem development lacks an overarching theoretical framework. Most past theoretical work has focused on particular developmental periods (e.g., the transition to adolescence) and particular life domains (e.g., work). Consequently, although the literature has generated a laundry list of possible reasons why self-esteem might drop during adolescence (and why this might be particularly true for girls), there is no integrative model of how the various proposed processes work together to shape self-esteem development. We also do not know whether these same processes can be invoked to account for the drop in self-esteem during old age. Given the complexity of self-esteem development, such a model would necessarily incorporate biological, social, and psychological factors; account for reciprocal and dynamic causal influences; and include mechanisms of continuity as well as change (e.g., various forms of person–environment interaction). Our hope is that, by examining patterns of findings across developmental contexts (childhood to old age) and across life domains (work, relationships, health), the field will move toward an overarching theory of the life-course trajectory of self-esteem.

Recommended Reading

Harter, S. (1999). *The construction of the self: A developmental perspective.* New York: Guilford.
Robins, R.W., Trzesniewski, K.H., Tracy, J.L., Gosling, S.D., & Potter, J. (2002). (See References)
Trzesniewski, K.H., Donnellan, M.B., & Robins, R.W. (2003). (See References)

Acknowledgments—This research was supported by Grant AG022057 from the National Institute of Aging.

Notes

1. Address correspondence to Richard W. Robins, Department of Psychology, University of California, Davis, CA 95616-8686; e-mail: rwrobins@ucdavis.edu.
2. The focus of this article is on explicit (i.e., conscious) global evaluations of self-worth, not implicit (i.e., unconscious) or domain-specific (e.g., math ability) self-evaluations.
3. These two forms of change are conceptually and statistically distinct. Individuals in a sample could increase substantially in self-esteem but the rank ordering of individuals would be maintained if everyone increased by the same amount. Similarly, the rank ordering of individuals could change substantially over time without producing any aggregate increases or decreases (e.g., if the number of people who decreased offset the number of people who increased).

References

Erikson, E.H. (1985). *The life cycle completed: A review.* New York: W.W. Norton.
Ferrer, E., & McArdle, J.J. (2003). Alternative structural models for multivariate longitudinal data analysis. *Structural Equation Modeling, 10,* 493–524.
Foster, J.D., Campbell, W.K., & Twenge, J.M. (2003). Individual differences in narcissism: Inflated self-views across the lifespan and around the world. *Journal of Research in Personality, 37,* 469–486.
Kling, K.C., Hyde, J.S., Showers, C.J., & Buswell, B.N. (1999). Gender differences in self-esteem: A meta-analysis. *Psychological Bulletin, 125,* 470–500.
McGuire, S., Manke, B., Saudino, K., Reiss, D., Hetherington, E.M., & Plomin, R. (1999). Perceived competence and self-worth during adolescence: A longitudinal behavioral genetic study. *Child Development, 70,* 1283–1296.
Mroczek, D.K. (2001). Age and emotion in adulthood. *Current Directions in Psychological Science, 10,* 87–90.
Roberts, B.W., & DelVecchio, W.F. (2000). The rank-order consistency of personality from childhood to old age: A quantitative review of longitudinal studies. *Psychological Bulletin, 126,* 3–25.
Robins, R.W., Trzesniewski, K.H., Tracy, J.L., Gosling, S.D., & Potter, J. (2002). Global self-esteem across the lifespan. *Psychology and Aging, 17,* 423–434.
Trzesniewski, K.H., Donnellan, M.B., & Robins, R.W. (2001, April). *Self-esteem across the life span: A meta-analysis.* Poster session presented at the biennial meeting of the Society for Research on Child Development, Minneapolis, MN.

Trzesniewski, K.H., Donnellan, M.B., & Robins, R.W. (2003). Stability of self-esteem across the lifespan. *Journal of Personality and Social Psychology, 84,* 205–220.

Trzesniewski, K.H., & Robins, R.W. (2004). *A cohort-sequential study of self-esteem from age 25 to 96.* Poster presented at the Society for Personality and Social Psychology. Austin, Texas.

Trzesniewski, K.H., Robins, R.W., Roberts, B.W., & Caspi, A. (2004). Personality and self-esteem development across the lifespan. In P.T. Costa, Jr. & I.C. Siegler (Eds), *Recent advances in psychology and aging* (pp. 163–185). Amsterdam, the Netherlands: Elsevier.

Twenge, J.M., & Campbell, W.K. (2001). Age and birth cohort differences in self-esteem: A cross-temporal meta-analysis. *Personality and Social Psychology Review, 5,* 321–344.

This article has been reprinted as it originally appeared in *Current Directions in Psychological Science*. Citation information for this article as originally published appears above.

Gender Differences in Depression

Susan Nolen-Hoeksema[1]
Department of Psychology, University of Michigan,
Ann Arbor, Michigan

Abstract

From early adolescence through adulthood, women are twice as likely as men to experience depression. Many different explanations for this gender difference in depression have been offered, but none seems to fully explain it. Recent research has focused on gender differences in stress responses, and in exposure to certain stressors. I review this research and describe how gender differences in stress experiences and stress reactivity may interact to create women's greater vulnerability to depression.

Keywords

gender; depression; stress

Across many nations, cultures, and ethnicities, women are about twice as likely as men to develop depression (Nolen-Hoeksema, 1990; Weissman et al., 1996). This is true whether depression is indexed as a diagnosed mental disorder or as subclinical symptoms. Diagnosable depressive disorders are extraordinarily common in women, who have a lifetime prevalence for major depressive disorder of 21.3%, compared with 12.7% in men (Kessler, McGonagle, Swartz, Blazer, & Nelson, 1993).

Most explanations for the gender difference in depression have focused on individual variables, and studies have attempted to show that one variable is better than another in explaining the difference. In three decades of research, however, no one variable has single-handedly accounted for the gender difference in depression. In recent years, investigators have moved toward more integrated models, taking a transactional, developmental approach. Transactional models are appropriate because it is clear that depression impairs social and occupational functioning, and thus can have a major impact on an individual's environment. Developmental models are appropriate because age groups differ markedly in the gender difference in depression. Girls are no more likely than boys to evidence depression in childhood, but by about age 13, girls' rates of depression begin to increase sharply, whereas boys' rates of depression remain low, and may even decrease. By late adolescence, girls are twice as likely as boys to be depressed, and this gender ratio remains more or less the same throughout adulthood. The absolute rates of depression in women and men vary substantially across the life span, however.

In this review, I focus on two themes in recent research. First, because women have less power and status than men in most societies, they experience certain traumas, particularly sexual abuse, more often than men. They also experience more chronic strains, such as poverty, harassment, lack of respect, and constrained choices. Second, even when women and men experience the same stressors, women may be more likely than men to develop depression because of gender differences in biological responses to stressors, self-concepts, or coping styles.

Frequent stressful experiences and reactivity to stress are likely to have reciprocal effects on each other. Stressful experiences can sensitize both biological and psychological systems to future stress, making it more likely that individuals will react with depression. In turn, reactivity to stress is associated with impaired problem solving, and, as a result, with the accumulation or generation of new stressors, which may contribute to more depression.

STRESSFUL LIFE EVENTS

Women's lack of social power makes them more vulnerable than men to specific major traumas, particularly sexual abuse. Traumas may contribute directly to depression, by making women feel they are helpless to control their lives, and may also contribute indirectly, by increasing women's reactivity to stress. Women's social roles also carry a number of chronic strains that might contribute directly or indirectly to depression. Major changes in the frequency of traumatic events and in social roles coincide with the emergence of gender differences in depression in adolescence, and may help to explain this emergence.

Victimization

Women are the victims of sexual assault—defined as being pressured or forced into unwanted sexual contact—at least twice as often as men, and people with a history of sexual assault have increased rates of depression (see Weiss, Longhurst, & Mazure, 1999). Sexual assault during childhood has been more consistently linked with the gender difference in depression than sexual assault that first occurs during adulthood. Estimates of the prevalence of childhood sexual assault range widely. Cutler and I reviewed the most methodologically sound studies including both male and female participants and found rates of childhood sexual assault between 7 and 19% for females and between 3 and 7% for males (Cutler & Nolen-Hoeksema, 1991). We estimated that, in turn, as much as 35% of the gender difference in adult depression could be accounted for by the higher incidence of assault of girls relative to boys. A few studies have examined whether depression might be an antecedent rather than a consequence of sexual assault. Depression does appear to increase risk for sexual assault in women and men, but sexual assault significantly increases risk for first or new onsets of depression.

Childhood sexual assault may increase risk for depression throughout the life span because abuse experiences negatively alter biological and psychological responses to stress (Weiss et al., 1999). Children and adolescents who have been abused, particularly those who have been repeatedly abused over an extended period of time, tend to have poorly regulated biological response to stress. Abuse experiences can also negatively alter children's and adolescents' perspectives on themselves and others, contributing to their vulnerability to depression (Zahn-Waxler, 2000).

Chronic Strains

Women face a number of chronic burdens in everyday life as a result of their social status and roles relative to men, and these strains could contribute to their higher rates of depression (see Nolen-Hoeksema, 1990). Women make less money than men, and are much more likely than men to live in poverty. Women are more likely than men to be sexually harassed on the job. Women often have full-time paid jobs and also do nearly all the child care and domestic work of the home. In addition, women are increasingly "sandwiched" between caring for young children and caring for sick and elderly family members. This role overload is said to contribute to a sense of "burn out" and general distress, including depressive symptoms, in women.

In the context of heterosexual relationships, some women face inequities in the distribution of power over important decisions that must be made, such as the decision to move to a new city, or the decision to buy an expensive item such as a car (Nolen-Hoeksema, Larson, & Grayson, 1999). Even when they voice their opinions, women may feel these opinions are not taken seriously, or that their viewpoints on important issues are not respected and affirmed by their partners. My colleagues and I measured chronic strain by grouping inequities in workload and heterosexual relationships into a single variable, and found that this variable predicted increases in depression over time, and partially accounted for the gender difference in depression (Nolen-Hoeksema et al., 1999). Depression also contributed to increased chronic strain over time, probably because it was associated with reductions in perceptions of control and effective problem solving.

Gender Intensification in Adolescence

Social pressure to conform to gender roles is thought to increase dramatically as children move through puberty. For girls, this may mean a reduction in their opportunities and choices, either real or perceived. According to adolescents' own reports, parents restrict girls' more than boys' behaviors and have lower expectations for girls' than for boys' competencies and achievements. Girls also feel that if they pursue male-stereotyped activities and preferences, such as interests in math and science or in competitive sports, they are rejected by their peers. For many girls, especially white girls, popularity and social acceptance become narrowly oriented around appearance.

This narrowing of acceptable behavior for girls in early adolescence may contribute to the increase in depression in girls at this time, although this popular theory has been the focus of remarkably little empirical research (Nolen-Hoeksema & Girgus, 1994). There is substantial evidence that excessive concern about appearance is negatively associated with well-being in girls, but these findings may apply primarily to white girls. In addition, very little research has examined whether appearance concerns and gender roles are risk factors for depression or only correlates.

REACTIVITY TO STRESS

Even when women and men are confronted with similar stressors, women may be more vulnerable than men to developing depression and related anxiety disorders such as posttraumatic stress disorder (Breslau, Davis, Andreski, Peterson, & Schultz, 1997). Women's greater reactivity compared with men's has been attributed to gender differences in biological responses, self-concepts, and coping styles.

Biological Responses to Stress

For many years, the biological explanations for women's greater vulnerability to depression focused on the direct effects of the ovarian hormones (especially estrogen and progesterone) on women's moods. This literature is too large and complicated to review here (but see Nolen-Hoeksema, 1990, 1995). Simply put, despite widespread popular belief that women are more prone to depression than men because of direct negative effects of estrogen or progesterone on mood, there is little consistent scientific evidence to support this belief. Although some women do become depressed during periods of hormonal change, including puberty, the premenstrual period of the menstrual cycle, menopause, and the postpartum period, it is unclear that these depressions are due to the direct effects of hormonal changes on mood, or that depressions during these periods of women's lives account for the gender differences in rates of depression.

More recent biological research has focused not on direct effects of ovarian hormones on moods, but on the moderating effects of hormones, particularly adrenal hormones, on responses to stress. The hypothalamic-pituitary-adrenal (HPA) axis plays a major role in regulating stress responses, in part by regulating levels of a number of hormones, including cortisol, which is released by the adrenal glands in response to chemicals secreted by the brain's hypothalamus and then the pituitary. In turn, cortisol levels can affect other biochemicals known to influence moods. People with major depressive disorder often show elevated cortisol responses to stress, indicating dysregulation of the HPA response.

An intriguing hypothesis is that women are more likely than men to have a dysregulated HPA response to stress, which makes them more likely to develop depression in response to stress (Weiss et al., 1999). Women may be more likely to have a dysregulated HPA response because they are more likely to have suffered traumatic events, which are known to contribute to HPA dysregulation. In addition, ovarian hormones modulate regulation of the HPA axis (Young & Korszun, 1999). Some women may have depressions during periods of rapid change in levels of ovarian hormones (the postpartum period, premenstrual period, menopause, and puberty) because hormonal changes trigger dysregulation of the stress response, making these women more vulnerable to depression, particularly when they are confronted with stress. The causal relationship between HPA axis regulation and the gender difference in depression has not been established but is likely to be a major focus of future research.

Self-Concept

Although the idea that girls have more negative self-concepts than boys is a mainstay of the pop-psychology literature, empirical studies testing this hypothesis have produced mixed results (Nolen-Hoeksema & Girgus, 1994). Several studies have found no gender differences in self-esteem, self-concept, or dysfunctional attitudes. Those studies that do find gender differences, however, tend to show that girls have poorer self-concepts than boys. Again, negative self-concepts could contribute directly to depression, and could interact with stressors to contribute to depression. Negative self-concept has been shown to predict increases in depression in some studies of children (Nolen-Hoeksema & Girgus, 1994).

One consistent difference in males' and females' self-concepts concerns interpersonal orientation, the tendency to be concerned with the status of one's relationships and the opinions others hold of oneself. Even in childhood, girls appear more interpersonally oriented than boys, and this gender difference increases in adolescence (Zahn-Waxler, 2000). When interpersonal orientation leads girls and women to subordinate their own needs and desires completely to those of others, they become excessively dependent on the good graces of others (Cyranowski, Frank, Young, & Shear, 2000). They may then be at high risk for depression when conflicts arise in relationships, or relationships end. Several recent studies have shown that girls and women are more likely than boys and men to develop depression in response to interpersonal stressors. Because depression can also interfere with interpersonal functioning, an important topic for future research is whether the gender difference in depression is a consequence or cause of gender differences in interpersonal strain.

Coping Styles

By adolescence, girls appear to be more likely than boys to respond to stress and distress with rumination—focusing inward on feelings of distress and personal concerns rather than taking action to relieve their distress. This gender difference in rumination then is maintained throughout adulthood. Several longitudinal and experimental studies have shown that people who ruminate in response to stress are at increased risk to develop depressive symptoms and depressive disorders over time (Nolen-Hoeksema et al., 1999). In turn, the gender difference in rumination at least partially accounts for the gender difference in depression. Rumination may not only contribute directly to depression, but may also contribute indirectly by impairing problem solving, and thus preventing women from taking action to overcome the stressors they face.

AN INTEGRATIVE MODEL

Women suffer certain stressors more often than men and may be more vulnerable to develop depression in response to stress because of a number of factors. Both stress experiences and stress reactivity contribute directly to women's greater rates of depression compared with men. Stress experiences and stress reactivity also feed on each other, however. The more stress women suffer, the more hyperresponsive they may be to stress, both biologically and psychologically. This hyperresponsiveness may undermine women's ability to control their environments and overcome their stress, leading to even more stress in the future. In addition, depression contributes directly to more stressful experiences, by interfering with occupational and social functioning, and to vulnerability to stress, by inciting rumination, robbing the individual of any sense of mastery she did have, and possibly sensitizing the biological systems involved in the stress response.

Important advances will be made in explaining the gender difference in depression as we understand better the reciprocal effects of biological, social, and psychological systems on each other. Key developmental transitions, particularly the early adolescent years, are natural laboratories for observing the establishment of these processes, because so much changes during these transitions, and these transitions are times of increased risk.

Additional questions for future research include how culture and ethnicity affect the gender difference in depression. The gender difference is found across most cultures and ethnicities, but its size varies considerably, as do the absolute percentages of depressed women and men. The processes contributing to the gender difference in depression may also vary across cultures and ethnicities.

Understanding the gender difference in depression is important for at least two reasons. First, women's high rates of depression exact tremendous costs in quality of life and productivity, for women themselves and their families. Second, understanding the gender difference in depression will help us to understand the causes of depression in general. In this way, gender provides a valuable lens through which to examine basic human processes in psychopathology.

Recommended Reading

Cyranowski, J.M., Frank, E., Young, E., & Shear, K. (2000). (See References)
Nolen-Hoeksema, S. (1990). (See References)
Nolen-Hoeksema, S., & Girgus, J.S. (1994). (See References)
Nolen-Hoeksema, S., Larson, J., & Grayson, C. (1999). (See References)
Young, E., & Korszun, A. (1999). (See References)

Note

1. Address correspondence to Susan Nolen-Hoeksema, Department of Psychology, University of Michigan, 525 E. University Ave., Ann Arbor, MI 48109; e-mail: nolen@umich.edu.

References

Breslau, N., Davis, G.C., Andreski, P., Peterson, E.L., & Schultz, L. (1997). Sex differences in post-traumatic stress disorder. *Archives of General Psychiatry, 54*, 1044–1048.
Cutler, S., & Nolen-Hoeksema, S. (1991). Accounting for sex differences in depression through female victimization: Childhood sexual abuse. *Sex Roles, 24*, 425–438.
Cyranowski, J.M., Frank, E., Young, E., & Shear, K. (2000). Adolescent onset of the gender difference in lifetime rates of major depression. *Archives of General Psychiatry, 57*, 21–27.
Kessler, R.C., McGonagle, K.A., Swartz, M., Blazer, D.G., & Nelson, C.B. (1993). Sex and depression in the National Comorbidity Survey I: Lifetime prevalence, chronicity, and recurrence. *Journal of Affective Disorders, 29*, 85–96.
Nolen-Hoeksema, S. (1990). *Sex differences in depression*. Stanford, CA: Stanford University Press.
Nolen-Hoeksema, S. (1995). Gender differences in coping with depression across the lifespan. *Depression, 3*, 81–90.
Nolen-Hoeksema, S., & Girgus, J.S. (1994). The emergence of gender differences in depression in adolescence. *Psychological Bulletin, 115*, 424–443.
Nolen-Hoeksema, S., Larson, J., & Grayson, C. (1999). Explaining the gender difference in depression. *Journal of Personality and Social Psychology, 77*, 1061–1072.
Weiss, E.L., Longhurst, J.G., & Mazure, C.M. (1999). Childhood sexual abuse as a risk factor for depression in women: Psychosocial and neurobiological correlates. *American Journal of Psychiatry, 156*, 816–828.
Weissman, M.M., Bland, R.C., Canino, G.J., Faravelli, C., Greenwald, S., Hwu, H.-G., Joyce, P.R., Karam, E.G., Lee, C.-K., Lellouch, J., Lepine, J.-P., Newman, S.C., Rubio-Stipc, M., Wells, E.,

Wickramaratne, P.J., Wittchen, H.-U., & Yeh, E.-K. (1996). Cross-national epidemiology of major depression and bipolar disorder. *Journal of the American Medical Association, 276,* 293–299.

Young, E., & Korszun, A. (1999). Women, stress, and depression: Sex differences in hypothalamic-pituitary-adrenal axis regulation. In E. Leibenluft (Ed.), *Gender differences in mood and anxiety disorders: From bench to bedside* (pp. 31–52). Washington, DC: American Psychiatric Press.

Zahn-Waxler, C. (2000). The development of empathy, guilt, and internalization of distress: Implications for gender differences in internalizing and externalizing problems. In R. Davidson (Ed.), *Wisconsin Symposium on Emotion: Vol. 1. Anxiety, depression, and emotion* (pp. 222–265). Oxford, England: Oxford University Press.

Section 5: Critical Thinking Questions

1. What are different ways to measure personality over time? Is one method preferable to another? In which instances might it be more beneficial to examine personality in a given moment in time, rather than across a lifespan?

2. What does it mean to explore mechanisms that explain the association between personality and risk (e.g., depression) and resilience (e.g., health)? What are different models that can be used? Which models do you think are most informative?

3. Is it important to show that men are different from women (e.g., Nolen-Hoeksema, 2001)? Or that those with high self-esteem are different from those with low self-esteem (e.g., Robins and Trzesniewski, 2005)? Provide arguments for and against research that examines such differences.

4. What does Rothbart (2007) mean when she says that, "Temperament and experience together "grow" a personality? Explain.

5. Is personality "fixed"? Discuss the conditions (situation, age, motivation) under which dispositional characteristics may change. Have you ever observed a change in someone's personality? What do you think caused the change? Has your own personality ever changed? Why?

This article has been reprinted as it originally appeared in *Current Directions in Psychological Science*. Citation information for this article as originally published appears above.

Section 6: Social Psychology

How we perceive ourselves in relation to our social world plays an important role in our choices, behaviors, and beliefs. At the same time, the opinions, attitudes, and views of others can have a strong impact on our behavior and the way we view ourselves. Social psychology is the scientific study of how thoughts, emotions, and behaviors are affected by the social environment. While not exhaustive, the articles in this section reflect current trends in the field of social psychology across three main domains: social cognition (how perception, memory, and thinking are influenced by the social environment); interpersonal relations (how people manage their behavior and the behavior of other people); and group dynamics (interactions within and between groups). Together the articles address issues of social influence, social perception, and social interaction.

Taking a social neuroscience perspective, Carnagey, Anderson, and Barthalow (2007) report on different pathways to explain the well-documented relation between media violence and aggression-related outcomes. They report that through the use of neurocognitive tools such as functional magnetic resonance imaging (fMRI), scientists can now examine the effects of violent media exposure on specific neural structures that support processes such as emotional regulation, memory, and executive functioning. In addition to the media, individuals learn about their social world from information that is inherent in a social structure. Bigler & Liben (2007) examine the development of stereotyping and prejudice in young children and theorize that intergroup biases are largely under environmental control. They argue that cultural environments may be explicitly structured to make differences between groups perceptually salient to young children. Sometimes differences between groups are less apparent, however. According to DePaulo and Morris (2006), certain groups are unacknowledged, but are stigmatized nonetheless. They report on the negative stereotypes held against people who are single. In their research, they show that people characterize married and coupled people as mature, stable, happy, and loving. In contrast, single people are characterized as immature, maladjusted, lonely, and self-centered. In their article, the authors speculate on possible explanations for "singlism." Other areas of social psychology examine the differences between automatic and controlled processes. Although we believe that much of our social behavior is under our control, research shows that much of our behavior may actually be unconsciously driven by situational cues. Bargh and Williams (2006) review research showing that things in our environment that are outside of our conscious awareness can affect our perceptions of others, our behaviors, and our social relationships. There are positive and negative consequences of automaticity in social life. In the final article of this section, Payne (2006) discusses a phenomenon called "weapon bias," wherein race stereotypes can lead people to claim to see a weapon (e.g., the person is holding a gun) where there is none (e.g., the person is actually holding a cell phone). His paper provides some interesting speculations of why people intentionally and unintentionally use stereotypes in their decisions.

Media Violence and Social Neuroscience: New Questions and New Opportunities

Nicholas L. Carnagey[1]
Wake Forest University

Craig A. Anderson
Center for the Study of Violence, Iowa State University

Bruce D. Bartholow
University of Missouri–Columbia

Abstract

Decades of research have demonstrated that exposure to violence on television can cause increases in aggression. The recent emergence of violent video games has raised new questions regarding the effects of violent media. The General Aggression Model (GAM) predicts that exposure to violent media increases aggressive behavior through one of three primary pathways (arousal, cognitions, and affect). Past psychophysiological research has supported GAM but has been limited to examining arousal-related variables. Recent advances in social neuroscience have opened the door to investigations of exposure to violent media on cognitive and affective components and their neurocognitive underpinnings. Neuroscience tools have the potential to provide answers to the new questions posed by recent advances in media technology.

Keywords

aggression; brain imaging; fMRI; media violence; violent video games

It is no secret that we are surrounded by electronic media. In a matter of years, through the development of the Internet, satellite television, cell phones, iPods, and video game systems, entertainment media have become more available than ever. As media technology has advanced, the amount of time that children and adolescents spend with it has increased. On average, American children now spend more than 5 hours a day consuming screen media (television, films, video games)—nearly as much time as they spend in school. Similar increases in media consumption have been reported in Europe and Asia. In addition, the most popular screen media consumed by children and adolescents contain considerable amounts of violence (Anderson et al., 2003). Such high levels of exposure to violent media in modern society have led to a combination of scientific intrigue and public concern. Although media technology is arguably causing changes in society at a faster pace than scientists can examine it, other technological advancements are benefiting the scientists' cause. Recent developments in neuroscience have allowed scientists to understand the interaction between the psychological and physiological mechanisms like never before. This article reviews the findings of past research on violent media and explores how the development of violent video games presents social scientists with new empirical questions, as well as how developments in social neuroscience can provide novel approaches to address those questions.

VIOLENT MEDIA EXPOSURE AND AGGRESSION

Children's exposure to violent media (e.g., television, movies, music, video games) has been a social concern for decades. For example, news reports linked Clint Eastwood's "Dirty Harry" film character to copycat killings involving forced ingestion of Drano. More recently, violent video games have been linked to numerous school killings (e.g., Columbine High School) and other violent crime sprees (e.g., in California, Michigan, Minnesota, and Ohio). Most studies examining violent media have focused on the effects of violent television and movies on viewers' aggression. The most recent comprehensive review of the effects of violent media found "unequivocal evidence that media violence increases the likelihood of aggressive and violent behavior in both immediate and long-term contexts" (Anderson et al., 2003, p. 81). Figure 1 (originally from the Anderson et al. review), shows that violent media are linked to increased aggression, regardless of the type of study design used to investigate its effects.

Although comparably fewer studies have specifically focused on violent video games, existing research demonstrates that they also cause increases in aggressive behavior (e.g., Anderson et al., 2004). For example, one recent experiment (Anderson, Gentile, & Buckley, 2007) found that brief exposure to a violent

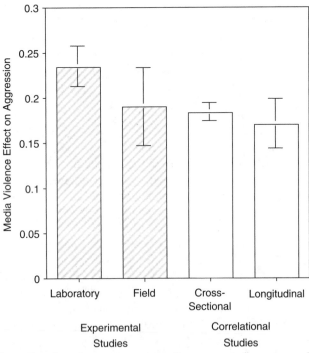

Fig. 1. Effects of media violence on aggression for two types of experimental studies and two types of correlational studies. Effect sizes are presented in terms of r (correlation coefficient). Vertical capped bars indicate 95% confidence intervals. Because the bars do not include the zero line, the effect of media violence on aggression is statistically significant for each type of study. This figure originally appeared in Anderson et al. (2003).

children's video game increased delivery of high-intensity noise blasts to an opponent by over 40%. This effect occurred for elementary school children and for college students.

Beyond these basic findings, violent video games have presented scientists with a host of new questions. Video games are a qualitatively different form of media than television and film, primarily because video games are more interactive and immersive. Players of violent video games actually engage in virtual violent actions, receive direct rewards for those actions, closely identify with the characters they control, and actively rehearse aggressive behavioral scripts.

GENERAL AGGRESSION MODEL

There also are strong theoretical reasons to believe that exposure to violent media can increase aggression-related outcomes. The General Aggression Model (GAM; see Fig. 2) is an integration of several prior models of aggression (e.g., social learning theory, social cognitive theory, cognitive neoassociation, excitation transfer; see Anderson & Carnagey, 2004). Although GAM is not specifically a model of media effects, it is easily applied to this domain. Theoretically, violent media could affect

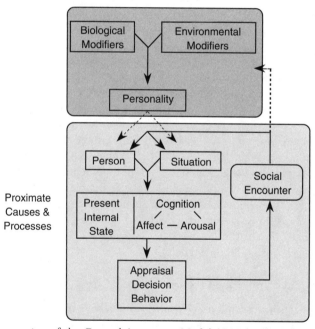

Fig. 2. An overview of the General Aggression Model (GAM). GAM describes how a cyclical pattern of interaction between personal factors (e.g., knowledge structures, trait aggression) and situational factors (e.g., provocation, recent exposure to violent media) influences the likelihood of aggressive behavior in the current situation and the development of aggressive personality over time. These input variables influence behavior ultimately by affecting decision processes through three primary routes: cognitive, affective, and physiological arousal. Although GAM is a comprehensive model of aggression, its theoretical constructs can be specifically applied to the effects of violent media.

one, two, or all three aspects of a person's present internal state. Recent research has demonstrated that violent video games can temporarily increase aggressive thoughts, aggressive affect, and physiological arousal (e.g., Anderson et al., 2004), and can reduce arousal to subsequent depictions of violence (e.g., Carnagey, Anderson, & Bushman, 2007). Exposure to violent media can increase aggressive behavior by influencing any combination of these internal states.

PHYSIOLOGICAL CONSEQUENCES OF MEDIA-VIOLENCE EXPOSURE

Media Violence and Arousal-Related Variables

Media-violence researchers have long used physiological tools to better understand the relationship between violence exposure and aggression. Most of this research has focused on the potential effects of violent media on arousal. Numerous models have linked physiological arousal with human aggression. For example, excitation transfer theory (e.g., Zillmann, 1983) states that arousal elicited by external sources (e.g., exercise) may be misattributed as anger in situations involving provocation and may thereby increase the chances of producing anger-motivated aggressive behavior. Recent meta-analyses have demonstrated that playing violent video games can increase physiological arousal and anger (e.g., Anderson et al., 2004). Thus, one route by which playing violent video games can increase aggression is through increased physiological arousal.

In addition to arousal-facilitated aggression, other research links violent media to physiological desensitization to violence. In this context, physiological desensitization refers to a reduction in physiological reactivity upon later exposure to violence. Most people have an automatic aversive emotional response to scenes of violence, often assessed by changes in heart rate and skin conductance. Such negative emotional responses help inhibit aggressive behavior and inspire helping behavior. Past research has shown that, following exposure to either violent television (e.g., Thomas, Horton, Lippincott, & Drabman, 1977) or to violent video games (Carnagey, Anderson, & Bushman, 2007), participants show reduced skin conductance and heart-rate reactivity when encountering subsequent depictions of real violence. In other words, exposure to virtual violence produces desensitization to actual violence, which has been linked to increased aggression and reduced helping.

Media Violence and Social Neuroscience

Until very recently, research on physiological mechanisms underlying the effect of violent media has been restricted to indicators of arousal. However, most social-cognitive models of human aggression clearly make predictions about cognitive and affective influences on aggression as well. Contemporary measures of physiological responding permit researchers to address the other routes to aggression (i.e., cognitive and affective) depicted in GAM. Through the use of neurocognitive tools such as event-related brain potentials (ERPs) and functional magnetic resonance imaging (fMRI), scientists can now examine the effects of exposure to violent media on specific neural structures that support processes such as emotional regulation, memory storage and retrieval, and executive functioning. These tools eventually will provide a more comprehensive understanding of the impact of violent media on the consumer by giving insight into the interaction between neural and psychological processes.

Although research examining the neurocognitive effects of exposure to violent media is currently scarce, a growing literature is emerging. For example, Bartholow, Bushman, and Sestir (2006) demonstrated that individuals with a history of high exposure to violent video games have different physiological reactions to scenes of real violence than do individuals with a low exposure history. Participants with varying degrees of exposure to violent video games were presented with a series of negative photos, half violent and half nonviolent, included among a set of more numerous neutral photos while ERPs were recorded. ERPs are scalp-recorded voltage fluctuations that represent neural activity associated with various information-processing operations. The P300 component of the ERP, which is a positive voltage deflection occurring approximately 300 to 600 milliseconds after stimulus onset, has been shown to be positively related to activation of the aversive motivational system (e.g., Ito, Larsen, Smith, & Cacioppo, 1998). Results demonstrated that high exposure to violent video games was associated with decreased amplitude of the P300 elicited by images of real violence and that this reduced brain activity predicted increased aggression in a later task. This work extends the concept of violence desensitization to the cognitive domain.

Other emerging evidence demonstrates that different neural regions are activated when one views violent scenes than when one views nonviolent scenes (Murray et al., 2006). Children were shown violent and nonviolent scenes from commercially released movies while fMRI data were collected. Violent scenes activated a network of brain regions (e.g., posterior cingulate cortex, hippocampi) involved in processing emotional stimuli, episodic memory retrieval, detecting threats in the environment, memory encoding, and motor programming. This combination of activation in areas linking memory and emotion to motor activation suggests that viewing media violence could integrate existing aggression-related thoughts and feelings, potentially facilitating aggressive behavior by increasing the strength or accessibility of aggressive behavior scripts in memory.

There is recent evidence that exposure to violent media may be linked to decreases in the activity of brain structures needed for regulation of aggressive behavior and to increases in the activity of structures needed to carry out aggressive plans. The anterior cingulate cortex (ACC), located in the medial frontal lobe, has been linked to aggressive and antisocial behavior (e.g., Sterzer, Stadler, Krelbs, Kleinschmidt, & Poustka, 2003). The ACC appears to be vital for various executive functions, including inhibition, performance monitoring, and possibly error correction, and serves as an interface between cognition (the dorsal ACC) and emotion (the rostral ACC; see Bush, Luu, & Posner, 2000). Recent work by Weber, Ritterfeld, and Mathiak (2006) used fMRI to test potential links between exposure to violent games, ACC activity, and aggression. Participants played a violent video game while fMRI data were collected. Game play was recorded and analyzed frame by frame to determine when participants were engaging in violent and nonviolent actions so that neural activations could be time locked to those actions. Results demonstrated that engaging in virtual violence led to decreased activity in the rostral ACC and increased activity in the dorsal ACC. The rostral ACC results indicate suppression of affective information processing. These results are the first to provide neural evidence distinguishing the impact of exposure to violent media on cognitive and affective processes.

Chronic consumption of violent media has also been linked to suppression of the ACC. In a recent study (Matthews et al., 2005), two groups of adolescents, one with disruptive behavior disorder with aggressive features and a clinically normal group, provided self-report data on their exposure to violent media and then completed a modified Stroop task while fMRI data were collected. In the classic Stroop task, participants respond to the color of printed words. Congruent trials require little executive control because the color and text of the word are the same (e.g., "RED" printed in red type). In contrast, incongruent trials (e.g., "RED" printed in blue type) require executive control to overcome the prepotent tendency to read the word and respond to the written color name. Incongruent Stroop task trials are known to elicit enhanced activity in the ACC (see Botvinick, Braver, Barch, Carter, & Cohen, 2001). Results from these Stroop tasks demonstrated that both the subjects with disruptive behavior disorder and the clinically normal subset who self-reported high exposure to violent media showed reduced ACC function in comparison with clinically normal subjects who self-reported low exposure to violent media.

Taken together, the results reported by Weber et al. (2006) and Matthews et al. (2005) form an important bridge linking the perpetration of virtual violence with reduced activation of a neural mechanism known to be important for self-control and for evaluation of affect. These findings strongly suggest that focusing on the activity of prefrontal cortical structures important for executive control could provide important mediational links in the relationship between exposure to violent media and increased aggression.

FUTURE DIRECTIONS: SOCIAL NEUROSCIENCE AND VIOLENT VIDEO GAMES

As this brief review illustrates, recent developments in social neuroscience have the potential to provide more insight into the effects of exposure to violent media by examining the affective and cognitive components of GAM at a neural level. These new advances also have the potential to address numerous unanswered questions. One such unanswered question is whether violent video games have a larger effect on children than on adults. For numerous reasons (e.g., children's brains, particularly the frontal cortex, are not fully developed; children's social scripts are more malleable), the theoretical response would be "yes." However, existing empirical evidence is sparse and unclear. Approaching this question from a social-neuroscience perspective, particularly within the framework of a longitudinal, developmental design, could shed needed light on the neurocognitive systems underlying the effects of violent media as well as on how those systems are shaped, perhaps permanently, by repeated exposure to violent media as the brain develops. Advances in neural-imaging technology also could increase our understanding of the brain structures that are at work (and those that are relatively silent) when someone is intentionally trying to harm another individual and how activations and deactivations in these structures during consumption of violent media relate to aggressive behavior.

Also, neuroimaging tools could assist in testing the causal association between brain activations while engaging in acts of virtual violence and subsequent real-life aggression. Initial results suggest that, although video-game players are aware that they are engaging in fictitious actions, preconscious neural mechanisms might not differentiate fantasy from reality. This suggests that engaging in virtual violence (i.e., playing violent video games) could impact neural systems in a manner comparable with engaging in actual violence. This question remains to be rigorously tested in future brain imaging research.

Finally, a question that has emerged in both the public-policy arena and the scientific community is whether aggression-related variables are affected more by exposure to violent video games than by exposure to violent television. There are a host of theoretical reasons to expect that exposure to violent video games would have a larger impact. From a social-neuroscience perspective, the interactive and immersive nature of violent video games could more strongly engage neural systems associated with activation of aggressive behavioral scripts and could more strongly suppress executive structures that would normally inhibit aggressive and violent actions. Neuroimaging tools could provide unique insight regarding the neural impact of exposure to passive television violence in comparison with exposure to interactive video-game violence. With next-generation media technology becoming more immersive, it is important to understand the impacts of such violent virtual immersion sooner rather than later.

Recommended Reading

Cacioppo, J.T., Berntson, G.G., Sheridan, J.F., & McClintock, M.K. (2000). (See References)
Gentile, D.A. (2003). (See References)
Kirsch, S.J. (2006). (See References)
Roberts, D.F., Foehr, U.G., & Rideout, V. (2005). (See References)

Note

1. Address correspondence to Nicholas L. Carnagey; e-mail: ncarnagey@gmail.com.

References

Anderson, C.A., Berkowitz, L., Donnerstein, E., Huesmann, L.R., Johnson, J., & Linz, D., et al. (2003). The influence of media violence on youth. *Psychological Science in the Public Interest, 4*, 81–110.
Anderson, C.A., & Carnagey, N.L. (2004). Violent evil and the general aggression model. In A. Miller (Ed.), *The social psychology of good and evil* (pp. 168–192). New York: Guilford Press.
Anderson, C.A., Carnagey, N.L., Flanagan, M., Benjamin, A.J., Eubanks, J., & Valentine, J.C. (2004). Violent video games: Specific effects of violent content on aggressive thoughts and behavior. *Advances in Experimental Social Psychology, 36*, 199–249.
Anderson, C.A., Gentile, D.A., & Buckley, K.E. (2007). *Violent video game effects on children and adolescents: Theory, research, and public policy.* New York: Oxford University Press.
Bartholow, B.D., Bushman, B.J., & Sestir, M.A. (2006). Chronic violent video game exposure and desensitization to violence: Behavioral and event-related brain potential data. *Journal of Experimental Social Psychology, 42*, 532–539.

Botvinick, M.M., Braver, T.S., Barch, D.M., Carter, C.S., & Cohen, J.D. (2001). Conflict monitoring and cognitive control. *Psychological Review, 108,* 624–652.

Bush, G., Luu, P., & Posnter, M.I. (2000). Cognitive and emotional influences in anterior cingulate cortex. *Trends in Cognitive Sciences, 4,* 215–222.

Cacioppo, J.T., Berntson, G.G., Sheridan, J.F., & McClintock, M.K. (2000). Multilevel integrative analysis of human behavior: Social neuroscience and the complementing nature of social and biological approaches. *Psychological Bulletin, 126,* 829–843.

Carnagey, N.C., Anderson, C.A., & Bushman, B.J. (2007). The effect of video game violence on physiological desensitization to real-life violence. *Journal of Experimental Social Psychology, 43,* 489–496.

Gentile, D.A. (Ed). (2003). *Media violence and children.* Westport, CT: Praeger.

Ito, T.A., Larsen, J.T., Smith, N.K., & Cacioppo, J.T. (1998). Negative information weighs more heavily on the brain: The negativity bias in evaluative categorizations. *Journal of Personality and Social Psychology, 75,* 887–900.

Kirsh, S.J. (2006). *Children, adolescents, and media violence: A critical look at the research.* Thousand Oaks, CA: Sage Publications.

Matthews, V.P., Kronenberger, W.G., Want, Y., Lurito, J.T., Lowe, M.J., & Dunn, D.W. (2005). Media violence exposure and frontal lobe activation measure by functional magnetic resonance imaging in aggressive and nonaggressive adolescents. *Journal of Computer Assisted Tomography, 29,* 287–292.

Murray, J.P., Liotti, M., Mayberg, H.S., Pu, Y., Zamarripa, F., & Liu, Y., et al. (2006). Children's brain activations while viewing televised violence revealed by fMRI. *Media Psychology, 8,* 25–37.

Roberts, D.F., Foehr, U.G., & Rideout, V. (2005). *Generation M: Media in the lives of 8–18 year-olds.* Menlo Park, CA: Kaiser Family Foundation.

Sterzer, P., Stadler, C., Krebs, A., Kleinschmidt, A., & Poustka, F. (2003). Reduced anterior cingulated activity in adolescents with antisocial conduct disorder confronted with affective pictures. *NeuroImage, 19*(Suppl. 1), 123.

Thomas, M.H., Horton, R.W., Lippincott, E.C., & Drabman, R.S. (1977). Desensitization to portrayals of real life aggression as a function of television violence. *Journal of Personality and Social Psychology, 35,* 450–458.

Weber, R., Ritterfeld, U., & Mathiak, K. (2006). Does playing violent video games induce aggression? Empirical evidence of a functional magnetic resonance imaging study. *Media Psychology, 8,* 39–60.

Zillmann, D. (1983). Arousal and aggression. In R. Geen & E. Donnerstein (Eds.), *Aggression: Theoretical and empirical reviews* (Vol. 1, pp. 75–102). New York: Academic Press.

This article has been reprinted as it originally appeared in *Current Directions in Psychological Science*. Citation information for this article as originally published appears above.

Developmental Intergroup Theory: Explaining and Reducing Children's Social Stereotyping and Prejudice

Rebecca S. Bigler[1]

University of Texas at Austin

Lynn S. Liben

The Pennsylvania State University

Abstract

Social stereotyping and prejudice are intriguing phenomena from the standpoint of theory and, in addition, constitute pressing societal problems. Because stereotyping and prejudice emerge in early childhood, developmental research on causal mechanisms is critical for understanding and controlling stereotyping and prejudice. Such work forms the basis of a new theoretical model, developmental intergroup theory (DIT), which addresses the causal ingredients of stereotyping and prejudice. The work suggests that biases may be largely under environmental control and thus might be shaped via educational, social, and legal policies.

Keywords

stereotyping; intergroup; children; prejudice

Young children are often perceived as being untainted by the negative social biases that characterize adults, but many studies reveal that stereotyping and prejudice exist by the age of 4. Contemporary theories explain how cognitive processes predispose children to acquire and maintain social stereotypes and prejudice (see Aboud, 2005; Martin, Ruble, & Szkrybalo, 2002). However, they fail to account for why some dimensions of human variation rather than others (e.g., gender but not handedness) become foundations for social stereotyping and prejudice, and they skirt the issue of whether biases are inevitable and, if not, how they might be prevented. A new theoretical model of social stereotyping and prejudice, *developmental intergroup theory* (DIT; Bigler & Liben, 2006), addresses both these issues. The theory's name reflects its grounding in two complementary theoretical approaches: *intergroup theory,* referring to social identity (Tajfel & Turner, 1986) and self-categorization theories (Turner, Hogg, Oakes, Reicher, & Wetherell, 1987), and *cognitive-developmental theory,* referring to Piagetian and contemporary approaches to cognitive development. We describe empirical foundations and then mechanisms by which children single out groups as targets of stereotyping and prejudice, associate characteristics with groups (i.e., stereotypes), and develop affective responses (i.e., prejudices). Elsewhere (Bigler & Liben, 2006) we focus on how DIT handles developmental differences (e.g., how the development of multiple classification skills during childhood affects stereotyping; see Bigler & Liben, 1992) and individual differences (e.g., the consequences of individual differences in attitudes; see Liben & Signorella, 1980). Here, we focus on how DIT conceptualizes group-level effects.

EMPIRICAL FOUNDATIONS

Causes of stereotypes and prejudice are difficult to study in the everyday world both because messages about social groups are pervasive and because it is impossible or unethical to assign individuals experimentally to most relevant groups (e.g., gender, race, social class). DIT thus draws heavily on research that circumvents these constraints by creating and manipulating *novel* social groups (e.g., Bigler, 1995; Bigler, Jones, & Lobliner, 1997; Bigler, Brown, & Markell, 2001). As in classic intergroup studies, group membership and environmental conditions are experimentally manipulated, permitting conclusions about causal effects of various factors on the development of stereotyping and prejudice.

In a typical study, participants are 6- to 11-year-old summer-school students who are unacquainted with each other when school begins. They are initially given tasks measuring factors (e.g., cognitive-developmental level, self-esteem) hypothesized to affect intergroup attitudes. Novel groups are created, usually by assigning children to wear different colored tee shirts. Characteristics of the groups (e.g., proportional size, purported traits) and their treatment within the classroom (e.g., labeling, segregation) are then manipulated. After several weeks, children's intergroup attitudes are assessed. One study, for example, tested children's intergroup attitudes as a function of adults' labeling and functional use of color groups (Bigler et al., 1997). In experimental classrooms, teachers used color groups to organize classroom desks, bulletin boards, and activities. In control classrooms, teachers ignored the color groups. After several weeks, children completed measures of their perceptions of trait variability within and between color groups, evaluated group competence and performance, and were assessed for behavioral biases and peer preferences. In-group biases developed only in experimental classrooms.

COMPONENT PROCESSES OF DIT

Three core processes (double-bordered rectangles in Fig. 1) are hypothesized to contribute the formation of social stereotyping and prejudice: (a) establishing the psychological salience (EPS) of different person attributes, (b) categorizing encountered individuals by salient dimensions, and (c) developing stereotypes and prejudices (DSP) of salient social groups.

Establishing the Psychological Salience of Person Attributes

Virtually all explanations of social stereotyping rest on categorization. However, there are almost endless bases on which humans might be parsed into groups. How and why are some of the available bases for classification—and not others—used by children to sort individuals? The first component of DIT addresses why some attributes become salient for categorization.

Drawing from constructive theories, we assume that individuals are motivated to understand their physical and social worlds and thus actively seek to determine which of the available bases for classifying people are important. Given the vast diversity of potentially important categories and the complexity of the cues that mark such categories, we reject the idea that evolution "hard wired"

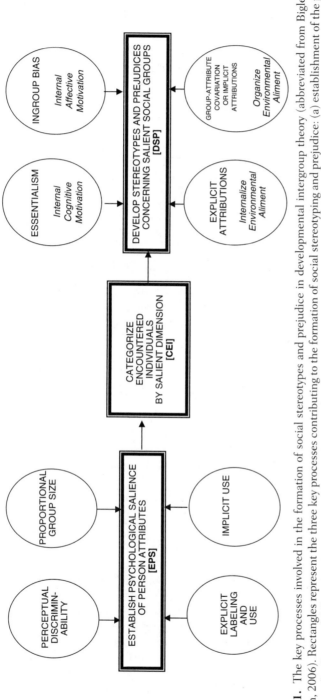

Fig. 1. The key processes involved in the formation of social stereotypes and prejudice in developmental intergroup theory (abbreviated from Bigler & Liben, 2006). Rectangles represent the three key processes contributing to the formation of social stereotyping and prejudice: (a) establishment of the psychological salience of different person attributes, (b) categorization of encountered individuals by salient dimensions, and (c) development of stereotypes and prejudices of salient social groups. Ovals represent the factors that shape the operation of core processes, including four factors that shape the establishment of psychological salience (perceptual discriminability, proportional group size, explicit labeling and use, and implicit use) and four factors that shape the development of stereotypes and prejudice (essentialism, ingroup bias, explicit attributions, and implicit attributions).

specific dimensions as salient bases for classification. We instead suggest that evolution led to a flexible cognitive system that motivates and equips children to infer—from environmental data—which bases of classification are important within a given context.

One relevant factor is the child's tendency to note perceptually salient dimensions of objects and people (Fig. 1., top left oval feeding EPS). Research indicates that young children tend to focus on perceptually salient attributes in person-perception tasks: Perceptually salient features such as race, gender, age, and attractiveness typically become the basis for their social stereotyping, whereas perceptually indistinct features (e.g., some nationalities and political affiliations) typically do not (e.g., Rutland, 1999). Cultural environments may be explicitly structured to make some classification schemes perceptually salient (e.g., requiring Jews to wear yellow stars in Nazi Germany or socializing males and females to wear different hair styles and clothing).

Further, we argue that proportional group size (Fig. 1, top right oval feeding EPS) affects the psychological salience of social groups for children (as for adults; Brewer & Brown, 1998). Proportionally smaller (minority) groups are more distinctive than proportionally larger (majority) groups, thus making minority groups more likely to become the targets of stereotypes and prejudice.

DIT also proposes that the psychological salience of grouping criteria (e.g., gender, color, reading ability) increases when adults label groups or group members, either as a matter of routine (e.g., beginning the day by stating "Good morning girls and boys" [or, "reds and blues"]) or in the service of organizing the environment (e.g., assigning different desks or bulletin boards to each group; Fig. 1, bottom left oval feeding EPS). This outcome holds even when groups are distinguished in a completely neutral (as opposed to stereotypic) manner (e.g., asking children to sit alternately by gender).

We also posit that implicit mechanisms increase the salience of social categories (Fig. 1., bottom right oval feeding EPS). Unlike explicit mechanisms in which categories are directly labeled, implicit mechanisms present some social grouping without explanation, thereby providing a cognitive puzzle for children to solve. One particularly powerful example is de facto segregation. Although segregation has long been linked to stereotyping and prejudice, the explanatory mechanism traditionally offered is unfamiliarity. Under this view, intergroup contact promotes familiarity, thereby increasing intergroup liking (Pettigrew & Tropp, 2000). We propose an additional inferential, constructive process in which children observe the characteristics along which humans are sorted. They notice perceptual similarities among those who live, work, and socialize together and then infer that the social divisions they observe must have been caused by meaningful, inherent differences between groups.

Thus, rather than explaining children's tendency to classify others along some dimension because of reinforcement or imitation, we suggest that children see a dimension used and then construct hypotheses about its importance. Consider a father directing his child to "Ask that lady if we are in the correct line." In traditional social learning theory, this event would not be expected to shape the child's gender stereotyping: The statement involves neither reward nor punishment, nor conveys the father's gender attitudes. In DIT, however, it would be

Table 1. *Key Factors Hypothesized to Affect the Formation of Social Stereotypes and Prejudice in Developmental Intergroup Theory (DIT) and Studies Offering Relevant Empirical Data*

DIT factor	Relevant empirical work	Key manipulations	Major conclusions
Perceptual discriminability	Bigler, 1995; Bigler et al., 1997	Groups were perceptually marked or unmarked.	Higher bias when groups were perceptually marked
Proportional group size	Brown & Bigler, 2002	Groups were equal or unequal in size.	Higher bias when groups were unequal in size
Explicit labeling and use	Bigler et al., 1997, 2001; Patterson & Bigler, 2006	Groups were labeled or ignored by teachers.	Higher bias when groups were labeled by teachers
Implicit use	Bigler, 2004	Groups were segregated or integrated within classrooms.	Higher bias when groups were segregated
Explicit attributions	Patterson, 2007	Groups were labeled as excelling or not at tasks.	Higher bias when groups were linked to positive traits
Implicit attributions	Bigler et al., 2001; Brown & Bigler, 2002	Groups were associated with positive or negative traits via classroom posters.	Higher bias when groups were linked to positive traits

expected to make gender salient, thereby inspiring the child to devise hypotheses about gender's importance. Studies consistent with our hypothesized mechanisms are identified in Table 1.

Categorizing Encountered Individuals by Salient Dimensions

Because children categorize stimuli as they attempt to structure knowledge and reduce cognitive complexity (Mervis & Rosch, 1981), we propose that they will classify encountered individuals into groups using those dimensions that are psychological salient. The degree and way in which the categorization process operates will be affected by the individual child's classification skill (which undergoes age-related change) and environmental experience (e.g., the number of encounters with exemplars). The mere act of categorization triggers processes involved in the construction of social stereotypes.

Developing Stereotypes and Prejudices Concerning Salient Social Groups

The process of categorization is hypothesized to result in constructivist, cognitive-developmental processes (enumerated later) that attach meaning to social groups in the form of beliefs (i.e., stereotypes) and affect (i.e., prejudice). DIT outlines the factors that guide children's acquisition of the content of their social stereotypes and the nature of their affective responses to social groups.

We propose that both internally and externally driven processes lead children to attach meaning to psychologically salient groups. The former are constructive processes through which children actively interpret and recall objects and events in the external world in relation to their current cognitive and affective schemata. Internally driven processes involve the self-generation (rather than passive learning) of links between social categories and (a) attributes (e.g., traits, behaviors, roles) and (b) affect (e.g., liking). In these processes, children go above and beyond the veridical information available in the environment to infer beliefs about the attributes associated with particular social categories. For example, cognitive-developmental psychologists have suggested that some categories, particularly those found in the natural world, are structured by *essentialist* thinking (see Gelman, 2003). Essentialism is the belief that members of a category share important, non-obvious qualities (Fig. 1., top left oval feeding DSP). Thus, children are likely to presume that visible markers of group membership denote other, unseen, inherent qualities (e.g., believing that African Americans and European Americans have different blood types, see Gelman, 2003). Obviously, such beliefs are based not on empirical evidence; instead they reflect the imposition of an internalized group schema onto the world.

With respect to prejudice, the processes are conceptualized as ones in which children actively generate more positive affective links to in-groups than to out-groups. Among adults, the mere act of categorizing individuals into social groups is often sufficient to produce intergroup prejudice and discrimination (Tajfel & Turner, 1986). Children, too, show prejudice within many intergroup contexts, viewing their in-group as superior to out-groups, despite the fact that such beliefs are neither modeled by adults nor objectively true (Fig. 1., top right oval feeding DSP). When stereotype content is acquired via self-generative or constructive processes, children fabricate category–attribute links that favor their own group (Bigler et al., 1997).

Children's cognitive processes are applied to what they encounter in the world. Children are exposed to explicit statements linking social groups to attributes—for example, "African Americans are hostile" and "girls are shy" (Fig. 1., bottom left oval feeding DSP). Explicit remarks are powerful because they operate at two levels simultaneously by employing labels that inherently mark the social groups as important and by providing information about attributes associated with the group. Although public remarks like these have undoubtedly diminished, they still occur, especially among peers. That is, children may "teach" attributions that they have detected (a process described next) or invented, as in the popular children's rhyme: "Girls go to college to get more knowledge; boys go to Jupiter to get more stupider." They may also explicitly teach prejudice without reference to attributes (e.g., "I hate girls").

In addition, children's environments (both macro- and micro-level) are characterized by covariations between social categories and attributes. Illustratively, the occupation of President of the United States shows a perfect correlation to race and gender: All Presidents have been White men. This high-profile correlation is likely to be detected by children, even when it is not explicitly pointed out. The nonverbal behavior that adults direct toward members of social groups or show in response to the presence of group members (e.g., Whites becoming nervous or socially withdrawn in the presence of African Americans) is another source of implicit information likely to cause prejudice.

Importantly, these nonverbal behaviors are likely to be unconscious and, as a consequence, adults are unlikely to explain their behaviors to children. We posit that children's attention to such correlations plays a role in shaping the content of stereotypes and, in turn, prejudice (Fig. 1., bottom right oval feeding DSP). Studies providing empirical data relevant to the role of explicit and implicit links in the formation of stereotype content are summarized in Table 1.

The veridical presence of correlations between social categories and some attributes has led some psychologists to claim that stereotypes are accurate generalizations (see Lee, Jussim, & McCauley, 1995). We agree that the detection of group–attribute correlations plays a role in stereotyping, but we view as incomplete approaches holding that stereotypes are *merely* the reflections of true category–attribute relations or that children learn stereotypes *primarily* through environmental models (e.g., via mechanisms described by social-learning theory). Both approaches fail to account for the fact that children and adults typically develop stereotypic views and prejudices concerning groups that are meaningless (and thus uncorrelated with any observable traits or behaviors). Furthermore, such approaches fail to acknowledge that individuals show systematic biases (e.g., illusory correlations) when processing information about social groups (Brewer & Brown, 1998; Martin et al., 2002). In addition, virtually limitless category-to-attribute correlations are available to the child. It seems unlikely that a child could calculate the correlations between (a) each possible social group within an environment and (b) the traits, roles, and activities that co-vary with each of those groups. We think it unlikely, for example, that children calculate the relation between a person's height and the likelihood of being a nurse, between hair color and the likelihood of being gentle, or between religion and the likelihood of using an ironing board. Yet, most children detect the correlation between gender and each of these characteristics, and thus some statistical learning of group-to-attribute relations appears to occur. We argue (as do researchers who study infants' and young children's attention to statistical information in the service of language learning) that some processes must narrow the scope of the problem so that children's attention is directed toward only a subset of possible correlations. DIT suggests such processes, outlining the factors that serve to make some (but not other) attributes the basis for children's social categorization.

IMPLICATIONS

The approach reviewed here implies that certain social policies will affect stereotyping and prejudice formation among children. Specifically, DIT predicts that the psychological salience of particular social groups for children will increase to the extent that societies (a) exaggerate the perceptual discriminability of groups, (b) foster numeric imbalance across multiple contexts, (c) call attention to groups by labeling them or by explicitly and routinely using group membership as a basis for some action, and (d) present conditions (like segregation) that implicitly convey the importance of group membership.

Importantly, most of the factors that serve to make social groups psychologically salient are under social control. Laws, for example, explicitly constrain adults' use of social categories to label children in some ways (e.g., federal law forbids routinely labeling children's race in classrooms) and might be extended to others (e.g., forbidding routine labeling of gender). Laws likewise affect the implicit use of social categories (e.g., by allowing vs. prohibiting single-sex and single-race schools). Once categorization along some particular dimension occurs, stereotyping and prejudice are likely to follow. When groups are labeled, treated, or sorted differently, children come to conceptualize groups as different in meaningful ways and to show preferential bias toward their own in-group. Children are also likely to internalize the stereotypic beliefs explicitly communicated in their environment and to detect covariations between social groups and attributes that would have otherwise gone unnoticed.

Additional research is needed to add to the empirical base for DIT shown in Table 1 and reviewed elsewhere (Bigler & Liben, 2006) and to test means for countering stereotypes and prejudices that have already developed. For example, whereas DIT suggests minimizing attention to group categories to avoid the formation of stereotypes, it might be necessary to actively draw children's attention to groups and to relevant cognitive processes (e.g., reconstructive memory; illusory correlations) when helping children to overcome stereotypes they already harbor. Our hope is that DIT will prove useful not only for understanding the emergence and evolution of stereotypes and prejudices long reported in the social-psychological literature (Brewer & Brown, 1998) but also for developing policies that will reduce their early emergence and their myriad negative consequences.

Recommended Reading

Aboud, F.E. (2005). (See References)
Bigler, R.S., & Liben, L.S. (2006). (See References)
Martin, C.L., Ruble, D.N., & Szkrybalo, J. (2002). (See References)

Note

1. Address correspondence to Rebecca S. Bigler, Department of Psychology, 1 University Station A8000, University of Texas at Austin, Austin, TX 78712; e-mail: bigler@psy.utexas.edu.

References

Aboud, F.E. (2005). The development of prejudice in childhood and adolescence. In J.F. Dovidio, P. Glick, & L.A. Rudman (Eds.), *On the nature of prejudice: Fifty years after Allport* (pp. 310–326). New York: Blackwell.
Bigler, R.S. (1995). The role of classification skill in moderating environmental influences on children's gender stereotyping: A study of the functional use of gender in the classroom. *Child Development, 66*, 1072–1087.
Bigler, R.S. (2004, January). The role of segregation in the formation of children's intergroup attitudes. In S. Levy (Chair), *Integrating developmental and social psychological research on prejudice processes.* Symposium conducted at the 5th annual meeting of the Society for Personality and Social Psychology, Austin, TX.
Bigler, R.S., Brown, C.S., & Markell, M. (2001). When groups are not created equal: Effects of group status on the formation of intergroup attitudes in children. *Child Development, 72*, 1151–1162.
Bigler, R.S., Jones, L.C., & Lobliner, D.B. (1997). Social categorization and the formation of intergroup attitudes in children. *Child Development, 68*, 530–543.

Bigler, R.S., & Liben, L.S. (1992). Cognitive mechanisms in children's gender stereotyping: Theoretical and educational implications of a cognitive-based intervention. *Child Development, 63*, 1351–1363.

Bigler, R.S., & Liben, L.S. (2006). A developmental intergroup theory of social stereotypes and prejudice. In R.V. Kail (Ed.), *Advances in child development and behavior* (Vol. 34, pp. 39–89). San Diego: Elsevier.

Brewer, M.B., & Brown, R.J. (1998). Intergroup relations. In D.T. Gilbert, S.T. Fiske, & G. Lindsey (Eds.), *The handbook of social psychology* (Vol. 2, 4th ed., pp. 554–594). New York: McGraw-Hill.

Brown, C.S., & Bigler, R.S. (2002). Effects of minority status in the classroom on children's intergroup attitudes. *Journal of Experimental Child Psychology, 83*, 77–110.

Gelman, S.A. (2003). *The essential child.* New York: Oxford University Press.

Lee, Y.T., Jussim, L.J., & McCauley, C.R. (Eds.). (1995). *Stereotype accuracy: Toward appreciating group differences.* Washington, DC: American Psychological Association.

Liben, L.S., & Signorella, M.L. (1980). Gender-related schemata and constructive memory in children. *Child Development, 51*, 11–18.

Martin, C.L., Ruble, D.N., & Szkrybalo, J. (2002). Cognitive theories of early gender role development. *Psychological Bulletin, 128*, 903–933.

Mervis, C., & Rosch, E. (1981). Categorization of natural objects. *Annual Review of Psychology, 32*, 89–115.

Patterson, M.M. (2007). *Negotiating (non) normality: Effects of consistency between views of one's self and one's social group.* Unpublished doctoral dissertation, University of Texas at Austin.

Patterson, M.M., & Bigler, R.S. (2006). Preschool children's attention to environmental messages about groups: Social categorization and the origins of intergroup bias. *Child Development, 77*, 847–860.

Pettigrew, T.F., & Tropp, L.R. (2000). Does intergroup contact reduce prejudice?: Recent meta-analytic findings. In S. Oskamp (Ed.), *Reducing prejudice and discrimination* (pp. 93–114). Mahwah, New Jersey: Erlbaum.

Rutland, A. (1999). The development of national prejudice, in-group favouritism and self-stereotypes in British children. *British Journal of Social Psychology, 38*, 55–70.

Tajfel, H., & Turner, J.C. (1986). The social identity theory of intergroup behaviour. In S. Worchel & W.G. Austin (Eds.), *Psychology of intergroup relations* (pp. 7–24). Chicago: Nelson.

Turner, J.C., Hogg, M.A., Oakes, P.J., Reicher, S.D., & Wetherell, M.S. (1987). *Rediscovering the social group: A self-categorization theory.* Oxford: Blackwell.

This article has been reprinted as it originally appeared in *Current Directions in Psychological Science*. Citation information for this article as originally published appears above.

The Automaticity of Social Life

John A. Bargh[1] and Erin L. Williams

Yale University

Abstract

Much of social life is experienced through mental processes that are not intended and about which one is fairly oblivious. These processes are automatically triggered by features of the immediate social environment, such as the group memberships of other people, the qualities of their behavior, and features of social situations (e.g., norms, one's relative power). Recent research has shown these nonconscious influences to extend beyond the perception and interpretation of the social world to the actual guidance, over extended time periods, of one's important goal pursuits and social interactions.

Keywords

social cognition; automaticity; unconscious

Automaticity refers to control of one's internal psychological processes by external stimuli and events in one's immediate environment, often without knowledge or awareness of such control; automatic phenomena are usually contrasted with those processes that are consciously or intentionally put into operation. Given the historical focus of social psychology on social problems (e.g., discrimination, aggression), it is important to understand the extent to which such negative outcomes might occur without the person's awareness or despite his or her good intentions.

But just because social psychologists tend to study social problems does not mean that automatic processes produce only negative outcomes. To the contrary, much current automaticity research has focused on how nonconscious processes contribute to successful self-regulation and adaptation. As traditional approaches to self-regulation have emphasized the role of conscious, controlled, or executive processes in overcoming impulsive reactions or bad habits, the potential role of nonconscious self-regulatory processes has been somewhat overlooked until recently. But because only conscious, controlled processes can "time-travel"—when the person remembers the past or anticipates the future—nonconscious processes become essential for keeping the individual grounded adaptively and effectively in the present (Bargh, 1997). In terms of contemporary dual-process approaches to cognition, then, nonconscious processes appear to serve a default, background regulatory function, freeing the conscious mind from the concerns of the immediate environment.

SOCIAL PERCEPTION

Much of the early automaticity research in social psychology focused on social perception—the degree to which people's impressions of others are driven by automatic biases. A widely studied source of such bias has been the accessibility of social-behavior representations (i.e., trait constructs such as "intelligent" or "shy"). The automatic use of a given construct to interpret the meaning of someone else's behavior occurs either when one has frequently used that construct in the past (i.e., chronic accessibility) or when one has recently used that construct in some unrelated context (i.e., priming or temporary accessibility). Priming manipulations typically seek to passively and unobtrusively activate the construct in question by having the participant think about or use it in an early phase of the experiment (e.g., a "language test") that is ostensibly unrelated to what follows.

In general, early automaticity research showed that several different forms of social representations become automatically activated in the course of social perception, triggered by the presence of their corresponding features in the environment. The race-, gender-, or age-related features of another person can automatically trigger group stereotypes associated with them; one's consistent affective reactions toward social objects (specific individuals, groups) can become automatically activated upon the mere perception of those objects; and features of one's significant others (e.g., mother, close friend) can automatically activate the specific mental representations of these individuals (see review in Wegner & Bargh, 1998).

Indeed, most automatic effects on social life are mediated by the nonconscious activation of social representations—either *preconsciously* through direct activation by strongly associated stimuli in the environment (as in racial stereotyping effects) or *postconsciously* through recent, conscious use in an unrelated context (as in most category-priming effects). Given the important mediational role played by these structures, current research has focused on discovering the types of information stored within them (e.g., evaluations, goals, trait concepts), as it is these contents that then automatically guide thought and behavior.

THE PERCEPTION–BEHAVIOR LINK

Under the hypothesis that whatever representations become active in social perception will also tend to directly influence behavior, initial tests of automatic social behavior used the same priming methods as in the prior social-perception research to subtly activate trait constructs. However, instead of being asked for their impressions of a target person, participants were put into a situation in which they had the opportunity to act (or not) in line with the primed construct. In an initial study, participants who had been unobtrusively exposed to (i.e., primed with) instances of the concept "rude" were considerably more likely to interrupt a subsequent conversation than were those primed with the concept "polite" (Bargh, Chen, & Burrows, 1996; see Fig. 1).

The logic of the perception–behavior link is that it should apply to any knowledge structure automatically activated in the course of social perception. Social or group stereotypes are one well-researched example. In the course of social perception, people tend to automatically encode minority-group members in terms of their associated stereotypes. Because stereotypes become automatically activated by the mere perception of group features (e.g., skin color) in an individual, the activated stereotype should produce stereotype-consistent behavioral tendencies.

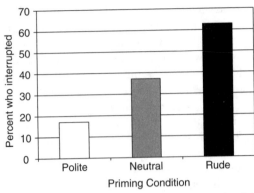

Fig. 1. Percentage of participants primed with the concept "polite," the concept "rude," or a neutral concept who interrupted a conversation between the experimenter and a confederate (Bargh, Chen, & Burrows, 1996, Experiment 1). From "Automaticity of Social Behavior: Direct Effects of Trait Construct and Stereotype Priming on Action," by J.A. Bargh, M. Chen, & L. Burrows, 1996, *Journal of Personality and Social Psychology, 71,* page 235. Copyright 1996 by the American Psychological Association. Reprinted with permission.

Over the past decade, many studies have obtained just this result. Subtle priming of the stereotype of the elderly (which includes the notions that the elderly are forgetful, as well as physically slow and weak) caused college students to walk more slowly when leaving the experimental session (in one study) and to subsequently have poorer memory for the features of a room (in another)—both effects predicted from the content of that stereotype. Stereotypes associated with social roles produce similar effects: Priming the professor stereotype led to students answering a greater number of questions correctly in a trivia game (see review in Dijksterhuis & Bargh, 2001).

NONCONSCIOUS GOAL PURSUIT

Another potential mechanism by which the social environment can directly influence social behavior is through the activation and operation of *goal representations* that have become strongly associated with a particular situation. If an individual repeatedly chooses to pursue a certain goal in a situation, then eventually merely encountering that situation is enough to automatically activate the goal and put it into operation (see Bargh, Gollwitzer, Lee-Chai, Barndollar, & Troetschel, 2001). For example, a parent who chose to forego her own interests and instead pursue her child's best interests, when there was a conflict between the two, eventually would come to act in her child's interests without having to think or consciously decide to; another person who tended to put her own interests first would eventually, over time, automatically pursue her own goals instead of those of her child.

Tests of this model have used the same priming procedures as discussed above to activate a variety of goal representations; the effects of the primed goals are then assessed across a variety of dependent measures. These have included not only cognitive and behavioral consequences of the goal pursuit but also classic qualities of motivational states, such as persistence in the face of obstacles and resumption of interrupted tasks. This research has shown that when a goal is activated outside of the participant's awareness, the same outcomes are obtained as in previous research on conscious goal pursuit. For example, in one study, subliminal priming of a cooperation goal produced the same increase in cooperative behavior as did explicit, conscious instructions to cooperate (Bargh et al., 2001). Importantly, participants showed no signs of being aware either of the activation of the goal or of its operation over time to guide their behavior. In the cooperation-goal study, for example, participants in the conscious-cooperation condition could accurately report on how cooperative they had just been; those in the nonconscious (primed) cooperation condition could not.

APPLICATIONS TO SPHERES OF SOCIAL LIFE

Close Relationships

Much recent work on the automaticity of social life has focused on close relationships. Because of the importance of the goals one typically pursues with close relationship partners (e.g., intimacy, belonging, achievement) and the high frequency of interacting with them, the significant others in one's life are likely to become external triggers of nonconscious goal pursuits. Across five studies, Fitzsimons and Bargh (2003) found that priming the representations of participants' close others (e.g., spouses, parents, colleagues) caused the participants to behave in line with the goals stored within those representations. People waiting at an airport were more likely to donate time to help the experimenter after being asked questions about their friends than they were after being asked about their coworkers; participants in a laboratory study who had earlier indicated having a goal to make their mother proud of them outperformed others on a subsequent verbal task, but only after subliminal priming of the representation of their mother.

Situational Features

Are there automatic influences on social behavior toward people one does not already know well? In general, it is the function of social norms to provide guidelines for how to behave toward strangers and new acquaintances. One is generally expected to act in a mildly positive manner toward strangers, to not harm them, and to assist them to the extent they truly need help and one has the ability to help.

Routine settings and situations also have particularized norms for conduct that are automatically activated when one enters those settings. In harmony with the hypothesis that the mental representation of "library" contains within it action components that automatically guide appropriate action in that setting, Aarts and Dijksterhuis (2003) found that showing participants a picture of a library and instructing them to go to the library after the experimental session caused them to speak more softly during the experiment, compared to control participants.

Social Structure (Power)

Sociostructural variables, such as where one fits in the organizational or power hierarchy of a group, can also have implicit, automatic effects on thought and behavior. Generally, the non-conscious activation of the concept of power seems to produce greater concern with one's own goals and less concern with the outcomes of others, consistent with the traditional lore that "power corrupts." Fortunately, not everyone has such self-centered automatic goals when in positions of power. Chen, Lee-Chai, and Bargh (2001) showed that there are those who instead automatically pursue the goal of helping and advancing the outcomes of those in their charge. Across several experiments, Chen et al. (2001) found that when these communally-oriented people (as determined by their responses to an initial questionnaire taken some months before the experimental session) were primed with power-related stimuli, they became *less* selfish than usual and more concerned with the outcomes of other participants, compared to a control condition.

(NONCONSCIOUSLY) MOTIVATED COGNITION

One burgeoning area of research involving automatic social phenomena is *motivated cognition*—especially self-protective motives. Spencer, Fein, Wolfe, Fong, and Dunn (1998) demonstrated that threatening participants' self-esteem (through false task-failure feedback) automatically caused an increase in their tendency to stereotype others. Apparently (and depressingly), the denigration of others appears to be an automatic and reflexive response to personal failures and threats to one's self-esteem.

But there are grounds for hope. Moskowitz, Gollwitzer, Wasel, and Schaal (1999) showed that automatic stereotype influences can be effectively countered if the individual possesses an automatic goal to be egalitarian and fair toward others. However, egalitarian participants did, however, show the same evidence of stereotype activation as did the other participants. Apparently, then, the stimulus of a minority-group member automatically started two processes at the same time: the activation of the stereotype and the activation of the egalitarian motive, with the latter functioning to shut down or inhibit the former before it could influence judgments. Moskowitz et al. (1999) have thus identified a positive form of automatic motivated cognition and shown how it is possible for chronically good intentions to prevail.

BENEFITS OF NONCONSCIOUS SELF-REGULATION

From Freud onward, scholars of successful adaptation and self-regulation have regarded nonconscious phenomena as mainly problematic—sources of negative outcomes (e.g., psychopathology, bad habits) and certainly not a help to adaptive functioning. However, recent theoretical analyses of intuition have emphasized the importance of immediate, automatic influences on choices and decision making. These have been touted as the mechanisms underlying the "gut feelings" or "hunches" that, far from being random or illusory, do a fairly good job of directing us (see Dijksterhuis & Nordgren, in press; Lieberman, 2000).

In general, the nonconscious nature of these judgment- and behavior-guiding processes makes them a boon to effective self-regulation, because of their immediacy, efficiency, and reliability. It would seem to make good sense for as much guidance of current behavior to occur outside those conscious limits as possible.

CONCLUSIONS AND FUTURE DIRECTIONS

The automatic influences on social life are many and diverse. Other people, their characteristic features, the groups they belong to, the social roles they fill, and whether or not one has a close relationship with them have all been found to be automatic triggers of important psychological and behavioral processes. So too have features of standard situations, which become automatically associated with general norms and rules of conduct, as well as with one's own personal goals when in those situations.

One new line of research concerns how specific emotions such as anger, guilt, and happiness prime (i.e., nonconsciously influence) judgments and behavior (e.g., Lerner, Small, & Loewenstein, 2004). Most people are aware of the powerful influences that emotions can have over immediate behavior and judgments but remain unaware that these influences can carry over into unrelated contexts in which decisions and behavioral choices are made. Indeed, most priming studies depend on the fact that mental representations activated in one context take time to return to a deactivated state and are more likely to have an influence while active than they are at other times. The carry-over effects of recent emotional experiences are likely to prove a common source of automatic influences in everyday life.

Research programs are moving beyond first-generation questions of whether nonconscious influences exist and what forms they might take to second-generation questions of how priming operates in the stimulus-rich real world. For instance, laboratory research has shown that a given priming stimulus can provoke, in parallel, a variety of immediate automatic responses (e.g., in perception, in motivation). But in unconstrained real-world settings, people are bombarded with thousands of such stimuli every day, from advertisements to items in store windows to individuals one passes while walking down a busy street. Which of these will exert nonconscious influences, and which will not?

Another direction for research is determining how the various kinds of automatic effects interact with each other. The responses suggested by nonconscious influences may be in conflict with each other, such that one cannot possibly act on every preconsciously generated behavioral impulse. Models of how these conflicts are resolved, utilizing both nonconscious and conscious means, are now beginning to enter the literature (e.g., Morsella's PRISM model; Morsella, 2005); further research on how these parallel potentialities are transformed into one-at-a-time responses by individuals is urgently needed.

Finally, the recent discovery of *mirror neurons* (e.g., Rizzolatti, Fogassi, & Gallese, 2001), and what they have revealed about the hard-wired nature of the perception–behavior link in humans, is a tremendously important development in the history of psychology. These neurons, located in the premotor cortex of higher primates, have the intriguing property of becoming active both when a person watches an action being performed and when the person performs that action him- or herself. Social cognitive neuroscience research has already shown just how deeply and fundamentally—dare we say, automatically—our minds are connected to each other and to the larger social world.

Recommended Reading

Bargh, J.A., & Chartrand, T.L. (1999). The unbearable automaticity of being. *American Psychologist, 54*, 462–479.
Chaiken, S., & Trope, Y. (Eds., 1999). *Dual-process theories in social psychology.* New York: Guilford.
Gladwell, M. (2004). *Blink: The power of thinking without thinking.* New York: Little, Brown.
Myers, D.G. (2002). *Intuition: Its powers and perils.* New Haven, CT: Yale University Press.
Wilson, T.D. (2002). *Strangers to ourselves.* Cambridge, MA: Harvard University Press.

Acknowledgments—Preparation of this manuscript was supported in part by Grant R01-MH60767 from the National Institute of Mental Health (USA). We thank Ap Dijksterhuis and Ezequiel Morsella for comments and advice on an earlier version.

Note

1. Address correspondence to John A. Bargh, Department of Psychology, Yale University, P.O. Box 208205, New Haven, CT 06520; e-mail: john.bargh@yale.edu.

References

Aarts, H., & Dijksterhuis, A. (2003). The silence of the library: Environment, situational norms, and social behavior. *Journal of Personality and Social Psychology, 84*, 18–28.
Bargh, J.A. (1997). The automaticity of everyday life. In R.S. Wyer (Ed.), *Advances in social cognition* (Vol. X, pp. 1–61). Mahwah, NJ: Erlbaum.
Bargh, J.A., Chen, M., & Burrows, L. (1996). Automaticity of social behavior: Direct effects of trait construct and stereotype priming on action. *Journal of Personality and Social Psychology, 71*, 230–244.
Bargh, J.A., Gollwitzer, P.M., Lee-Chai, A.Y., Barndollar, K., & Troetschel, R. (2001). The automated will: Nonconscious activation and pursuit of behavioral goals. *Journal of Personality and Social Psychology, 81*, 1014–1027.
Chen, S., Lee-Chai, A.Y., & Bargh, J.A. (2001). Relationship orientation as a moderator of the effects of social power. *Journal of Personality and Social Psychology, 80*, 173–187.
Dijksterhuis, A., & Nordgren, L.F. (in press). A theory of unconscious thought. *Perspectives on Psychological Science.*
Dijksterhuis, A., & Bargh, J.A. (2001). The perception-behavior expressway: Automatic effects of social perception on social behavior. In M.P. Zanna (Ed.), *Advances in experimental social psychology* (Vol. 33, pp. 1–40). San Diego: Academic Press.
Fitzsimons, G.M., & Bargh, J.A. (2003). Thinking of you: Nonconscious pursuit of interpersonal goals associated with relationship partners. *Journal of Personality and Social Psychology, 84*, 148–164.
Lerner, J.S., Small, D.A., & Loewenstein, G. (2004). Heart strings and purse strings: Carry-over effects of emotions on economic transactions. *Psychological Science, 15*, 337–341.
Lieberman, M.D. (2000). Intuition: A social cognitive neuroscience approach. *Psychological Bulletin, 126*, 109–137.
Morsella, E. (2005). The functions of phenomenal states: Supermodular interaction theory. *Psychological Review, 112*, 1000–1021.

Moskowitz, G.B., Gollwitzer, P.M., Wasel, W., & Schaal, B. (1999). Preconscious control of stereotype activation through chronic egalitarian goals. *Journal of Personality and Social Psychology, 77*,
167–184.
Rizzolatti, G., Fogassi, L., & Gallese, V. (2001). Neurophysiological mechanisms underlying the
understanding and imitation of action. *Nature Reviews Neuroscience, 2*, 661–670.
Spencer, S.J., Fein, S., Wolfe, C.T., Fong, C., & Dunn, M.A. (1998). Automatic activation of stereotypes: The role of self-image threat. *Personality and Social Psychology Bulletin, 24*, 1139–1152.
Wegner, D.M., & Bargh, J.A. (1998). Control and automaticity in social life. In D. Gilbert, S. Fiske, &
G. Lindzey (Eds.), *Handbook of social psychology* (4th ed, pp. 446–496). Boston: McGraw-Hill.

This article has been reprinted as it originally appeared in *Current
Directions in Psychological Science*. Citation information for this article
as originally published appears above.

Weapon Bias: Split-Second Decisions and Unintended Stereotyping

B. Keith Payne[1]
University of North Carolina at Chapel Hill

Abstract

Race stereotypes can lead people to claim to see a weapon where there is none. Split-second decisions magnify the bias by limiting people's ability to control responses. Such a bias could have important consequences for decision making by police officers and other authorities interacting with racial minorities. The bias requires no intentional racial animus, occurring even for those who are actively trying to avoid it. This research thus raises difficult questions about intent and responsibility for racially biased errors.

Keywords

implicit; attitude; stereotyping; prejudice; weapon

The trouble with split-second decisions is that they seem to make themselves. It is not simply that snap decisions are less accurate than "snail" decisions; it is easy to understand why people might make random errors when thinking fast. If you only have 30 seconds, it is probably a bad idea to do your taxes, pick a stock, or solve any problem beginning with "Two trains leave the station . . ." The real puzzle is when snap judgments show systematic biases that differ from our considered decisions. Should I consider those decisions my decisions if they differ from *my* intentions? Who is responsible?

These questions are asked most loudly when decisions have immense consequences, as when a split-second decision has to be made by a surgeon, a soldier, or a police officer. Four New York City police officers had to make that kind of decision while patrolling the Bronx on a February night in 1999. When the officers ordered Amadou Diallo to stop because he matched a suspect's description, Diallo reacted unexpectedly. Rather than raising his hands, he reached for his pocket. The Ghanaian immigrant may have misunderstood the order, or maybe he meant to show his identification. The misunderstanding was mutual: One officer shouted, "Gun!" and the rest opened fire. Only after the shooting stopped was it clear that Diallo held only his wallet.

Many in the public were outraged. Some accused the NYPD of racial bias. Congress introduced legislation. Protests followed the officers' acquittal, in which the defense successfully argued that at the moment of decision, the officers believed their lives were in danger and that they therefore did not have the conscious intent, the *mens rae* (literally, "guilty mind") to commit a crime. The court did not consider the mechanisms that might produce such a belief.

The death of Amadou Diallo dragged into the spotlight some of the disquieting questions that have run through implicit social cognition research for some time. Can stereotypes about race influence such split-second decisions? And can that kind of race bias take place without intent to discriminate? To answer these questions, it is necessary to move away from the particulars of the Diallo case and toward controlled studies in which causes and mechanisms can be identified. What are the psychological factors that would lead a person, in the crucial moment, to shout, "Gun"?

THE WEAPON BIAS

To study these questions, we developed a laboratory task in which participants made visual discriminations between guns and harmless objects (hand tools). A human face flashed just before each object appeared: a black face on some trials, a white face on others (see Fig. 1). The task for participants was to ignore the faces and respond only to the objects (Payne, 2001). There were two versions of the experiment. In one version, participants responded at their own pace. In the other version they had to respond within half a second on each trial. In the self-paced condition, accuracy was very high regardless of race. However, participants detected guns faster in the presence of a black face. This suggested that the black face readied people to detect a gun but did not distort their decisions.

In the snap-judgment condition, race shaped people's mistakes. They falsely claimed to see a gun more often when the face was black than when it was white (Fig. 2). Under the pressure of a split-second decision, the readiness to see a weapon became an actual false claim of seeing a weapon.

These effects are not bound to the details of a particular experimental paradigm. Several independent lab groups have reported strikingly similar results

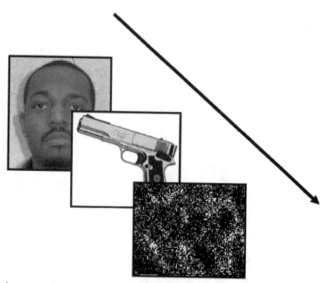

Fig. 1. Schematic illustration of weapons-priming procedure. On each trial, a white or black face appears first, followed by a gun or hand tool, followed by a visual mask. Participants' task is to indicate, as quickly as possible, whether they saw a gun or a tool.

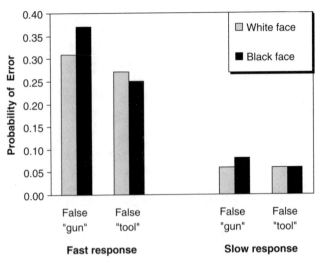

Fig. 2. Probability of falsely identifying a "gun" or "tool" depending on the race of the person shown prior to the object and whether participants were under time pressure to respond. Data adapted from Payne (2001).

using a variety of different procedures. For example, one procedure presented photos of black and white men who appeared on a computer screen holding a variety of objects such as guns, bottles, or cell phones (Correll, Park, Judd, & Wittenbrink, 2002). Participants were told to "shoot" any armed person by pressing one button, and to "not shoot" unarmed persons by pressing a different button. Another procedure presented pictures of white and black men popping out from behind obstacles, again holding either guns or harmless objects (Greenwald, Oakes, & Hoffman, 2002). During some phases of the study, participants were instructed to shoot if a white person, but not a black person, was armed. In other phases, the instructions were reversed. All of these procedures have provided evidence of race bias in both response times and errors. Although the samples in these studies have often been convenience samples, the data suggest that the bias is widespread. Responses made by African American participants in one study were indistinguishable from those of European American participants: both groups were biased toward claiming weapons in black hands more than in white hands (Correll et al., 2002).

Though participants did not need to use race to make their judgments, these studies provide no proof that the bias is unintentional in the strong sense of happening despite intentions to the contrary. Another study tested whether intentional use of race was necessary to produce bias (Payne, Lambert, & Jacoby, 2002). In a baseline condition, participants completed the weapon task under instructions to ignore the faces altogether. A second group was told that the faces might bias them and was instructed to try to avoid being influenced by race. Finally, a third group was also told about the biasing potential of the faces but was instructed to intentionally use the race of the faces as a cue to help them identify guns.

Results showed that although participants' goals affected their self-reported intentions, such goals did not improve their performance. Reliable race bias emerged in all three conditions and was in fact greater in both the "avoid race bias" and the "use race bias" conditions than in the baseline condition. Ironically, directing attention to race had exactly the same effect whether participants attended to race with the intent to discriminate or with the intent to avoid discrimination. In this and other studies, the weapon bias seems largely independent of intent. This is important because it means that the bias can coexist with conscious intentions to be fair and unbiased.

WHAT DRIVES THE WEAPON BIAS?

Why is it that people use stereotypes in their decisions both when they intend to and when they intend not to? And if we are not to turn intelligent people into caricatures or automatons, shouldn't intentions play a role somewhere? Integrating intentional and unintentional aspects of behavior is the job of dual-process theories, which attempt to explain when, how, and why behavior is driven by automatic versus intentionally controlled aspects of thought. My collaborators and I have proposed a particular dual-process theory to account for both intentional control over decisions and the patterns of unintended bias seen in snap judgments (Payne, 2001; Payne, 2005; Payne, Lambert, & Jacoby, 2002).

The first factor is a stereotypic association that, for some people, links African Americans to violence and weapons. These stereotypic links can include both purely semantic associations and emotions such as fear or anger. These associations serve as an impulse that automatically drives responses whenever a person is unable to control a response. The second factor is the degree of intentional control participants have over how they respond (see Fig. 3). To predict whether someone will show the weapon bias, it is critical to know the answers to two questions. First, what is the person's automatic impulse that will drive responses when behavioral control fails? Second, how likely is it that control will fail? Research using a variety of behavioral and neuroscience methods has provided support for the key claims.

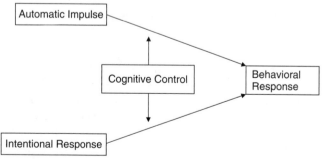

Fig. 3. A dual-process model of weapon bias. When people have full control of their behavior, they respond as intended. When control is impaired, automatic impulse drives responses.

Behavioral Evidence

Evidence for the role of stereotypic associations comes from studies of individual differences. One study found that individuals with more negative self-reported attitudes toward blacks showed greater race bias in their weapon claims (Payne, 2001). In another study, weapon bias correlated with individual differences in perceptions of cultural stereotypes about African Americans (Correll et al., 2002). To avoid the limitations of self-reports, a recent study had participants complete two popular implicit-attitude measures in addition to the weapons task (Payne, 2005). Because implicit measures assess attitudes indirectly, without asking for a self-report, they avoid problems of introspection and social-desirability bias that affect explicit or self-report measures. Individuals with more negative implicit attitudes toward Blacks showed greater weapon bias. Finding consistent correlations using multiple measures provides converging evidence for the important role of stereotypic associations.

The finding that people with stronger stereotypes tend to show greater weapon bias is deceptively simple. It is deceptive because it tempts us to conclude that automatic stereotyping is all there is to the story. But that conclusion leaves out the important factor of how much intentional control people have over their responses. In the first studies described above, there was only one key difference between the snap-judgment and the slow-judgment conditions: how much time participants had to respond. Snap judgments didn't change people's stereotypes. Snap judgments allowed those stereotypes to spill out into overt behavioral errors.

Time pressure is only one way to limit control over responses. Govorun and Payne (2006) showed similar effects as a result of self-regulation depletion. When people are required to self-regulate in one way, they are less likely to control themselves in other ways (Muraven & Baumeister, 2000). We depleted resources for one group of participants by requiring them to persist for several hundred trials on the tedious Stroop color-naming task. The Stroop task presents color words (e.g., *red, green*) in font colors that are either congruent or incongruent with the word meanings. When participants name the font color, incongruent word meanings interfere, requiring cognitive control. A nondepleted group saw a few trials of the Stroop task but did not exert sustained effort. The depleted group showed greater weapon bias, a result of reduced control over their responses.

Neuroscience Evidence

Several studies have examined the neural underpinnings of the weapon bias. Event related potentials (ERP) are more useful than other methods such as functional magnetic resonance imaging or positron emission tomography for this split-second effect because ERPs have greater temporal resolution. ERP studies examine fluctuations in electrical brain activity as a person processes information. Because different ERP components reflect specific cognitive functions, researchers can use those components to reveal processes underlying behavior.

One informative study examined an ERP component called error-related negativity (ERN), which is associated with detecting conflicts between goals and ongoing mental activity (Amodio et al., 2004). Conflict detection is a critical part of mental control because detecting a conflict between current and intended states is necessary for implementing self-control. Individuals showing the greatest ERN activity showed the fewest false weapon claims, and this effect was mediated by the ability to control responses.

A second study using ERP methods found several additional ERP components associated with weapon biases (Correll, Urland, & Ito, 2006). Of particular interest were two components, known as the P200 and the N200. The P200 is associated with emotional reactions to threatening stimuli, whereas the N200 is associated with conflict detection and cognitive control—similar to what was found with the ERN. Consistent with the two-factor theory, participants with greater P200 responses to black individuals, and those with lesser N200 responses, showed greater race bias.

Modeling the Weapon Bias

The evidence reviewed here converges to suggest that both automatic stereotype activation and failures of control are important in the weapon bias. Dual-process theories are commonly tested by comparing implicit and explicit tests, on the assumption that implicit tests measure only automatic responses and explicit tests measure only controlled responses. That assumption is not likely to be realistic, however, as virtually any task reflects a combination of automatic and controlled components (Jacoby, 1991). An alternative approach is to use a formal model to separate component processes within the same task. The value in this approach is that each component process can be studied individually without confounding underlying processes with different test formats.

My collaborators and I have used the process-dissociation procedure (Jacoby, 1991) as a tool to model automatic and controlled factors in the weapon bias. By that model, if a process is automatic, it influences responses regardless of whether it is consistent with intent or inconsistent with intent. In contrast, when a process is controlled, it influences responses only when intended, but not otherwise. When a black face precedes a gun, stereotypes and intent are in concert. Responding based on either will lead to the correct response. When a black face precedes a harmless object, stereotypes and intent are in opposition. The relationships among intentional control, automatic stereotyping, and behavioral responses can be formalized using algebraic equations (Jacoby, 1991; Payne, 2001). We can then decompose responses into numeric estimates of two processes: automatic stereotyping and cognitive control.

Applying the model to the studies just reviewed sheds light on the factors driving the weapon bias. For example, time pressure (Payne, 2001) and self-regulation depletion (Govorun & Payne, 2006) affected only the controlled component but not the automatic component. In other cases, differences in automatic stereotype activation were key. For example, implicit measures of race attitudes correlated with the automatic but not the controlled component (Payne, 2005). The evidence from these studies supports the two-factor account of the weapon bias and provides a means of measuring the underlying factors. The utility of modeling the underlying processes becomes apparent when considering strategies to reduce the race bias.

REDUCING WEAPON BIAS

Bias-reduction strategies might take either of two approaches. On one hand, they can try to change the automatic impulse. On the other hand, they can try to maximize behavioral control. One intriguing study compared police officers and civilians drawn from the same communities and found that both groups showed weapon bias, though officers showed somewhat less bias than civilians (Correll, Park, Judd, Wittenbrink, Sadler, & Keesee, 2006). Even more important, the officers with the most firearms training showed the least race bias. This finding suggests that the routine training that officers receive may effectively reduce weapon bias. There is evidence that practice in identifying weapons may have beneficial effects on both controlled and automatic components of responses and that these benefits extend to police officer volunteers (Plant & Peruche, 2005; Plant, Peruche, & Butz, 2005).

Finally, a recent study shows that although people cannot simply will the weapon bias away, certain specific strategies may be able to eliminate the automatic component of the bias. Stewart and Payne (2006) had participants form simple plans that linked racial categories to specific counterstereotypic thoughts (Gollwitzer, 1999). For example, participants made the plan, "when I see a black face I will think 'safe.'" Unlike participants who simply tried to avoid bias, those who formed specific plans showed no automatic race bias. Together, these studies offer clues to how and why specific strategies may succeed or fail.

IMPLICATIONS AND FUTURE DIRECTIONS

Research on the weapon bias has been consistent in answering several basic questions. Race can bias snap judgments of whether a gun is present, and that bias can coexist with fair-minded intentions. Although overt hostility toward African Americans is probably sufficient to produce this bias, it is not necessary. The bias happens not just because of racial animus but because of stereotypical associations that drive responses when people are unable to fully control them.

The answers to these questions suggest many more questions. One question is how well, and under what conditions, these findings generalize to the decisions police and other authorities make. Samples of police officers provide some evidence that the effect generalizes to a critical population. However, all of the existing studies have used computer tasks, even the most realistic of which do not capture the complexity facing an actual police officer. Future studies might incorporate manipulations of suspects' race into real-time, three-dimensional simulations of the sort that are used in police firearms training.

A second question concerns the mechanisms underlying the weapon bias. Evidence suggests that both emotional responses to and semantic associations with race play a role (Correll, Urland, & Ito, 2006; Judd, Blair, & Chapleau, 2004). But it is unknown under what conditions one or the other is likely to be influential. Do emotional and semantic responses act in identical ways, or do they have different consequences? And do the mechanisms of control differ for emotional versus semantic responses?

Another important question concerns how people attribute responsibility for biases that demonstrably contradict intent. I received two letters shortly after the first paper on the topic was published. A retired police officer rejected the conclusion that race may bias weapon decisions, concerned that the research might lead to unjustified allegations that police, who must make the best decisions they can under terrible conditions, are prejudiced. A second letter writer objected to the conclusion that the weapon bias may happen without intent, concerned that the research might be used to excuse race bias among police officers rather than holding them accountable for their decisions. It is difficult to dismiss the worries of either writer, though they are polar opposites. Each expresses some of the thorny possibilities that may reasonably follow from a complex situation. Do ordinary people consider this a case of diminished capacity and therefore diminished responsibility? Or do they perceive the bias to reflect hidden malice? Are their judgments biased by their own racial attitudes or their attitudes toward police?

Empirical research will not settle the hard normative questions of ethics and responsibility. But it can shed light on how ordinary people actually reason about such unintended biases. Because juries and other decision-making bodies are made up of these same people, the answers are important for how social and political institutions will treat unintended race biases. Understanding the psychology of the weapon bias is a prelude to a better-informed conversation about the hard questions.

Recommended Reading

Payne, B.K. (2001). Prejudice and perception: The role of automatic and controlled processes in misperceiving a weapon. *Journal of Personality Social Psychology, 81*, 181–192.

Payne, B.K., Jacoby, L.L., & Lambert, A.J. (2005). Attitudes as accessibility bias: Dissociating automatic and controlled components. In R. Hassin, J. Bargh, & J. Uleman (Eds.), *The new unconscious*. Oxford, England: Oxford University Press.

Note

1. Address correspondence to Keith Payne, Department of Psychology, University of North Carolina, Chapel Hill, Campus Box 3270, Chapel Hill, NC 27599; e-mail: payne@unc.edu.

References

Amodio, D.M., Harmon-Jones, E., Devine, P.G., Curtin, J.J., Hartley, S.L., & Covert, A.E. (2004). Neural signals for the detection of unintentional race bias. *Psychological Science, 15*, 225–232.

Correll, J., Park, B., Judd, C.M., & Wittenbrink, B. (2002). The police officer's dilemma: Using race to disambiguate potentially threatening individuals. *Journal of Personality and Social Psychology, 83*, 1314–1329.

Correll, J., Park, B., Judd, C.M., Wittenbrink, B., Sadler, M.S., & Keesee, T. (2006). *Across the thin blue line: Police officers and racial bias in the decision to shoot*. Unpublished manuscript, University of Chicago.

Correll, J., Urland, G.L., & Ito, T.A. (2006). Event-related potentials and the decision to shoot: The role of threat perception and cognitive control. *Journal of Experimental Social Psychology, 42*, 120–128.

Gollwitzer, P.M. (1999). Implementation intentions: Strong effects of simple plans. *American Psychologist, 54*, 493–503.

Govorun, O., & Payne, B.K. (2006). Ego depletion and prejudice: Separating automatic and controlled components. *Social Cognition, 24*, 111–136.

Greenwald, A.G., Oakes, M.A., & Hoffman, H.G. (2002). Targets of discrimination: Effects of race on responses to weapon holders. *Journal of Experimental Social Psychology, 39*, 399–405.

Jacoby, L.L. (1991). A process dissociation framework: Separating automatic from intentional uses of memory. *Journal of Memory and Language, 30*, 513–541.

Judd, C.M., Blair, I.V., & Chapleau, K.M. (2004). Automatic stereotypes vs. automatic prejudice: Sorting out the possibilities in the Payne, 2001 weapon paradigm. *Journal of Experimental Social Psychology, 40*, 75–81.

Muraven, M., & Baumeister, R.F. (2000). Self-regulation and depletion of limited resources: Does self-control resemble a muscle? *Psychological Bulletin, 126*, 247–259.

Payne, B.K. (2001). Prejudice and perception: The role of automatic and controlled processes in misperceiving a weapon. *Journal of Personality Social Psychology, 81*, 181–192.

Payne, B.K. (2005). Conceptualizing control in social cognition: How Executive Functioning Modulates the Expression of Automatic Stereotyping. *Journal of Personality and Social Psychology, 89*, 488–503.

Payne, B.K., Lambert, A.J., & Jacoby, L.L. (2002). Best laid plans: Effects of goals on accessibility bias and cognitive control in race based misperceptions of weapons. *Journal of Experimental Social Psychology, 38*, 384–396.

Plant, E.A., & Peruche, B.M. (2005). The consequences of race for police officers' responses to criminal suspects. *Psychological Science, 16*, 180–183.

Plant, E.A., Peruche, B.M., & Butz, D.A. (2005). Eliminating automatic racial bias: Making race non-diagnostic for responses to criminal suspects. *Journal of Experimental Social Psychology, 41*, 141–156.

Stewart, B.D., & Payne, B.K. (2006). *Counterstereotypical thought plans reduce automatic stereotyping.* Unpublished manuscript, Ohio State University.

This article has been reprinted as it originally appeared in *Current Directions in Psychological Science*. Citation information for this article as originally published appears above.

The Unrecognized Stereotyping and Discrimination Against Singles

Bella M. DePaulo[1]
University of California, Santa Barbara
Wendy L. Morris
McDaniel College

Abstract

A widespread form of bias has slipped under our cultural and academic radar. People who are single are targets of singlism: negative stereotypes and discrimination. Compared to married or coupled people, who are often described in very positive terms, singles are assumed to be immature, maladjusted, and self-centered. Although the perceived differences between people who have and have not married are large, the actual differences are not. Moreover, there is currently scant recognition that singlism exists, and when singlism is acknowledged, it is often accepted as legitimate.

Keywords

singles; stigma; discrimination; stereotypes; relationships

For years, we have been studying what we call *singlism*, the stigmatizing of adults who are single. We have found evidence of singlism in the negative stereotypes and discrimination faced by singles (DePaulo, 2006; DePaulo & Morris, 2005a; DePaulo & Morris, 2005b). Although singlism is a nonviolent, softer form of bigotry than what is often faced by other stigmatized groups such as African Americans or gay men and lesbians, the impact of singlism is far ranging. Unlike more familiar isms such as racism, sexism, or heterosexism, singlism is not often recognized, and when it is pointed out, it is often regarded as legitimate.

WHO IS "SINGLE?"

We can define singles as legally single or socially single, though the two often overlap. According to the U.S. Census Bureau, over 40% of adults are legally single, including people who are divorced or widowed and those who have always been single. In everyday interactions, what matters most often is whether a person is socially single or socially coupled. People who are in sexual partnerships regarded as serious by themselves and others are socially coupled. Impressions of seriousness are shaped by factors such as the length of time the twosome has been together, the regularity and exclusivity with which they see each other, whether they seem to intend to stay together, and whether they live together.

EVIDENCE OF SINGLISM

Negative Stereotypes of the Socially Single

We asked nearly 1,000 undergraduates to list the characteristics that came to mind when they thought about people who were married (in one condition) or single (in the other). Married people were more likely than singles to be described as mature, stable, honest, happy, kind, and loving. Singles were more often called immature, insecure, self-centered, unhappy, lonely, and ugly (but also, on the positive side, independent). The perceived differences between single and married people were often quite large. For example, married people were described as caring, kind, and giving almost 50% of the time, compared to only 2% of the time for singles (Morris, DePaulo, Hertel, & Ritter, 2006).

Next, we wanted to know whether singles are perceived even more negatively after they have passed the age at which most people marry. Groups of undergraduates and community members rated descriptions of single and married people. The targets were described as men or women and as 25 or 40 years old. All groups rated the singles as less socially mature, less well-adjusted, and more self-centered and envious than the married people (though also more independent and career-oriented). As we expected, the differences favoring married people were even greater when the targets were described as 40 years old than when they were described as 25. Still, though, there were significant differences even at the younger age.

Why should 25-year-olds be derogated simply because they are not yet married? As of the year 2004, at least half of all American women, and even more men, had not married by age 25. Maybe, we thought, young adults needed to show that they were at least working at coupling, to avoid getting stigmatized.

In another experiment, undergraduates read profiles describing students who were currently coupled, currently single, previously coupled, or always single. Working at coupling did matter. Students who were described as having current or past relationship experience were regarded as more socially mature, better-adjusted, and less self-centered than the others.

Discrimination Against Singles

Discrimination against single people is often legal. As of 2004, 23 states offered no protections from marital-status discrimination, and others offered only partial protections. Employers can legally subsidize health benefits for spouses of married employees (and sometimes domestic partners), while offering no comparable benefits to a parent, sibling, or friend of their single employees. That amounts to unequal compensation for the same work. Similarly, a married person in need of care can receive it from a spouse who is covered by the Family and Medical Leave Act (FMLA), but singles who need care do not have anyone in their own generation who is eligible for FMLA benefits.

Single men are paid less than their married male colleagues even when they are of similar age and have comparable work experience. Marriage also brings increased tax benefits and social security benefits and discounts on automobile insurance, travel packages, and club memberships (reviewed in DePaulo, 2006).

We have also found experimental evidence of housing discrimination against singles (Morris, Sinclair, & DePaulo, 2006). In three studies, participants read descriptions of three applicants for a rental property and indicated their preferred lessee. Rental agents were much more likely to choose a married couple (60%) over a cohabiting romantic couple (23%) or a pair of friends (17%). Undergraduates' preference for the married couple was even stronger: 80% chose the married couple, as compared to just 12% choosing the cohabiting couple and 8% who chose the friends. Undergraduates also overwhelmingly favored a married couple (70%) over a single woman (18%) or a single man (12%). The preferences of the rental agents are particularly significant, as they raise the possibility that singles may be at a disadvantage when trying to find housing. Future research should explore this.

Byrne and Carr's (2005) analysis of a nationally representative sample found that people who have always been single and are not cohabiting with a romantic partner are more likely than married people to report experiencing (for example) poorer service in restaurants or condescending attitudes in everyday life. The authors controlled for many factors such as age, race, sexual orientation, and health, making a convincing case that singles really are slighted in their interpersonal experiences. But we still wondered whether singles themselves think they are discriminated against based upon their relationship status.

SINGLISM IS UNACKNOWLEDGED

What is especially interesting about singlism is that most people are unaware that singles are stigmatized at all. When we asked adults to list any groups to which they belonged that might be targets of negative stereotypes or discrimination, only 4% of singles spontaneously mentioned singles as such a category. When explicitly asked whether they thought singles might be a stigmatized group, only 30% of singles and 23% of coupled people said that they were. This level of awareness is low compared to the 100% of gay people, 90% of obese people, 86% of African Americans, and 72% of women who acknowledged their groups' stigma (Morris, 2005).

The practice of singlism is often considered acceptable. While many are outraged by discrimination based on race, gender, or sexual orientation, few people feel any injustice has occurred when a single person is targeted. When participants in an experiment read about housing discrimination against singles, they thought the practice was more legitimate and fair than when they read that the housing discrimination targeted a member of a recognized stigmatized group such as an African American person, a gay person, or an obese person (Morris, Sinclair, & DePaulo, 2006).

WHY ARE SINGLES STIGMATIZED?

Unfounded Stereotypes or Accurate Perceptions?

What if marriage really does transform people, such that they become strikingly happier than they were when they were single and much happier than their peers who have always been single? Then negative perceptions of single people as unhappy would seem more like accurate assessments than like unfair characterizations.

Meta-analytic reviews (summarized by DePaulo & Morris, 2005a) are sometimes said to support the claim that getting married makes people happier, because currently married people score higher on happiness than other groups. But the biggest differences are between the currently married and those who were previously married but are currently divorced or widowed. Getting married cannot account for those differences, because currently married, divorced, and widowed people all got married. The smallest difference ($r = .09$) is between the currently married and those who have always been single.

Nor can it be said that getting married and staying married makes people happy. The meta-analytic reviews summarize studies in which the single, married, and previously married people are all different people. So, the people who stayed married may have been happier than the other people even before they got married. A recent review suggests that happiness may indeed come first in the causal chain leading to other life outcomes (Lyubomirsky, King, & Diener, 2005).

Definitive causal statements about marriage and happiness can never be made, because people cannot be randomly assigned to get married or stay single. Still, longitudinal research can provide an answer to an important question: When people marry, do they become happier than they were when they were single?

An 18-year longitudinal study of thousands of German adults analyzed by Richard Lucas and his colleagues suggests that the long-term answer is no (Lucas, 2005; Lucas, Clark, Georgellis, & Diener, 2003). People who got married and stayed married experienced a small increase in happiness around the year of the wedding, but then their happiness returned to the level it was before. People who married and later divorced were already becoming less happy as the wedding day approached, a trend that did not reverse until the year before the divorce became final. (Their happiness then continued to increase; on the average, though, divorced people did not become as happy as they had been when they were single.)

People who stayed single throughout the study started out slightly less happy (0.2 points on an 11-point scale) than the people who would eventually get married and stay married. However, their mean happiness level was always squarely on the happy end of the scale (never more than 0.6 points lower than the continuously married). It was never as low as that of the divorced people the year before their divorce became official (and it was slightly higher than that of the divorced people for most other years, too). Also, the mean happiness level of the single people was never as low as that of the widowed people right after they were widowed.

The pattern of results is similar for health. People who have always been single are typically just as healthy, or only slightly less healthy, than people who have always been married. When there is a difference related to marital status, it is likely to be the previously married, not the continuously single, who are disadvantaged (DePaulo, 2006; Rook & Zettel, 2005).

Crandall and Warner (2005) argue that negative evaluations are indicative of prejudice, regardless of whether they are accurate. Claims about the transformative power of marriage, though, seem to be grossly exaggerated or just plain wrong. Getting married does not make people lastingly happier or definitively healthier.

Can Singlism Be Explained from an Evolutionary Perspective?

Evolutionary psychologists Pillsworth and Haselton (2005) have noted that we need "adaptations that promote successful mating, such as the basic desire to find a mate and have sex" (p. 98). Thus, people pay attention to whether others are single or coupled because this information is relevant to reproduction. However, the cultural assumption that coupling is the key to happiness is more difficult to explain. As Pillsworth and Haselton note, "the evolutionary perspective does not suggest that coupling will result in a healthier or more satisfying life for any particular individual. . . . In the modern world, coupling does not guarantee an on-average fitness benefit to couple members or their children" (p. 101).

A Cultural Lag in Perceptions?

As recently as the mid-20th century, there were big differences between single and married adults. Then, having sex or children outside of marriage was considered shameful. Women were more dependent on marriage for financial security. Adults married younger, and divorced less often, than they do now. In contrast, Americans today spend more years of their adult lives single than married. Many women earn enough to support themselves and sometimes children, too. Because of advances in birth control and reproductive technology, women can have sex without having children, and they can have children without having sex. Perhaps, then, the negative appraisals of single people are signs of cultural lag: Perceptions of single people have not yet caught up with their rapidly changing place in society (Byrne & Carr, 2005).

Singles as a Threat to Cultural Beliefs

DePaulo (2006) suggests that there is more than just cultural lag at work. In contemporary American society, there is a glorification of marriage and coupling that many single and married people accept uncritically. According to the marital mythology, finding a soul-mate is a transformative experience: Marrying that all-purpose, all-important partner can make a person happy and healthy and fulfill all emotional and social needs. The marital mythology is powerfully attractive, offering as it does a seemingly simple path to a rewarding and meaningful life. Singles—especially those who clearly lead fulfilling lives—challenge that belief system. Singlism serves to maintain cultural beliefs about marriage by derogating those whose lives challenge those beliefs.

THE PARADOX OF SINGLEHOOD

Singles are targeted with stereotyping and discrimination, and married people are glorified. Yet, paradoxically, getting married does not result in lasting improvements in well-being, and people who have always been single are not very different in health or happiness from people who have been continuously married. How is this possible?

Singles often maintain a diversified relationship portfolio, rather than investing so much in just one person. Even in their later years, when others expect them to be lonely and alone, they often enjoy networks of supportive relationships (Zettel, 2005). Social scientists who study adult relationships have focused overwhelmingly on romantic relationships. Perhaps it is time to give relationships with friends, siblings, and everyone else their due.

Single people who have the resources and opportunities to do so can pursue their passions and excel at work that they love. They can embrace solitude as well as interpersonal engagement. If singles are increasingly living their lives fully, rather than marking time waiting for "the one," then the paradox begins to resolve itself. Maybe singles more often respond to stereotyping and discrimination with resilience than with victimization. Much more research will be needed to know for sure.

FUTURE RESEARCH

In our own work, we found evidence of singlism in the United States and Germany (Hertel, Schütz, DePaulo, Morris, & Stucke, in press). But as Pillsworth and Haselton have noted, "In most cultures around the globe, your spouse is not your best friend, or even your primary social partner" (p. 102). How are singles perceived in those cultures? Even within the United States, there is much left to learn about how singlism is shaped by factors such as gender, ethnicity, sexual orientation, and social class.

Reams of research reports have examined marital status as a predictor of well-being. Marital status, though, may be a poor proxy for more important predictors. Do people have the degree of social connectedness that they need and want, whether that is attained by cohabitation, embeddedness in a network of friends, or some other means? Are they living a life that they find engaging and meaningful?

The development of a new field of study offers great promise. Many of the most fundamental questions about singles and singlism have yet to be addressed, or even framed. The answers are likely to have implications for public policy and even for the way people conduct their everyday lives.

Recommended Reading

Byrne A., & Carr, D. (2005). (See References)
DePaulo, B. (2006). (See References)
DePaulo, B.M., & Morris, W.L. (2005a). (See References)
DePaulo, B.M., & Morris, W.L. (2005b). (See References)
Gillis, J.R. (1997). The perfect couple. In J.R. Gillis, *A world of their own making* (pp. 133–151). Cambridge, MA: Harvard University Press.

Note

1. Address correspondence to Bella M. DePaulo, P.O. Box 487, Summerland, CA 93067; e-mail: depaulo@psych.ucsb.edu.

References

Byrne, A., & Carr, D. (2005). Caught in the cultural lag: The stigma of singlehood. *Psychological Inquiry, 16*, 84–91.

Crandall, C.S., & Warner, R.H. (2005). How a prejudice is recognized. *Psychological Inquiry, 16*, 137–141.

DePaulo, B. (2006). *Singled out: How singles are stereotyped, stigmatized, and ignored, and still live happily ever after*. New York: St. Martin's Press.

DePaulo, B.M., & Morris, W.L. (2005a). Singles in society and in science. *Psychological Inquiry, 16*, 57–83.

DePaulo, B.M., & Morris, W.L. (2005b). Should singles and the scholars who study them make their mark or stay in their place? *Psychological Inquiry, 16*, 142–149.

Hertel, J., Schütz, A., DePaulo, B.M., Morris, W.L., & Stucke, T.S. (in press). She's single, so what? How are singles perceived compared to people who are married? *Journal of Family Research*.

Lucas, R.E. (2005). Time does not heal all wounds: A longitudinal study of reaction and adaptation to divorce. *Psychological Science, 16*, 945–950.

Lucas, R.E., Clark, A.E., Georgellis, Y., & Diener, E. (2003). Reexamining adaptation and the set point model of happiness: Reactions to changes in marital status. *Journal of Personality and Social Psychology, 84*, 527–539.

Lyubomirsky, S., King, L., & Diener, E. (2005). The benefits of frequent positive affect: Does happiness lead to success? *Psychological Bulletin, 131*, 803–855.

Morris, W.L. (2005). The effects of stigma awareness on the self-esteem of singles (Doctoral dissertation, University of Virginia, 2005). *Dissertation Abstracts International, 66*(03), 1785B.

Morris, W.L., DePaulo, B.M., Hertel, J., & Ritter, L. (2006). *Perception of people who are single: A developmental life tasks model*. Manuscript submitted for publication.

Morris, W.L., Sinclair, S., & DePaulo, B.M. (2006). *The perceived legitimacy of civil status discrimination*. Manuscript submitted for publication.

Pillsworth, E.G., & Haselton, M.G. (2005). The evolution of coupling. *Psychological Inquiry, 16*, 98–104.

Rook, K.S., & Zettel, L.A. (2005). The purported benefits of marriage viewed through the lens of physical health. *Psychological Inquiry, 16*, 116–121.

Zettel, L.A. (2005). Aging alone: Do the social support resources of never-married individuals place them at risk? *Dissertation Abstracts International, 65*(10), 5441B.

Section 6: Critical Thinking Questions

1. Several authors in this section report on the interaction between automatic and controlled social processes. What features of one's social environment can trigger automatic judgments? Give some examples of when automatic social judgments can facilitate or impair decision-making tendencies.

2. Given the aggression research reported by Carnagey, Anderson, and Barthalow (2007), what do you feel is the best way to reduce levels of aggression in society? In what ways can individuals limit media violence, and in what ways can the film/video-game industry limit it?

3. Bigler & Liben (2007) speculate that intergroup biases are largely under environmental control. What do they mean by this? Can their theory be used to explain "singlism" as described by DePaulo & Morris (2006)? What kinds of subtle, possibly nonconscious ways have you witnessed prejudice against single people?

4. In what way(s) can social neuroscience advance our understanding of stereotyping and outcomes of stereotyping (aggression, weapon bias)? Are there

alternative ways of interpreting the evidence? What additional evidence would help to evaluate the alternatives?

5. Do you think that college students, in general, are more or less susceptible to making snap judgments about others than older adults? Why? Are they more or less likely to be affected by snap judgments? Why?

This article has been reprinted as it originally appeared in *Current Directions in Psychological Science*. Citation information for this article as originally published appears above.